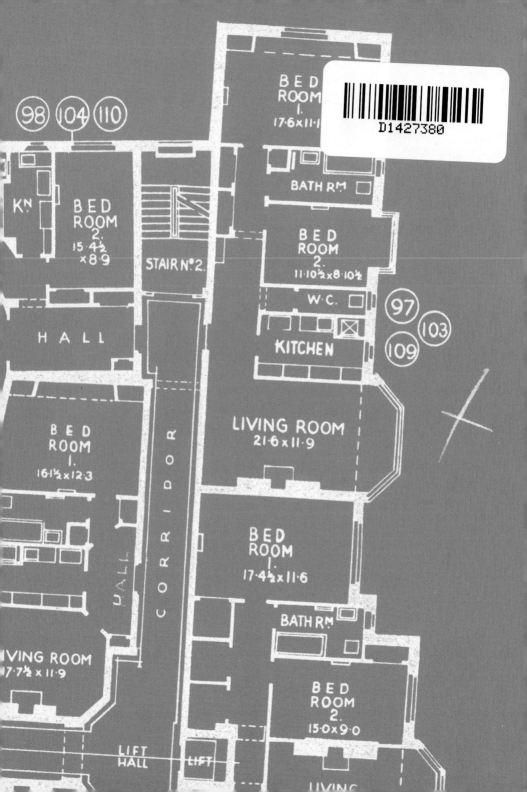

JAMES COURAGE

diaries

JAMES COURAGE DIARIES

edited by
Chris Brickell

transcribed by
Natasha Smillie

OTAGO UNIVERSITY PRESS
Te Whare Tā o Te Wānanga o Ōtākou

CONTENTS

FOREWORD

MOST OF WHAT I KNEW about James Courage I learned from Bill Pearson while writing the latter's biography. The men were close friends in London in the early 1950s, and Pearson admired Courage for his willingness to defy the strictures of the day and write fiction about his homosexuality, something he himself had tried and failed to do in his only novel, *Coal Flat*.

Despite Courage's defiant honesty, I had received the impression from Pearson (though I'm not now certain exactly why) that he was buttoned down and bland. Chris Brickell's selections from Courage's diaries are a delightful surprise. They reveal him to be a truly engaging man, a complex personality and an astute observer with a gentle, whimsical sense of humour, a dry slightly acerbic wit when warranted and an artist's appreciation of art. Almost everything he writes is from the position of sympathetic participant. He is candid about himself, unsparing of his own faults, but still capable of being forgiving and tolerant of himself and others. One senses that he possessed that core of 'passionate integrity' – James K. Baxter's description of his pacifist father, Archie – that compels good people to take stands against a crushing mainstream. Courage indeed.

Courage's descriptions of living through London's Blitz are immediate and gripping. The reader experiences with him the fear, frustration, exhaustion, boredom and claustrophobia that he and so many others endured. As a record of a drawn-out reign of terror and trauma it resonates with many similar situations, and contemporary readers may identify with versions of these experiences in a world dominated by Covid-19 restrictions.

Some of Courage's diary entries hold together as vignettes, nearly perfect, with the impact and narrative structure of quality flash fiction. He is adept at developing an ordinary, mundane comment or observation into a revelation with universal qualities, mixing the everyday with the exceptional, the theatrical and the sexual. He offers new and interesting glimpses of figures from New Zealand literature we believe we are familiar with – D'Arcy Cresswell, Charles Brasch and a memorable dinner with Denis Glover. And there is always the sense that although London, primarily, is where he has his existence, New Zealand is never far away, ready to catch him by surprise, be it the smell of damp and rotting wood that reminds him of a bush stream, or thatch that suggests a raupō roof.

Despite the persecution and discrimination Courage experienced as a gay man, he is entirely cognisant of his own worth and integrity, and prepared to make the case for the rightness of his orientation. It's clear that what he writes here in terms of relationships, physical, spiritual and emotional, is more often than not rehearsal for his novels, particularly *A Way of Love*. In that regard, this edition represents another important addition to the growing body of work that reveals just how much twentieth-century New Zealand arts and letters owes to the persecuted gay men within its midst. How truly buttoned down and bland we would be without, to name just a few, D'Arcy Cresswell's flamboyant resistance to the status quo, Frank Sargeson's genre-bending short fiction, Douglas Lilburn's experimental compositions or Charles Brasch's poetry and cultural philanthropy.

Thanks to Chris Brickell's careful editorial work, James Courage is revealed to be both a significant writer and a sensitive, brave and engaging New Zealander we should be proud to own and celebrate. The moment is right for him to be fully inducted into the literary mainstream.

Paul Millar
Professor of English
University of Canterbury

James (left) and companions in Auckland in 1920.

S20-578e, MS-0999/173, Hocken Collections

INTRODUCTION

Have eaten some cherries out of a paper bag, smoked a cigarette, written up this spasmodic journal and am now going to bed.[1]*

JAMES FRANCIS COURAGE was a prolific and idiosyncratic diarist. He began making notes about his life in 1920, at the age of 16, and carried on until 1963, the year of his death. His 14 private journals have attracted less attention than his novels, short stories and plays, but they have an immediacy that is not often found in his formal writings. Courage's 'spasmodic' diary entries captured the smallest details of lives and places: the fine-grained aspects of his daily routine in Christchurch, and later in England after he moved there in 1922, as well as the impact of global events. He wrote about his travels by ocean liner during the 1930s, the effects of World War II on the inhabitants of inner-city London where he was a fire warden for an apartment building, and his treatment for tuberculosis. The diaries also reveal what it was like to be homosexual in a world that was not always accepting, how Freudian psychotherapy changed Courage's view of himself and how publishers' decisions affected his often-tenuous self-esteem.

A sensitive soul, Courage was a wry observer with a knack of capturing an atmosphere. As David Hall points out in a review of the novel *The Call Home*, his writing was always 'alert, deeply felt and vividly expressed'.[2] This is obvious in the descriptions of his earliest years. James, the first of five children – he was followed by Constance ('Tiny'), John, Patricia and Sally – was born on 9 February 1903 on a farm station near the North Canterbury

---

* Endnotes for the Introduction begin on page 42.

A young James Courage, c. 1912. The original image, about two centimetres square, is cut out of a class photograph.

S19-601a, MS-0999/176, Hocken Collections

RIGHT: Classmates from Christ's College, late 1910s.

S20-569, MS-0999/180, Hocken Collections.

town of Amberley. 'Behind the homestead were the smooth-rounded tops of the downs, their slopes rich with silvery-yellow tussock grass,' he later wrote in 'A Present for K', an unpublished memoir.[3] 'I knew every gorse-bush, stone, tree, and almost every grass-blade of that country when I was a boy, you know. Particularly that strange scrubby hinterland behind the beach, which was then covered with thick rabbit-scratched turf and with manuka bushes flattened into streamers by the perpetual wind.'[4]

Courage applied his descriptive skills to his mother, Zoë, 'a handsome, brown-haired, merry-natured woman' with 'a real love of life, a vivacity, a gay heart'.[5] James's father, Frank, was a less amenable character. A 'tall, dry-looking man with a high-bridged Roman nose, a firm steel-lipped mouth', Frank suffered from 'what he called "a liver", and was frequently quite volcanic in anger'. Only occasionally did he loosen up, sing from his repertoire of songs and, 'as carefree as a lark', waltz Zoë around the living room.[6]

At first James and his younger sister Constance attended lessons in the nursery at home. They would stand on the fender of the fireplace and rest their chins on the mantelpiece, staring intently at pieces of cardboard with the alphabet written on them. Brother and sister were not initially good scholars, frequently bursting into tears and having to stand in the corner. Eventually their mother would release them from their torment and they would run out into the garden with a palpable sense of relief.[7] Soon the family home needed rebuilding and the siblings moved to Christchurch with Zoë. They attended Dunelm, C.L. Wiggins' preparatory school in Durham Street, and young James learned to love poetry.[8] In 1916 he was enrolled at Christ's College near the Botanic Gardens, boarded at Flowers House hostel over the road and enjoyed amateur dramatics. 'There is nothing so fascinating as acting on the stage, if one is really interested in it,' Courage wrote in his diary. 'After my success as Dick Bultitude in *Vice Versa* I got so many compliments it nearly turned my head.'[9] He took on female roles, too, including Clara Manners in *A Pair of Lunatics*, a short play about an evening ball in a psychiatric institution with 'two hundred dancers, and almost every one of them mad!'[10]

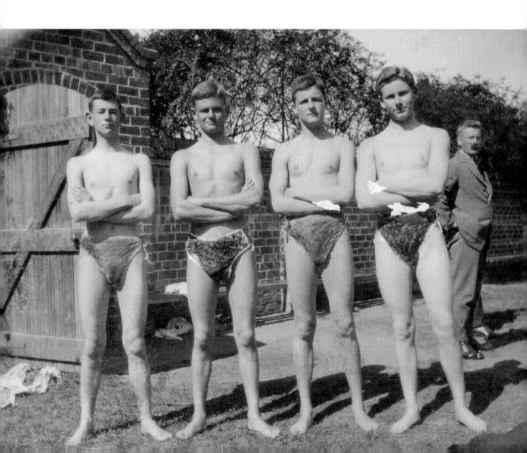

ABOVE: 'Our camp', James and his friends' tent site in Peel Forest.

S14-604f, MS-0999/186, Hocken Collections

RIGHT: A friend of Courage, probably Ronnie Peter, at Peel Forest, c. 1920.

S07-008n, MS-0999/117, Hocken Collections

From their early years until 1921, James and Constance spent holidays at Mt Somers with their grandmother, Ida Peache.[11] Each trip from Christchurch began on a southbound passenger train that stopped at a series of country towns; at Tinwald the travellers boarded an old carriage hitched to the back of a goods train. In 'The Promising Years', a second unpublished autobiographical manuscript, James wrote of arriving at Mt Somers: 'After a hot dusty day, in trains full of smuts, the sight of melting amethyst mountains against a greenish evening sky sent a grateful chill through my veins, a shiver which I felt mingle deliciously with the tremors of pleasure I was enjoying at the prospect of seeing my grandmother again and of hearing her silvery voice.'[12]

The children adored Ida, whom Constance described as hospitable, broad-minded and fond of young people.[13] At Mt Somers the young Courages settled themselves into a holiday routine. They walked, rode horses, fished for trout and watched the sun go down after dinner: 'a red-hot penny that seared the mountain-edge'.[14] One summer they went camping with friends in Peel Forest, some 50 kilometres away. This was a chance to escape the strictures of polite Canterbury society and experiment with new personae. James stood under a mataī tree dressed in a shawl, skirt and stockings, the ensemble held together at the back by a rosette. He hated having his photo taken, but this time a companion managed to persuade him. One friend, most likely Ronnie Peter, whom a relative later described as 'rather camp', posed self-importantly next to a large bonfire in the making.[15] Ronnie, who later moved to England, told Courage that the holiday at Peel Forest 'comes back to my mind as I write, happy days full of sunshine and laughter, how can I forget them?'[16]

James Courage dresses up in Peel Forest, c. 1920.

S20-578b, S20-578c, MS-0999/117, Hocken Collections

When James finished up at Christ's College in 1921, he talked with his father about what he might do next. Frank wanted his son to become a farmer but conceded there might be merit in 'the profession of letters'. It would make no man wealthy, of course, 'but if you have any talent you'd best cultivate it ... Your uncle went to Oxford, though nobody ever discovered what he did there. However, it has turned out some fine men in the past.'[17] In 1922 James set sail for England in the company of an aunt who was travelling there on holiday. He marvelled at life on board ship, 'at once so free and at once so confined, and for a long time the days resolved themselves into so many stretches of lying in a chair with my eyes fixed on the sea, a sea boundless, green, and chilly'. There was plenty of time to dream of Oxford. 'I dwelt on the word until, from being a mere two-syllabled charm, it opened, like one of those little tight Japanese flowers I had seen in toy shops, into blossoms, delicate fantasies of towers, bells, meadows, I knew not what.'[18]

Courage was excited to arrive in the 'Old Country' at last. London was a revelation, a place of personal freedom and liberty.[19] Its busy streets offered a real contrast to sparsely populated Christchurch and the sleepy New Zealand countryside:

> Can't you imagine the London streets in the dusk – full of lights and hurrying people and men in the gutters trying to sell you bananas or apples or little toys; and then, further in, the glowing theatres and the lighted signs of Piccadilly Circus – most ingenious some of them – and somebody flying past in an opera hat and just around the corner coming on a beggar, one side of his face a great red scar, drawing with coloured chalks on the pavement the illuminated words 'To Live'.[20]

Courage immediately fell in love with Oxford, where he gained admission to St John's College. No longer a young boy who stared with bewilderment at letters propped up on the mantelpiece, he became proficient at writing short stories and plays and soon published prose in the university journals *Oxford Outlook*, *Cherwell* and *Isis*. He had struggled socially at Christ's College, but the company at St John's turned out to be vastly more congenial. Courage thrilled at the dynamism and comradeship of Oxford:

Lighting a cigarette I watched from my second storey a sauntering procession at the junction of Ship St and the Turl, a crowd of leisurely young men on their way to attend lectures, to visit friends, to drink coffee, to amuse themselves. The wind at the corner blew out their gowns and ruffled their hair; they shouted and ran through the traffic: they laughed and walked arm-in-arm. They were the real Oxford, these my friends and contemporaries: they had no doubt of that.[21]

'I was happier than I had been at any time since my actual boyhood,' Courage wrote. He strolled to the rooms of his friend Leonard for lunch and chatted about Oxford, politics, tennis and life in New Zealand.[22] Archie was another friend, 'playing the piano; in rowing shorts; stealing my teapot; the way he said "Dinkums, Buddy." He was so easy to like.'[23] Emlyn Williams, a young bisexual Welshman who later became a successful playwright and actor, invited him to a rowdy twentieth birthday party with a bottle of liqueur and dancing on the tables to music from a gramophone.[24] When not studying or socialising, Courage wandered into the Ashmolean Museum to 'dream for hours' before the Greek statues.[25] He soon acquired a baby grand Bösendorfer piano, moved it into his Oxford flat and played it most days. That piano stayed with him his whole life.

In 1927 Courage graduated from Oxford with a Bachelor of Arts in English language and literature, and went to Greece for a holiday. His diary offers an account of new experiences, emotions and encounters on the tourist trail.[26]

One of the moments in my whole life I remember most brightly and when I seemed to live most intensely was on a certain evening in Athens. I stood alone in the Parthenon, looking through the columns east towards Lycabettus and Pentelikon, and from behind me the light of the setting sun turned the marble to an indescribable, glowing pink ... as I descended the Propylaeum I felt I had seen something I should never forget.[27]

Back in England, Courage gravitated towards London and breathed in its 'smoky air and smell of soot'.[28] Occasionally he was reminded of New Zealand: one autumn, 'I was walking through Cavendish Square when a smell of rich, rotten wood, wafted from heaven knows where, took me back in a flash to a bush-stream in the mountains of New Zealand. A damp, cool, primeval whiff.'[29] Courage spent many English summers in hotels or hired cottages in the Cornish town of St Ives, a quiet spot where he could write and admire the scenery. Waves broke 'gently on the rocks just below my bedroom balcony' and the smell of burning gorse on the hills 'brought back old New Zealand days!'[30]

Two further trips sent Courage away from England. He travelled to Argentina at the end of 1930 and an extensive account of the sea voyage is filled with his usual lively prose: 'Reach Vigo harbour about five, and sail up between purple hills to a most lovely and theatrical-looking city with the lamps just beginning to be lit ... Drink again – lager beer, iced – with small but hilarious party of ghastly people in smoking room.'[31] In November 1933, having been treated for tuberculosis at Mundesley Sanitorium in Norfolk, Courage set sail to New Zealand on the *Rangitata* to recuperate. 'Home again. A most extraordinary experience after eleven years. Like dream-walking.'[32] He spent time with his beloved grandmother, turned 31, and at Hanmer Springs had his first flight in an aeroplane.[33] Courage visited his sister Constance, now married, who lived on a farm near the small settlement of Goose Bay on the Canterbury coast south of Kaikōura.

His diaries say nothing of any erotic adventures back in New Zealand. Family lore has it that he told his mother about his attraction to men, she told Frank and then 'all hell broke loose'.[34] In April 1935 Courage returned to England via Sydney on the *Oronsay*, and was reassuringly greeted on a cold June day by 'oaks still with bronze leaves, the fields yellow with buttercups and the hawthorn still white'.[35] He would never return to the land of his birth.

● ● ●

JAMES COURAGE WAS a prolific writer. His diaries contain some 400,000 words, of which 90,000 are reproduced in this edition. Most of the early entries are included here, except some long transcriptions of other authors' writing – pieces of novels and poetry – which Courage often copied into his own diaries. I have left out some short entries that break up the flow of larger themes, but the largest omission involves most of the two reams of paper, inscribed on both sides, that constitute the two parts of 'Diary of a Neurotic'. Here Courage recorded, in 1000 pages of granular and often repetitive detail, months of psychotherapy carried out between 1960 and 1962. I include a small representative selection of this material.

Courage's diaries sit in the Hocken Collections in Dunedin alongside his two other pieces of autobiographical writing. 'The Promising Years' dates from 1930, an account of school and home life and time spent at Oxford that draws its inspiration from Marcel Proust's seven-volume novel *À la recherche du temps perdu*.[36] 'A Present for K', from 1941, describes Courage's very early years and evokes the memory of a well-known New Zealand writer: 'I have today been working on the book about my own childhood in N.Z. Like Katherine Mansfield, whom I idolize, I want to make my "undiscovered country leap into the eyes of the Old World".'[37] 'A Present for K' was never submitted for publication, but Courage tried hard to find a home for 'The Promising Years'. Poet T.S. Eliot, who worked at Faber, could see the Proustian influences – and the general appeal – but in the end the firm turned down the manuscript.[38]

Although Courage found no takers for his memoirs, some of his 34 short stories attracted publisher interest, along with a few poems.[39] Of his several plays, *Private History* (1938), an exploration of romantic friendship and homosexuality in an English boys' boarding school, was performed in London and is easily the most accomplished. Courage had eight novels published. Many of these explore the frailties of human character and draw their inspiration from Courage's relatives and friends. Five are set in Canterbury: *The Fifth Child* (1948), *Desire Without Content* (1950), *Fires in the Distance* (1952), *The Young Have Secrets* (1954) and *The Call Home* (1956). They focus on tense dynamics between son and mother, son and father, or husbands and wives, and several rest upon a psychoanalytic framework.[40] As Elizabeth Caffin puts it, '[T]he social setting is fixed and unquestioned, the context is always the family and the tensions within that family are so fixed and unvarying that the novels easily mingle in the mind.'[41] The remaining three novels – *One House* (1933), *A Way of Love* (1959) and *The Visit to Penmorten* (1961) – are set in England: the first in rural Wiltshire, the second in London and the third in Cornwall. *The Young Have Secrets, The Fifth Child* and *A Way of Love*, the latter the first published gay novel written by a New Zealander, were reprinted.[42]

Courage's writing career depended on contributions from his family. Frank granted him a modest allowance that got him started in England and sent money at frequent intervals over the years. An aunt died about 1933 and left Courage a considerable sum.[43] By the end of the 1930s he felt he had a moral obligation to earn an income: 'I fully admit that, as a *rentier*, living almost wholly on unearned income, I am a sinner.'[44] He began as a reliever in Wilson's Bookshop in Hampstead, and soon a more permanent position became available.[45] He enjoyed the work at first.[46] Each day he did a long stint in the shop, came home, had dinner, slept for an hour and started writing.[47] Around this time Courage embraced socialism: 'I must seek in my writing to show the coming (not without humour, I hope) of a more equitable and fairer state of human society.'[48] The new philosophy caused some tension with his fervently conservative parents, who donated money to the National Party and decried Labour's 'socialism' and 'communism'.[49] His beloved grandmother was no more sympathetic, telling Courage in a letter that 'Jack has all the say and his master no hold' in Labour's New Zealand during the 1940s.[50]

A writing career involved more than philosophy and income support. As any author knows, the process has its own inherent pressures. Courage once told a journalist he found the process of writing 'rather more perspiration than inspiration'.[51] He could spend a considerable amount of time and 'much labour' crafting only two sentences, beginning 'all very cold at first, but gradually warming up to creation-heat'.[52] Often he found the process stressful and emotionally draining. 'I am so often in despair, full of apprehension and angst, and physically "crook" (good old NZ term) into the bargain. I often curse the day I ever decided to write a word,' he told fellow fiction writer and New Zealander Frank Sargeson in 1954.[53] It was not always easy to get back into the groove when writing stalled or publishers turned down a manuscript. In 1932 Courage responded to Faber's rejection of 'The Promising Years' with evident irritation. 'They say the MS "interested" them, but they had decided, after "careful consideration" not to make an offer for it. Publishers are queer cattle and no mistake. Surely if it "interested" *them*, it would interest other people too?'[54] The following year, after a fallow period, Courage 'started working on the new book (about the boy and his grandmother) and crawled back on to some self-esteem like a wet fly on to solid ground'.[55] His happiness was short-lived. This manuscript, 'Some Other Being', was also rejected for publication and has since disappeared.[56] 'Morning Sky', another iteration of the boy and grandmother theme written about 1940, is also unpublished but the typescript survives.[57]

Things looked up after the war. Courage contemplated his progress in 1954, by which point he had five books in print:

> *Although I'd always meant to be a writer I didn't really* get down *to writing until 1947 (when I was 44) … When I did begin, however, with* The Fifth Child, *one result of this long delay was that I saw my given subjects with a maturer eye than I would have had I published books (dealing with the same material) in my twenties (as would most intended writers). The subjects, insofar as they were based on early autobiography, had by that time also gained a remoteness that made it easier for me to discard inessentials in them. Furthermore, they'd accumulated a nice varnish or patina with time: most of the bitterness, for instance, was painted over with a kind of compassion – or at least a better understanding.*[58]

In the words of friend and poet Charles Brasch, whom Courage met in London in 1936, 'It was with the ending of the war, those more than six years of darkness, privation and fear, that Courage at last found himself as a writer, when he was in his early forties.'[59] Although Courage had no manuscripts accepted for publication during the war, his diaries continued to reveal the acuity of his perception. The sights, sounds and emotions associated with life on the home front formed the focus of many entries. Omens of terror became poetic: 'All the London barrage-balloons gleaming in the light of a clear September evening, with a pale half-moon behind them. The whole sky studded with silver buttons: a curious and even beautiful sight if it were not so suggestive of horror and menace to come. Even the moon, regarding the scene from the south-west, seemed to half-shut a pale and sinister eye-lid.'[60]

Courage's chronicles of wartime offer powerful insights into the seemingly endless lockdown Londoners endured. He took responsibility for switching off the lift in his Belsize Park apartment building during an air raid and helped usher other residents, groggy and in their nightwear, to the basement shelter during the 'dreadful nights ... made hideous with bombs and fires'.[61] His diaries tell of old men in pyjamas, and young married couples carrying out the rituals of their intimate lives in the semi-public gloom of the cellar. 'As for one's social life, it simply ceases to exist under these conditions of animal apprehension,' Courage wrote in 1940. 'One reverts to a kind of feral individualism: a beast in the jungle of a stone city.' By 1944 he and his acquaintances were exhausted. 'We all huddled into a cupboard under the stairs which smelled of mint and boot-polish. All-clear half an hour later. But the bomb stories had meanwhile lost their flavour: we spoke of other things.'[62]

The war took the lives of two of Courage's lovers. The first, Chris Huth, was a sailor whom he met in 1938. 'Blue eyes, shining black hair, bronzed skin ... Strange it is, the intense sense of privilege I have in loving anyone so personable.'[63] Courage sent Chris out to buy beer one winter's day in 1941 and watched through his window as the young man returned, 'his arms full of bottles, his sailor's cap on the back of his head, a real nautical roll in his walk – a Chris I'd never seen before: a real lad of the Lower Deck'.[64] The pair were separated some months later when Chris went away on active service and in February 1943 a devastating note arrived: Chris had died on active service. 'I shall remember this day all my life for the sad news it brought me,' Courage wrote in his diary:

For about an hour I hardly felt the shock. I even played the piano and read. Then when Mrs Timmons (who remembered Chris) arrived to cook my dinner I told her the news. Directly she said 'Oh, how terrible', the tears rushed into my eyes and I wept. Later in the evening I rang up Joan V. who knew Chris well. She told me that he died of wounds 'due to shell or bomb blast' on Dec. 11th last (two months ago) somewhere in the Mediterranean. The announcement had been in the papers but I had not seen it. Chris was 27.[65]

'Have thought of Chris every hour – almost every minute. I find it difficult to believe that he is dead,' Courage wrote a few days later.[66]

Later that year Ivan Alderson, a corporal who worked in the Air Ministry, committed suicide. 'The evidence given at the inquest and printed in the papers was to the effect that he was unhappy owing to the war and its enforced interruption of the true bent of his life, which was creation, not destruction (he had been the youngest qualified landscape gardener in England).'[67] Courage suspected Alderson's melancholy – and his *'inward nature'* – had also contributed to his death. 'Ivan has killed himself – my boy, my child, my love – he was 23. It happened on Friday night, two days ago; I knew only this evening. He must have died in a mental anguish I cannot contemplate. A difficult time. I cannot write about it.'[68]

• • •

WHEN JAMES COURAGE DESCRIBED his first voyage to England as 'at once so free and at once so confined', he might just as easily have been describing his own sexuality. His feelings about his 'homosexual temperament' were like two tectonic plates driving against one another: a deep sense of shame constantly pushed up against something akin to pride, warping and twisting it.[69] This is hardly surprising: public opinion on homosexuality in the first part of the twentieth century vacillated between silence, doctors' assumptions about nervous irregularities, and outright public hostility.[70] Courage experienced all of these. 'When an iconoclast like Wyndham Lewis dissects homosexuality he makes me feel an utter worm,'

Courage wrote in 1927.[71] At the same time he spoke out on behalf of the 'male invert', the man with an abiding desire for his own sex: 'All my life I shall fight against the unwritten, senseless, cruel law that brands sexual inverts as degenerates and beasts ... Sexual intercourse between males – *where both are inverts* – has every scrap of right to be considered as normal as that between men and women.'[72]

Courage's sentiments carried down the decades. In 1940 he wrote that sexuality is 'an animality shared by every human being' and ought not be considered sinful. The following year he attempted a novel, apparently untitled and never published, 'which shall accept homosexuality as a natural phenomenon like any other (which to me it is)'.[73] He drew inspiration from other authors, including Austrian philosopher Otto Weininger, who believed all people were inherently bisexual; the anonymous 'Anomaly', who described the complex psychology of the invert; and Greek poet Sappho, whose words on love between women were already legendary.[74] One evening Courage picked up a book 'containing fragments of Sappho' and 'was so profoundly stirred that I spent two hours writing an excessively erotic poem addressed to an unknown youth'.[75]

Mid-twentieth-century homosexual life was a matter of geography as well as philosophy, psychology and literature. Having a place of one's own, as Courage did, was a boon for those who wanted somewhere safe to take other men for sex and companionship. A private studio room or flat provided a refuge from social opprobrium and police harassment.[76] Courage took many lovers home over the years, and mentioned them in his diaries: Chris, Ivan, Dick, Ernest, Frank, Harry, Graham, Edward, Nigel, Stuart, men referred to only as A., K., M. and R., and various sailors whose names he did not record. In 1931 he 'completely lost [his] heart' to one young seaman: 'we became lovers. He was charming,' but left town the next day.[77] Courage moved apartments every few years, but he mostly lived in Hampstead or Belsize Park. These were not the parts of London most popular with homosexual men during the middle of the twentieth century, but they offered opportunities of their own.[78] Bedsitterland, as historian Matt Cook calls the inner-city London districts filled with apartments, gave rise to friendships, sex and socialising.[79] In 1931 Courage hosted a young chap by the name of Ernest, who stayed with him: 'An extraordinary time – half-dream, half nightmare. I lived his life – we ate and drank more than was good for us, went to the theatres and cinemas in the evenings, visited Madame Tussauds. His easiness of taking life as it comes, his complete lack of spiritual questioning, his physical strength – all have a terrible, heart-aching attraction for me.'[80]

In January 1930 Courage met Frank Fleet on board the Cornish Riviera Express train while travelling between London and St Ives and the chance encounter 'developed into the most passionate love-affair I've ever had'.[81] Fleet, whom Courage called 'Paco', was 'an athlete, and handsome; one of the sweetest creatures I've ever known, with something so touchingly lonely and child-like in him that it makes tears of gentleness start to the eyes'.[82] The men lived together in London for two months, a time Courage described as 'the happiest period of my life'.[83] Soon afterwards Fleet returned to Argentina, where Courage travelled to visit him in December. The affair inspired an unpublished novel titled 'A Traveller Came By', set partly in London and partly in Buenos Aires, in which Courage fashioned himself as Julia Somers, a pale-skinned piano player, and Fleet as an ambitious grain trader by the name of Roy Trevean.[84] These characters' early passion, like that of Courage and Fleet, dissipated after they travelled from England to Argentina. Fleet later married, but he and Courage remained friends and corresponded for 30 years.

Courage also stayed in touch with Fleet's friend Billy Thompson.[85] An openly homosexual man, Thompson provided invaluable support to Fleet who, by his own admission, had not entirely renounced his 'queer ways'.[86] Thompson later wrote to Courage about his own comfortable existence in Buenos Aires: 'I've been able to sort out my life with an intelligent Mother & afterwards my bro-in-law (100% normal man) brought along and entertained my queer friends.'[87] Courage appreciated the sentiment, although he preferred the terms 'invert', 'homosexual' – and even the obscure 'Uranian' – to 'queer', which he regarded as 'derogatory'.[88] He usually reserved 'queer' for disparaging other members of his 'fraternity': 'Heaven preserve me from the mercies of the queer world, particularly the younger element,' he told Brasch in 1958. 'They're still in the jungle – predatory, utterly amoral, frenziedly competitive ... What a crew.'[89]

A relationship with Stuart Hurrell, who worked in the insurance industry and took part in 'militant trade union activities', offered sustained support during the last decade of Courage's life.[90] The men met during the mid-1950s and quickly grew close, although they never actually lived together. Courage wrote that the pair understood one another 'very well', and Hurrell, who was about 12 years younger than Courage, cared for him in times of adversity.[91] The 'faithful' Hurrell picked up Courage from hospital appointments and, when he had a heart attack in June 1963, helped out on a daily basis.[92] Others noticed his efforts. 'As soon as you are able to convalesce at home I shall be round during the day (when Stuart can't manage) to do what I can,' wrote one friend.[93] 'I will call in as often as I can to help with chores and things, at least until Stuart is free in the evenings to keep you company.'[94]

'I'm fonder of S. than of anyone,' Courage wrote in his diary.[95] The two developed a comforting, familiar routine. 'S. came to see me last night, as he does every Friday ("our evening"). We drank whiskey and soda, our customary consolation and aphrodisiac.'[96]

We smoked cigarettes in bed afterwards. 'I wonder what lovers used before cigarettes were invented,' S. remarked.

'They had their little lamps – Psyche and Eros – to reveal themselves in the dark.'

'H'm, not very satisfactory,' said S., not much given to poetic overtones. 'Messy too.' He smoked his cigarette. 'You know, this ought to be the answer – lying here in peace.'

'Why aren't you always like this?', I asked later. 'I mean why don't you want sex more often?'

'All you think of is my body', he mocked.

'Nothing of the sort, you exasperating bastard.'[97]

Courage (right) and two friends, one of whom is probably Billy Thompson, at Mar del Plata, an Argentinian resort some 400 kilometres from Buenos Aires, in 1931.

S19-601c, MS-0999/179, Hocken Collections

Courage knew Hurrell had a life of his own too. This became doubly clear when he saw him hanging out with 'a crowd of second-rate youths I haven't much time for' in a nearby street. 'Told myself that S. was *with* them but not *of* them and that only I know his mind and body.' Never mind. 'Let him stay as he is, with mediocre chums for the weekend at the pub. I am not married to him.'[98] In the end, though, Hurrell came to have the same standing as Courage's siblings: along with Constance and John Courage, he received the sum of £500 in James's will. Courage named his London-based sister Patricia as executor and the recipient of his household effects and put Frank Fleet down for £100.[99]

Courage took other lovers and had quite a few friends, many of whom moved in queer and artistic circles. Playwright Emlyn Williams stayed in touch, while a number of New Zealand literary men spent time with Courage in London. They included historian, critic and biographer Eric McCormick, writer Bill Pearson, poet D'Arcy Cresswell and artist Rodney Kennedy as well as Sargeson and Brasch.[100] When Courage and Cresswell first met, the latter suggested they should 'pick up a sailor or guardsman and spend the night in mutual fornication *à trois*'.[101] A bemused Courage declined the offer and for some years he was not sure he 'even liked' Cresswell, a 'curious man'. Eventually he decided he probably did.[102] He was especially close to Brasch, who said of Courage, 'he is nearer to me than anyone in London'.[103] Brasch published some of Courage's stories in the literary magazine *Landfall*, of which he was the founding editor, and he relayed snippets of good news from New Zealand. 'Someone was asking this week why you had not published a book of stories. I think it was a student asking me, and he went on to say that one of the English lecturers at Otago considered your "After the Earthquake" *the* best N.Z. story.'[104]

Not all of Courage's close friends were homosexual men. He enjoyed a supportive friendship with poet Basil Dowling and his wife Margaret; he stayed with them for a while after his heart attack.[105] Other close female friends included Barbara Cooper, a secretary at *London Magazine*, and her sister Lettice Cooper, a novelist and one-time reviewer of Courage's work who shared his interest in psychoanalysis.[106] Courage also forged a close bond with his long-term housekeeper, Mrs Timmons, who comforted him after the death of his sailor lover Chris. Margaret Bassett, another intimate female friend, lived nearby and provided Courage with comfort and reassurance. He regarded her as his 'foster-mother'.[107] Very occasionally he even experienced something akin to a twinge of erotic feeling for her. '"You've got a big son of your own," I said teasingly when I kissed her a foster-son's "good night" on the cheek. The soft skin made me think I was kissing my mother – yet there was a faint stirring of sexual feeling also, unless I deceive myself.'[108] In a perceptive discussion of Courage's friendships with women, Christopher Burke writes: 'Even while [he] maintained an implacable and largely unceasing sexual attraction for men, some of his interactions with women record a sexual undercurrent that would be unthinkable in most contemporary accounts of gay experience today.'[109]

• • •

JAMES COURAGE'S WRITING about homosexuality marks him out among his New Zealand contemporaries. Sargeson's and Pearson's discussions of the topic were heavily coded and McCormick reflected on his own sexuality in his diaries but not his published work.[110] Cresswell wrote openly but misogynistically about homoeroticism during the 1930s, and his two volumes of memoir were packed with idiosyncratic interpretations of ancient Greece and Rome,[111] but Courage's work had greater public appeal and attracted much more attention.

His play *Private History* ran for a season at the Gate Theatre Club in London's Villiers Street and drew considerable acclaim.[112] It is the tale of Geoffrey Longman, a talented athlete who has a crush on a younger student called Gordon Danvers. The headmaster at Bradbourn School compares Longman to Otley, a boy earlier expelled for 'seducing' younger lads, and tries to get rid of Longman as well. Longman eventually leaves the school after his mother visits, declares her son's feelings for other boys 'disgusting' and takes him home with her. Eventually Longman falls in love with another

Students from the fictional Bradbourn School in Courage's play, *Private History*, staged at the Gate in 1938. This is one of several stage shots taken on the set by society photographer Angus McBean. *S19-601f, MS-0999/005, Hocken Collections*

man named Kit Brewster and they live together in cosy domesticity near the Cornish town of Falmouth. Staff at Bradbourn suggest Longman might have avoided becoming homosexual if only he had spent more time with girls during the holidays, and he himself wonders whether his 'nature' might otherwise 'have turned out differently'. This reflects Sigmund Freud's presumption that humans are born bisexual and become heterosexual only if they follow a successful process of socialisation.[113] Such a narrative sat awkwardly with Courage's own views during the 1930s. He regarded same-sex attraction as inborn and felt his play's discussion of 'induced homosexuality' was 'just a little "faked" in the interests of common opinion – not quite true to itself'.[114]

There is no doubt, however, that Courage judged 'common opinion' adroitly. 'The play is, for the Gate, a smash-hit,' he wrote in his diary. 'Quite sympathetic notices from all the papers, and a really excellent one from *The Times*. I feel, after all my anxiety, that it is all too good to be quite true.'[115] Reviewers greeted the performance enthusiastically, describing it as 'a powerful play extremely well-acted'. It struck them as 'very convincing' with a 'well-constructed plot' and 'poignantly truthful' characterisation, especially the 'shy affection and heartsick misery of Longman'.[116]

A few of Courage's novels also have queer characters, some of them coded and others more overt.[117] Mark, a lighthouse keeper in *The Young Have Secrets*, knows he will never marry, is suspicious of sex and feels himself 'betrothed to iconoclasm, curiosity and the damnation of my too-human nature'.[118] In *Fires in the Distance*, 25-year-old 'tomboy' Kathy is ambivalent about relationships with men and enjoys physical work on the family station in Canterbury; she is 'a bit mannish' but 'feminine enough underneath'.[119] Her 19-year-old brother Leo, inspired by Courage's friend Ronnie Peter, desires other men. His mother describes him as 'unnatural' and Kathy says he is 'vainer than a girl'.[120] Peter Fitzgerald in *The Call Home* still holds a candle for Norman, the book's protagonist, who has embraced a heterosexual life after his youthful boarding school romance with Peter.[121] *The Visit to Penmorten* tells of Gregory and Morgan who live together and bicker as many couples do: 'Stop it, Morgan. Behave yourself … Try not to act like a spoilt child for once.'[122]

Courage also engaged in gender-swapping. He intended Effie in *Desire Without Content* and Louise in *The Call Home*, both central characters, as stand-ins for men he knew in real life.[123] A letter to a friend hinted at the subterfuge:

My dear lost boy,

What *a surprise your sweet letter gave me. Such memories! Ah, those days at Morere Springs – wherever they may be – and you with your big manly form. Of course I loved every moment of it, but Mother (hush) must never know. I've hardly recovered yet. Read my other book,* Desire without Content, *and find out what it really is to be a woman. Yes, my sweet, I mean it. You men know nothing of us girls.*

Darling, do send me your poem. It might at least explain – though I doubt it – what on earth your letter was all about. I can hardly wait.

Meanwhile, let us keep our little secret, shall we? Nobody must know that you're just another girl, disguised. But how clever of you to choose such an unassuming name as Jim Harris: it puts everyone off the scent

including your bewildered
J.C.[124]

A Way of Love, published by Jonathan Cape in 1959, was Courage's queer tour de force. The book told of a love affair between London architect Bruce and a much younger man, Philip. A story of the lives of men 'of a certain kind', the novel described conversations and parties, rituals and expectations among those who lived 'in more or less full self-acceptance of their own natures as members of what I may call without exaggeration our immense league'.[125] Courage claimed *A Way of Love* 'was in me and had to come out', but his diaries reveal the compromises involved in getting it in print.[126] 'Outside prejudices and assumed disapproval kept getting in the way,' he said of the 19 months the book took to write, and he felt the need to balance competing perceptions that homosexuality was both 'a valid human theme' and 'a clinical phenomenon'.[127] He had originally intended Bruce as 'something of a hedonist in private life, a lover of youth in the fullest and most erotic sense', but the character turned out to be rather more sedate and discreet.[128] Courage told Sargeson he had written 'something near what I set out to write – a serious novel about homosexuality, neither jeering nor safely satirical in tone, but concerned in some degree with the heart and its deeper emotions', but he admitted to Brasch that the final version of the novel was 'not bold enough'.[129] The book ultimately ends in sadness: the relationship breaks apart as Philip leaves Bruce to marry.

All compromises aside, *A Way of Love* was a landmark novel for a New Zealand author and an exceedingly rare bird in the English context.[130]

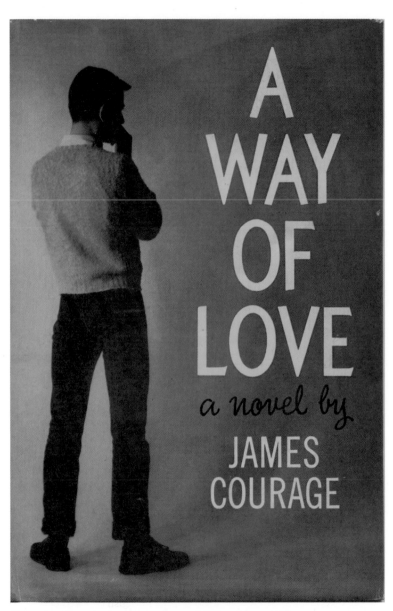

The jacket from the American edition of *A Way of Love*, 1959. Chris Brickell collection

Literary scholar Martin Dines describes it as the only novel published in England during the 1950s 'to be fully centred on a homosexual affair'.[131] Many readers adored *A Way of Love* and wrote to Courage to say so.

> *It's difficult to express appreciation of such a fine work, indeed almost impossible ... I like everything about this book ... I like the brevity of your descriptions, terse and vivid, conveying exactly what is required ... and the admirable treatment, sensitively handled with tender intimacy. It's so human. You have given life and compassion to a story which could have become a bawdy sensational theme ... Each time of reading only convinces me more of your talents as a most skilled and accomplished writer.*[132]

Conservative-minded cultural critics offered a less generous interpretation. M.K. Joseph, a poet and senior lecturer at Auckland University, wrote a hateful review for *Landfall*. Brasch was horrified. He had presumed Joseph to be a 'cool, judicious man', but the academic's conservative Catholicism quickly bubbled to the surface.[133] '[H]omosexual relations ... may be serious, destructive or pathetic: but any attempt to make them the subject of exalted lyricism must almost inevitably collapse into disgust or derision or (even worse) banality,' Joseph wrote. '*A Way of Love* is a quietly ruthless exposure of the pretensions of homosexuality, and a sad book, despite its appearance of an urbane and sensual exterior.'[134] A gay critic later described the review as 'a piece of pious prejudice'.[135] In 1961 a New Zealand 'interdepartmental committee' banned *A Way of Love* on the grounds of indecency. The committee also moved against Gore Vidal's openly homosexual book *The City and the Pillar*, and Jack Kerouac's Buddhist-hippy classic *The Dharma Bums*.[136] Courage's diary includes a quixotic note about it all:

> *I feel nervous about the ban today, but not at the moment depressed by it. Even if there were a Court case in N.Z. I wouldn't be there. But slight paranoid feelings do arise apropos of the N.Z. background, even so. A bit mephitic, though only what I'd expect; 'that dreadful book,' and so on. All the same I regret that it wasn't much more 'dreadful'. It was too timid by far, a mouse of a novel.*[137]

• • •

FOR MUCH OF HIS LIFE Courage struggled with his mental health. There were several nervous breakdowns, the first at the age of 14 after his 19-year-old uncle Robert made sexual advances to him in a cave. James felt sure he would face punishment – and possibly prison – if he told anybody what had happened.[138] Robert later developed schizophrenia and spent his final years at Ashburn Hall, a private psychiatric hospital in Dunedin.[139] (He inspired two literary characters: Mark in *The Young Have Secrets* and, in *Desire Without Content*, Effie's husband Lewis, who drowns the couple's baby in a fit of religious mania.[140]) At Oxford, Courage's own occasional depressive episodes marred an otherwise positive experience. Another breakdown came in 1950 when a combination of long days at the bookshop and a heavy writing schedule in the evenings became overwhelming.[141] Courage told his composer friend Douglas Lilburn that he 'collapsed into a nightmare' and was in and out of Napsbury Mental Hospital, north of London, 'hardly knowing what I was doing'.[142] In 1957 he spent more time in a psychiatric clinic.[143] There is no doubt Courage's writing-induced stress made matters worse: he felt his mental state was to some degree a reflection of his 'artistic gift'.[144] He described his other problems as 'depression, much anxiety, homosexual guilt, tension, stomach pains, inadequacy feelings'.[145] As he had written in 1929, 'What an extraordinary shuttle-cock is this thing called self-esteem!'[146]

Few medical treatments for depression and anxiety were available during the 1950s. Courage's physicians wrote out prescriptions for a supply of 'blue bombers': tablets of sodium amytal, a barbiturate derivative with sedating properties, but talking therapy was Courage's main form of treatment. In 1950 he went to psychiatrist Dr Ellis Stungo in Harley Street and then to 'F.B.' at Notting Hill Gate.[147] Seven years later he began to see Dr Edward Larkin, a Freudian analyst from Australia, three times a week. Larkin judged him 'a bit dotty' and 'slightly schizoid' but so intelligent as to possess 'a degree of near-genius'.[148] The sessions with Larkin continued for the rest of Courage's life.[149]

Courage had been interested in Freud's work since about 1930, but two decades later he became much more receptive to it. Freudian therapists encouraged patients to probe their early childhood memories and reinterpret their adult lives as the product of past dynamics. They suggested that sexual troubles were rooted in childhood and formed the basis of much adult neurosis. Courage's therapists helped him to fashion a suitable narrative.[150] In 'A Present for K', he presented his mother in a positive light and his father as moderately flawed, but years later his analysts led him to reimagine both parents as deeply malign. In therapy he claimed that Zoë abandoned him by handing him over to a nanny, and that Frank was a hostile, domineering tyrant. His mother's rejection 'castrated' him, Larkin said, and as a result Courage 'never developed the aggression, the genital drive' he ought to have had. 'It was all inhibited, resulting in a failure of development – a fixation – a regression.'[151] Frank Courage reminded young James of his 'failure' as a man when he eschewed farming in favour of writing. 'He simply regarded me as no good, ineffective, a sissy – no proper son for him to have engendered.'[152] Apparently the cause of Courage's homosexuality lay in these family troubles. Such a version of events spoke to ideas he was familiar with, if unconvinced by, when he wrote *Private History*.

A series of letters from his parents tell of ongoing family dynamics. Frank lived until 1955 and Zoë until 1967, and they wrote to their son while he was in therapy. Frank's letters were surprisingly warm and informal in tone, expressing concern about James's 'mental illness' and offering to pay the cost of a private 'nursing home'. 'Remember you have got me behind you as far as finance goes,' he wrote, and also suggested taking 'passage to N.Z. for a trip and see us all'.[153] Frank sent considerable sums of money through the early 1950s – hundreds of pounds in each instalment. His letters also told of his lambs, farm life and his own faltering health. One he closed with a friendly exhortation to 'keep your pecker up!' and another with 'your affectionate father'.[154] James felt awkward about these exchanges:

> Wrote to my father. I find it so difficult to be natural towards him, even writing at a distance of 12,000 miles: he is still the awful parent of my childhood, with a pipe, an explosive temper and a general attitude towards me in particular of 'you'll never be a man, or a success'. And now he writes of himself – 'I am pretty feeble. I get up at midday and walk about round the house, in the sun in the early afternoon … But at 87 one must expect these troubles.'[155]

Courage's correspondence with his mother was even more fraught. Many of Zoë's letters convey care and antagonism in equal measure. On the one hand, she worried about her son, whom she called 'Bim', and told him about her own 'long years of battling with nerves'. The solution to his mental state lay in changing his 'outlook on life and to make yourself take a calmer view of your illness'.[156] She knew, however, that James blamed her and Frank for his state of mind, which made her 'miserable and unhappy'.[157] As she wrote defensively, 'My children have always come first in my life as you very well know.'[158] James's long silences annoyed her. When he stopped replying to her letters she admonished him for 'being a great big silly' and then ramped up the pressure: 'Are you going to write to me again or are you still determined to break with me altogether and it's of your own making you know and I feel no guilt about the matter.' Zoë laid down an ultimatum. 'Please get over your sulks soon Bim and write to me. If you don't this will be the last letter you get from me my son.'[159]

In therapy, Larkin spent hours talking about Courage's parents but showed no interest in changing the direction of his patient's sexuality. Instead he attempted to convince him to understand and then accept it. This was not unusual among analysts during the 1950s; some homosexual men reported the same thing in New Zealand.[160] But Courage was not so sure. As he had done for years, he constantly vacillated between voicing self-acceptance, confessing shame, and harbouring a sneaky feeling that others, including Larkin, were judging him. Sometimes he defended his right to sexual pleasure and denounced social hypocrisies, but he also found it difficult to believe that Larkin was content to leave him to his desires.

Courage eased up on himself near the end of his life. His last two diaries acknowledge that readers enjoyed his novels and he began to obtain some validation from his fans' praise. In early 1962 he received a letter from an admirer whose friends had asked to borrow *A Way of Love*. 'The reaction in *every* case was most favourable.'[161] Three months later, at a dinner party, another guest thought the same book 'very fine, yet he's a married man of presumed normal sexuality (4 children) … I never get over the shock of surprise.'[162] Right at the end of the last diary, Courage wrote: 'Dr L. appears to think I'm improving, if only because I have (with him) less guilt about the homosexuality.' The final diary entry, written three days later, also hints that Courage made peace with his mental state: 'At least I think I can see where I'm going, in a blinkered sort of fashion. No masochism.'[163]

Even though Courage's psychological anxieties began to ease, other health problems loomed. His heart attack in mid-1963 was the start of the end: his 'rebellious heart' sent him to hospital again in August and he suffered a further, fatal cardiac arrest at home on 5 October.[164] His obituary in Wellington's *Evening Post* read: 'The death in London recently of the New Zealand author and playwright James Courage, aged 60, was greatly regretted by his countless friends and acquaintances, among them London-domiciled fellow-countrymen.'[165] His relatives re-established the tie to Courage's homeland: in accordance with his wishes they arranged for the return of his ashes and scattered them at the mouth of the Waipara River near Amberley.

• • •

MANY YEARS BEFORE he died, Courage pondered his diaries' future. In 1938 he supposed his private writings would be of little interest to other readers: they were surely 'too gauche, too complaining, too sexually unorthodox'.[166] Towards the end of his life he was not so sure. Courage learned that an acquaintance had destroyed the diaries and letters of a deceased friend, D., but this seemed wrong to him: 'I thought here of this journal of mine, which must one day be destroyed in similar fashion (perhaps by S.). Well, all this is as it should be, I suppose, though part of my mind revolts at the necessity for covering up the evidence of a man's homosexuality – or indeed his heterosexuality, come to that. Such a necessity simply indicates the neurosis of our repressive civilisation.'[167]

We are lucky that Courage did not have his diaries destroyed, although his sister Patricia imposed a 30-year embargo when she sent them to the

Hocken Library in 1975. In 2005, when that expired, I read some of them. I marvelled at the distinctive writing and evocative descriptions, and gazed with fascination at the sketch in the front of the second diary: a line drawing, deftly executed by a friend, showing the pensive young Courage with eyes downcast. He was shy – one acquaintance described his 'air of isolation and loneliness' – but carefully attuned to social comings and goings.[168] 'He was,' wrote Brasch, 'a good friend and excellent company, with an acute sense of humour, a lively witty talker about books, theatre, music, people and their foibles – good talk often sent him into bursts of delighted laughter; he had a novelist's interest in everything that was going on in the world.'[169] His beautifully articulated diaries encourage readers to explore the complex connections between the lives we lead and the stories we tell.[170]

Chris Brickell

EDITORIAL NOTE

I have made minimal corrections to James Courage's diary text. Most of his spelling was free of errors, although I have corrected the names of a few people and places. I have also standardised punctuation and line spacing throughout. Courage was inconsistent in his use of italics, underlining and speech marks. Publication titles, musical works and ships' names are now italicised; single quote marks are the norm. In a few places readers will notice words with a strikethrough: these represent text that Courage had crossed out but which remains legible. My own annotations are included as footnotes.

NOTES

1. James Courage (hereafter JC), Diary, 29 May 1937. The diaries are all held in the Hocken Collections in Dunedin (HC), under reference number ARC-0384 and individual folder numbers MS-0999/078 to MS-0999/091.

2. David Hall, 'Major Novelist', *NZ Listener*, 12 October 1956, 12. For an especially evocative description of melting snow, for instance, see JC, *The Call Home*, London: Jonathan Cape, 1956, 198.

3. JC, 'A Present for K', unpublished manuscript, MS-0999/069, HC, 4; JC, Diary, 21 April 1941.

4. JC to Charles Brasch, 15 July 1953, MS-0996-003/042, HC.

5. JC, 'Present for K', 12.

6. Ibid., 10, 11.

7. Ibid., 76–77.

8. John Lee, '"A Private History": Towards a biography of James Courage, expatriate New Zealand writer', MA thesis, Victoria University of Wellington, 2001, 23.

9. JC, Diary, 28 July 1920.

10. www.mtpocketstheatre.com/uploads/2/9/4/6/29463083/a_pair_of_lunatics.pdf, 2.

11. Constance Gray, *Quiet with the Hills: The life of Alfred Edward Peache of Mount Somers*, Christchurch: Pegasus Press, 1970, 209.

12. JC, 'The Promising Years', unpublished manuscript, MS-0999/056, HC, 127.

13. Gray, *Quiet with the Hills*, 207.

14. JC, 'The Promising Years', 145.

15. Lee, 'A Private History', 39.

16. Ronnie Peter to JC, 10 June 1923, MS-0999/110, HC. Peter and JC lost touch, and 20 years later JC wrote to his grandmother to find out what had become of his old friend: Ida Peache to JC, 1 June 1942, MS-0999/109, HC.

17. JC, 'The Promising Years', 207.

18. Ibid., 219, 209.

19. Christopher Burke, 'Speak to Me Stranger: Subjectivity, homosexuality and the preliberation narratives of James Courage', PhD thesis, Otago University, 2012, 141.

20. JC, Diary, 21 September 1923.

21. JC, 'The Promising Years', 211. Two pages in this manuscript are numbered 211; this refers to the second of those.

22. Ibid., 234, 219–24.

23. JC, Diary, 20 October 1927.

24. Emlyn Williams, *George: An early autobiography*, London: Hamish Hamilton, 1961, 387.

25. JC, Diary, 11 November 1923.

26. On the broader theme, see David Picard, 'Tourism, Awe, and Inner Journeys', in David Picard and Mike Robinson (eds), *Emotion in Motion: Tourism, affect and transformation*, Farnham: Ashgate, 2012, 1–20, esp. 4–5.

27. JC, Diary, 14 November 1927.

28. JC, Diary, 1 April 1931.

29. JC, Diary, 27 September 1930.

30. JC, Diary, 4 October 1927; 7 October 1927.

31. JC, Diary, 20 December 1930; 24 December 1930.

32. JC, Diary, 22 December 1933.

33. JC, Diary, 31 March 1934.

34. Virginia Clegg, 'Memories of James Courage': https://christchurchcitylibraries.com/Society/Culture/Holidays/CourageDay/JamesCourageMemories.pdf

35. JC, Diary, 5 June 1935.

36. JC, Diary, 27 May 1930.

37. JC, Diary, 21 April 1941. The full quote from Mansfield can be found in John Middleton Murry (ed.), *Journal of Katherine Mansfield*, London: Constable, 1962, 94.

38. JC, Diary, 30 July 1931; 20 February 1932.

39. The figure of 34 comes from Charles Brasch, 'Preface', in JC, *Such Separate Creatures: Stories chosen by Charles Brasch*, Christchurch: Caxton Press, 1973, 7–14, esp. 11.

40. Philip Steer, 'James Courage, 1903–1963', *Kotare*, 7(2), 2008, 226–33; Grant Harris, 'A Reading of the Novels of James Courage', MA thesis, Massey University, 1990, 5, 10.

41. Elizabeth Caffin, 'Introduction', in JC, *The Young Have Secrets*, Wellington: Unwin Paperbacks, 1985, xii.

42. Harris, 'Reading', 8; Lee, 'A Private History', 73.

43. Phillip Wilson, 'Expatriate Novelist', *NZ Listener*, 21 November 1952, 12.

44. JC, Diary, 20 May 1940.

45. JC to Brasch, 4 September 1941, MS-0996-003/042, HC.

46. JC, Diary, 6 September 1941.

47. Lee, 'A Private History', 74.

48. JC, Diary, 20 May 1940.

49. Frank Courage (hereafter FHC) to JC, 24 August 1952, MS-0996/146, HC; 30 August 1951, MS-0996/147, HC; 24 November 1954, MS-0996/147, HC.

50. Ida Peache to JC, 11 February 1946, MS-0999/109, HC.

51. 'N.Z. Novelist's Death in England', *Evening Post*, 15 October 1963, 4.

52. JC, Diary, 25 December 1930; 6 July 1958.

53. Cited in Lee, 'A Private History', 87.

54. JC, Diary, 19 May 1932.

55. JC, Diary, 18 Nov 1933.

56. Burke, 'Speak to Me Stranger', 237.

57. JC, 'Morning Sky', unpublished manuscript, MS-0999/072, HC.

58. JC, Diary, 5 May 1954.

59. Brasch, 'Preface', 10. Brasch also provides a brief account of his own friendship with JC.

60. JC, Diary, 18 September 1939.

61. JC, 'Present for K', 1.

62. JC, Diary, 9 September 1940; 14 June 1944.

63. JC, Diary, 6 July 1939.

64. JC, Diary, 26 January 1941.

65. JC, Diary, 13 February 1943.

66. JC, Diary, 14 February 1943.

67. JC, Diary, 10 December 1943.

68. JC, Diary, 10 October 1943.

69. On this dynamic see Jeffrey Escoffier, *American Homo: Community and perversity*, London: Verso, 2018, 93.

70. Chris Brickell, *Mates and Lovers: A history of gay New Zealand*, Auckland: Random House, 2008, ch. 2.

71. JC, Diary, 3 November 1927.

72. JC, Diary, 25 April 1929.

73. JC, Diary, 21 September 1940; 25 March 1941.

74. Otto Weininger, *Sex and Character*, New York: Howard Fertig, 2003; Anomaly, *The Invert and His Social Adjustment*, London: Bailliere, Tindall & Cox, 1927.

75. JC, Diary, 10 September 1927.

76. Matt Houlbrook, *Queer London: Perils and pleasures in the sexual metropolis, 1918–1957*, Chicago: University of Chicago Press, 2005, 111; 129.

77. Burke, 'Speak to Me Stranger', 187–89; see, for example, JC, Diary, 20 June 1931.

78. Houlbrook discusses the areas of London most popular with homosexual men: *Queer London*, passim.

79. Matt Cook, *Queer Domesticities: Homosexuality and home life in twentieth-century London*, Houndmills: Palgrave Macmillan, 2014, 152.

80. JC, Diary, 31 July–2 August 1931.

81. JC, Diary, 22 December 1950.

82. JC, Diary, 16 January 1930.

83. JC, Diary, 15 May 1932.

84. JC, 'A Traveller Came By', unpublished manuscript, MS-0999/068, HC.

85. On Ernest's sexual 'normality', see JC, Diary, 31 July–2 August 1931.

86. Frank Fleet to JC, 16 July 1957, MS-0999/142, HC.

87. Thompson to JC, 19 October 1954, MS-0999/149, HC.

88. JC, Diary, 8 June 1963.

89. JC to Brasch, 25 January 1958, MS-0996-003/042, HC.

90. JC, Diary, 3 December 1960.

91. JC, Diary, 18 June 1960.

92. JC, Diary, 18 June 1960.

93. Acuila to JC, June 1963, MS-0999/149, HC.

94. Acuila to JC, Thursday night, MS-0999/118, HC.

95. JC, Diary, 4 June 1961.

96. JC, Diary, 16 July 1960.

97. JC, Diary, 24 June 1961.

98. JC, Diary, 18 March 1963.

99. JC, Probate, CAHX 2989 CH171 644 CH213/1965, Archives New Zealand. Sally Courage was not named in the will.

100. Christopher Burke, '"And so he Died as he had Lived, in Exile and Alone": Friendship, narrative and the politics of remembering', *Journal of New Zealand Studies*, NS13 (2012), 89–104, esp. 96; Paul Millar, *No Fretful Sleeper: A life of Bill Pearson*, Auckland: Auckland University Press, 2010, 196–97.

101. JC, Diary, 2 December 1938.

102. JC to Brasch, 4 September 1941, MS-0996-003/042, HC.

103. Charles Brasch, *Charles Brasch: Journals 1938–1945*, Dunedin: Otago University Press, 2013, 158.

104. Brasch to JC, 5 July 1959, MS-0999/107, HC.

105. Burke, 'Speak to Me Stranger', 246.

106. Lettice Cooper reviewed JC's novel *Desire Without Content* for the *Yorkshire Post*: see the clipping in MS-0999/141, HC.

107. JC, Diary, 7 December 1960; for an extensive discussion, see Burke, 'Speak to Me Stranger', 260ff.

108. JC, Diary, 7 December 1960.

109. Burke, 'Speak to Me Stranger', 240.

110. For a discussion of homosexual undertones in Sargeson's work, see John Newton, 'Homophobia and the Social Pattern: Sargeson's queer nation', *Landfall 199*, 2000, 91–107; on Pearson's novel *Coal Flat*, see Millar, *No Fretful Sleeper*, ch. 17; on McCormick, see Brickell, *Mates and Lovers*, 97–101.

111. Brickell, *Mates and Lovers*, 116–17.

112. The play can be found at MS-0999/018, HC.

113. Jeffrey Weeks, *Sexuality and its Discontents: Meanings, myths and modern sexualities*, London: Routledge and Kegan Paul, 1985, 134–35.

114. JC, Diary, 5 October 1938.

115. JC, Diary, 19, 14 October 1938.

116. Reviews of *Private History*, MS-0999/005, HC.

117. R.A. Copland, 'The New Zealand Novels of James Courage', *Landfall*, 18(3), 1964, 242; Michael Wooliscroft, 'Courage, James (Francis)', in Robert Aldrich and Garry Wotherspoon (eds), *Who's Who in Contemporary Gay and Lesbian History: From World War II to the present day*, London: Routledge, 2002, 93–94.

118. JC, *The Young Have Secrets*, London: Jonathan Cape, 1954, 176; 180; 182.

119. JC, *Fires in the Distance*, London: Constable, 1952, 133; 205. Harris offers a good discussion of Kathy in 'A Reading of the Novels of James Courage', 56.

120. JC, *Fires in the Distance*, 177; 10.

121. JC, *The Call Home*, London: Jonathan Cape, 1956, 101–02. See the analysis in Harris, 'A Reading of the Novels of James Courage', 80.

122. JC, *The Visit to Penmorten*, London: Jonathan Cape, 1961, 47. For a brief discussion, see Christopher Burke, 'Turning the Inside Out: Pre-liberation literary worlds in the works of Frank Sargeson, James Courage and Bill Pearson', *Journal of New Zealand Literature*, 26, 2008, 95–117, esp. 107.

123. Burke, 'Speak to Me Stranger', 309; 354; Lee, 'A Private History', 95; JC to Brasch, 22 November 1956, MS-0996-003/042, HC.

124. JC to Jim Harris, 7 November 1951, MS-0999/155, HC.

125. JC, *A Way of Love*, New York: Putnam, 1959, 48; 145.

126. JC, Diary, 11 January 1958; 12 January 1959.

127. JC, Diary, 11 January 1958.

128. See the editorial notes in MS-0999/053, HC.

129. JC to Frank Sargeson, 23 February 1958, MS 0432-152, Alexander Turnbull Library; JC to Brasch, 16 September 1958, MS-0996-003/042.

130. On *A Way of Love*, see Harris, 'A Reading of the Novels of James Courage', ch. 8, and Peter Wells, 'Introduction: Modest achievements', in Peter Wells and Rex Pilgrim (eds), *Best Mates: Gay writing in Aotearoa New Zealand*, Auckland: Reed, 1987, 7–33.

131. Martin Dines, 'Is it a Queer Book? Re-reading the 1950s homosexual novel', in Nick Bentley, Alice Ferrebe and Nick Hubble (eds), *The 1950s: A decade of modern British fiction*, London: Bloomsbury, 2019, 111–40, esp. 129–30.

132. JC, Diary, 14 November 1961.

133. Brasch to JC, 24 February 1959, MS-0999/107, HC. For more on Joseph and his Catholic faith, see Millar, *No Fretful Sleeper*, 222–23.

134. M.K. Joseph, 'Review', *Landfall 50* (June) 1959, 178–79.

135. Bobby Pickering, 'The Conspiracy Against James Courage', *Pink Triangle*, 18 (December) 1980, 5.

136. Lee, 'A Private History', 101–03.

137. JC, Diary, 31 July 1962.
138. JC, Diary, 11 October 1960.
139. Gray, *Quiet with the Hills*, 207.
140. Robert called James 'White Mouse' (JC, Diary, 11 October 1960), as Mark did Walter in *The Young Have Secrets*. On the parallels between Lewis and Robert, see JC, Diary, 2 December 1949.
141. Wilson, 'Expatriate Novelist', 12–13.
142. Cited in Lee, 'A Private History', 78.
143. JC to Sargeson, 23 February 1958.
144. JC to Brasch, 12 July 1956, MS-0996-003/42, HC.
145. JC, Diary, 8 September 1960.
146. JC, Diary, 21 July 1929.
147. JC, Diary, 24 November 1950.
148. JC, Diary, 23 September 1957.
149. Charles Brasch to JC, 24 February 1961, MS-0999/107, HC.
150. Weeks, *Sexuality and its Discontents*, 132.
151. JC, Diary, 4 October 1960.
152. JC, Diary, 11 July 1960; 19 July 1960.
153. Frank Courage (hereafter FHC) to JC, 3 October 1950, MS-0999/147, HC.
154. FHC to JC, 21 October 1954, MS-0999/146, HC; 3 October 1950, MS-0999/147, HC.
155. JC, Diary, 5 May 1954.
156. Zoë Courage (hereafter ZFC) to JC, 6 August 1950, MS-0999/147, HC.
157. ZFC to JC, 28 October 1958, MS-0999/146, HC.
158. ZFC to JC, 4 June 1954, MS-0999/147, HC.
159. ZFC to JC, 4 December 1959, MS-0999/146, HC.
160. Brickell, *Mates and Lovers*, ch. 4.
161. JC, Diary, 23 January 1962.
162. JC, Diary, 23 April 1962.
163. JC, Diary, 14, 17 June 1963.
164. Brasch to JC, 9 August 1963, MS-0999/107, HC; Brasch, 'Preface', 8.
165. 'N.Z. Novelist's Death in England', *Evening Post*, 15 October 1963, 4.
166. JC, Diary, 15 August 1938.
167. JC, Diary, 23 January 1963.
168. Phillip Wilson, 'James Courage: A recollection', *Landfall*, 18(3), 1964, 234.
169. Brasch, 'Preface', 9.
170. Cook, *Queer Domesticities*, 15.

Journal

Sept. 2nd 1927 to

Nov. 6th 192

Sketch of myself by
R. de Bonneville

the
DIARIES

1920–1924

~DIARY~
~for 'MYSELF' and no other~
James Francis Courage

~1920~

Awake! for morning in the bowl of night
Has flung the stone that puts the stars to flight:
And lo! the Hunter of the East
Has caught
The Sultan's Turret in a noose of Light.*

---

*   A quotation from *The Rubaiyat of Omar Khayyam*, Edward FitzGerald's hugely popular
1859 translation of the work of a twelfth-century Persian poet.

21 March 1920

What do I live for? My music, yes. That is all I look forward to, the brief hour a day when I am at my piano and am happy. I daresay to many people this definition of happiness would seem absurd. However 'he enjoys himself' they say. The rest go *via trita via tuta* [the trodden way is the safe way], but I choose to go off from the beaten path.

I must have originality, I must have individuality. Individuality is a great comfort for no two people are exactly the same in this world. I wonder if they are after death. I believe in reincarnation, but not atheism. They are very different things, one would say. Think and see.

20 May 1920

I am staying with such a happy family. They are, to me, the very essence of married happiness and they have been married 25 years. Every morning he goes off to the office after kissing his wife and children most fondly. When he comes home they rush to meet him and bring him in by the fire where his slippers have been warming for him. They never have a quarrel and even if they have a little point of disagreement it is so soon patched up with a smile that it is hardly noticed. There are three children. The eldest is a nice boy of 23; I can see all the time they are afraid of his leaving them, & of getting married. But in the parents' eyes no girl is good enough for their son. They have a daughter of 12. Such a happy disposition and a sweet face.

28 July 1920

There is nothing so fascinating as acting on the stage, if one is really interested in it. After my success as Dick Bultitude in *Vice Versa* I got so many compliments it nearly turned my head. My absolute happiness was marred by the fact that I had made a stupid little mistake in a speech. That night I lay awake for hours trying to think how I could have come to make it. We

OPPOSITE: The first page of Courage's first diary, 1920.

S20-542j, MS-0999/078, Hocken Collections

~ DiaRY ~

~ For "MYSELF" and no other ~

James Francis Courage

~ 1920 ~

"Awake! for morning in the bowl
of night
Has flung the stone that puts the
stars to flight:
And lo! the Hunter of the East
has caught
The Sultan's Turret in a noose of
Light."

Leslie Blunt, R. Thompson, Tristram Reeves, Geoffrey Gray and James Courage on a school picnic, c. 1920. *S19-601b, MS-0999/179, Hocken Collections*

are now working on a play called *Holed Out in One*, it is very amusing and modern. I have got the part of Ruth Pemberton, I don't know how I shall get on, but my usual slight streak of effeminacy will no doubt help me.

I have now got a confession to make to myself. I am passionately fond of clothes. To have nice clothes and to look smart is one of my ambitions. It is in fact part of me, like my love for music and for beautiful things. My ideal house would have a great many beautiful things in it. But I must not delude myself into thinking that because I worship beauty I am an atheist. I am not, I worship God, I take all my troubles to him in my prayers and I ask him to help me. I heard a queer definition of confirmation the other day. It was 'What's the use of getting confirmed? I swear just as much after it as before it.' It reflects a peculiar mind.

The athletic contingent from Christ's College. *S20-578d, MS-0999/117, Hocken Collections*

28 February 1921

I have at last managed to attain an allowance for £80 per year for clothes and pocket money. It is highly satisfactory to me for I will be able to have heaps of neat clothes ~~and be quite à la mode~~. But I will have to be careful what I do with my money. Everyone thinks that when they first get an allowance but they never adhere to it & I don't expect for a second that I shall. I was chatting yesterday to a friend who had just had his fortune told. The fortune teller (a woman) had told him 'that he was not understood'. I smiled, she must have known something about men, and especially emotional men, for every man cherishes an inward belief that he is misunderstood. We both had a good laugh over it.

I am not so sure now that I am so fond of Betsy, I sometimes think she is vulgar and a little coarse, but always the essential woman, the flirt. What woman does not like to be clasped in a man's arms? To be kissed by him. They can't help liking it, it was born in them, it was in Eve and has probably ever since existed. But I make one stipulation – it must be the right man who does it. There is no such thing as Platonic friendship. No man can be a constant friend with an eligible woman without love entering into the question – it isn't possible. [PIECE OF PAGE CUT OUT]. But enough of love. Mr Empson played me an 'arabesque' of Debussy's to-day.* I have never heard anything so dainty, so elfin-like. Truly the greatest art shows the greatest ease for Empson played it superbly. I was entranced. Empson is [PIECE OF PAGE CUT OUT].

12 March 1921

I am extraordinarily conceited and I shall now put down my character as I see it. I am fickle. ~~My numerous flirtations show me that~~. I am not particularly generous, my spending of money proves that, but in some matters I am peculiarly indulgent. I am effeminate, yes, it hurts me to write it but I am, for I love clothes and pretty things, and have great opinions on art. I am sensual, I am self-centred, I am a snob, I try to think I am good looking but I have a hideous nose. [PIECE OF PAGE CUT OUT].

26 June 1921

My little sister was born last night, I went up to see her to-day.† Quite a cute kid, though as a rule I detest kids, on principle. They cry so. I saw dear mother just for a moment. I kissed her. Poor mother, there were tears in her eyes. I was just allowed to ask her how she was, but she looked so white and her face was so lined as she lay there among the pillows. I could hardly speak, I

---

* Prominent Christchurch pianist and teacher Ernest Empson (1880–1970).

† Although Sally does not subsequently appear in her brother's diaries or letters she inspired his novel *The Fifth Child*, a Christchurch-based story of a woman who has a baby in her forties, and her relationships with her earlier four children. As an adult, Sally lived in both England and New Zealand.

March 12th 1921 –

I am extroadinarily conceited
and I shall now put down my character
as I see it. I am fickle, ~~my various~~
~~feelings show me that~~. I am not
particularly generous, my spending of money
proves that, but in some matters I
am peculiarly indulgent. I am
effeminate, yes, it hurts me to write
it but I am, for I love clothes and
pretty things, and have great Opinions
on art. I am sensual, I am self-
centred, I am a snob, I long to think
I am good looking but I have a hideous
nose.

just bent down and kissed her soft cheek and went out. When I got into the drawing room, which was empty, I burst into tears. To think that all that pain was needed to bring such a beautiful thing into the world. It seems awfully hard.

19 September 1921

A few nights ago I went to hear Mischa Levitzki, the young pianist, play.* Having to go early, in order to get a seat, I took a book of Tennyson's poems with me to enable me to relapse into the mood for listening to wonderful music. Levitzki is a short man with a quick, graceful walk; his shoulders have a suspicion of a stoop but are broad and it is easy to see where the power of his tone and the breadth of his fortissimo passages comes from. He has short hair with a wave above his forehead, his eyes have a suggestion of Slav in their position and colouring, his mouth is a trifle sensual, and his nose is handsome and straight; he wore a dress suit and seemed pleased at his applause. His playing of course to me represents an ideal. His Chopin playing was quite the most wonderful thing I have ever heard. Ethereal beauty and lightness of touch made each composition more like a dream than a succession of sounds. The *Butterfly Etude* was absolutely wonderful and marvellous, and gave me a feeling of sad exhilaration, very close to tears. I came away in a dream with the sight of a slight figure seated at an enormous grand piano always before my eyes.

24 January 1922

I am staying at Stewart Island for a few days during my stay in Otago. It is very beautiful over here, the bush is quite unspoiled by the little civilisation that has been forced upon it. There are no cars, no trams, no paved streets, and only one telephone. But yet I love civilisation better, one has not the idea

---

* Ukrainian-born pianist Mischa Levitzki (1898–1941) toured Scandinavia and Europe, then the United States, Asia, Australia and New Zealand. He was only 23 when Courage heard him in Christchurch.

Ronnie Peter at Peel Forest, c. 1920. *S10-580b, MS-0999/181, Hocken Collections*

that nature is regarding one with the hostile eyes bestowed on a stranger.
Even the birds in the bush will someday run against civilisation, and the
wood-pigeon will lose the sheen of his burnished wings, and the tui will find
his little necklet of white feathers drooping as some complacent house-cat
creeps through the undergrowth.

30 May 1922

> Do you remember all the little things that gave us such shy pleasure
> The night we lay half scared of one another
> In the dry brusque oak leaves which seemed to smother
> Us and the autumn bark they had drifted against
> A yard deep. And the russet moon had glared at us and bathed your face
> And I covered you half-up with leaves, and you
> Pretended to be scared but I, I knew!

[SEVERAL PAGES CUT OUT]

25 July 1922

East Hill House, Dorchester

Here is an atmosphere of lavender and blue china; the lavender in a great warm garden surrounded by a dark red brick wall, the blue china arranged round the hall and drawing-room of a tall white house with a flat-headed tower at one corner. The whole is built on a slope and one looks down into a small valley, onto the top of cute red roofs and the most little of gardens. Altogether good! And then there is the aunt. Stately, with white hair and a strangely young face. Looks as if she ought to smell of jasmine; has a rich voice, constantly reminding one of very red wine or very pale diamonds. Rather the ideal widow. Without prejudice, about 38. Tried to initiate her into *Kitten on the Keys* last night, but she gave one shriek when I'd finished and lay on the sofa in a limp heap. And then her diamond voice said: 'No, I don't like it at all!; is it *really* meant to be a kitten running up & down?' I think I replied something about 'artistic cats with syncopated kits cavorting killingly'.

21 September 1923

Can't you imagine the London streets in the dusk – full of lights and hurrying people and men in the gutters trying to sell you bananas or apples or little toys; and then, further in, the glowing theatres and the lighted signs of Piccadilly Circus – most ingenious some of them – and somebody flying past in an opera hat and just around the corner coming on a beggar, one side of his face a great red scar, drawing with coloured chalks on the pavement the illuminated words 'To Live' ... I'm writing, you don't know how hard it is to be simple, not insipid but penetrating, trenchant and sympathetic. Words are delightful things to handle but they need such careful handling! And they have a way of lying dead there on the paper and refusing to get up and obey your ideas. Disconcerting!

11 November 1923

Oxford

... I am writing prose these days – short stories with a queer twist. I have eight; perhaps I may try and publish them together when I have twelve! Prose is more difficult to write than poetry, at least prose that satisfies me and is not obscure or affected or 'muddy'. Of course I still read Pater;* I go into the Ashmolean Museum and dream for hours before Hermes or the Discobolus-thrower or Myron's 'Satyr'. Then I rush home and put it all into a prelude of Scriabin or a devilish cold thing of Bach's! Ego! I have been reading Browning. The Heavens have fallen and *stayed* with me. At present I merely like him but I know that soon my liking will 'leap to the dream' (to have the pleasure of quoting myself) and become love. With Pater it was like that and with Bach. Slow at first and then the reward! About ten days ago I went to see [George Bernard] Shaw's *Heartbreak House* and heard G.B.S. give a very subtle speech. He said, 'There have been moments tonight when I've been tempted to commit suicide!' Last week I saw Wilde's *Important of Being Earnest* – rather funny but a *little* faded.

21 November 1923

I can't decide whether I am a hypocrite or merely so overwhelmingly selfish that things only have one side, and that the side that pleases or affects me ... My father allows me £700 a year at Oxford, yet, after receiving a letter from him, I can write to my mother, apropos 'his letter was as usual a cross between a moral-diatribe and a bargain hunter's catalogue'. Cruel, and so utterly shallow. I think I have worshipped people ever since I was fourteen. First Chopin then Rupert Brooke, then Katherine Mansfield, then Oscar Wilde, then who? Baudelaire perhaps. It has been James Elroy Flecker and Walter Pater. William H. Davies.†

---

*   Walter Pater (1839–1894), English essayist and critic.

†   Both poet Rupert Brooke (1887–1915) and James Elroy Flecker (1884–1915), an English novelist and playwright, died young; Charles Baudelaire (1821–1867) was a French poet and an essayist and art critic; William H. Davies (1871–1940) was a popular Welsh poet.

James Courage's passport photo from 1926.

S14-604b, Ms-0999/176, Hocken Collections

23 January 1924

I have been deep in the 'dead black waters' to-day: reached the point of comparing practical methods to take my own life. I have never before suffered such agony of the mind. [REST OF PAGE CUT OUT]

17 February 1924

I have been less introspective of late, thank God. It does make life such an eternal consciousness, not only of the flesh but through that (so close in my case) of the spirit. This evening I walked around St John's Gardens. A thought I have had many times before recurred to me. Am I destined to be a poet … ? If so I must have some abnormal striving of a spirit within me. And yet I cannot find anything tangible that is in itself intrinsically poetic or that it is in itself symbolic of anything that will lead to an end whose apparent name is poetry. Yet I am able to conceive the very mood in which great poets have written their greatest lines.

1927–1929

2 September 1927

This morning as I was sitting on the lawn I threw my cigarette into the grass and clover and watched the smoke sift about among the green stems. I could almost see them shrinking from the acrid fumes. One leaf began to brown. They are so sensitive, yet grow so quietly, drinking in the fresh sun! The tobacco smoke was stale, rank, foreign.

Later. I wish I had the *guts* to set my manuscript in front of me. As it is I only shilly-shally with the thought of writing. The physical act of pen-pushing is to me incredibly iconoclastic: I can't get down to it at all. The only comfort is that when I'm so reluctant to write I have an idea the matter is good, personal, individual, and I won't eventually be ashamed of it. Yet I evade the effort of creation like an invalid. I'm too listless.

3 September 1927

This morning I noticed an elegantly dressed woman sitting on a seat by the sea. She was shading herself with a large black Japanese parasol. But on her lap was a bloated bundle done up in a man's red cotton handkerchief – can it have been her lunch? Those elegant ankles ... and mutton sandwiches? I have seldom seen more painful examples of shapelessness than the trousers fat men wear when playing tennis.

5 September 1927

Encounter

Directly I saw him approaching up the road something inside me 'switched on'. I tried not to look at him; surveyed the magnolias in the garden. Then, just as he passed, I looked into his face and met a confident (yes!) smile. My heart quivered like a hot light, and the blood rushed into my face. I felt lusty but intensely embarrassed. I don't even know his name.

9 September 1927

Woke up this morning in a state of abysmal depression and dressed in a thoroughly suicidal mood. In the middle of breakfast I was suddenly visited by a flash of amazing, ecstatic happiness. Down and up. Wrote nothing yesterday and don't feel like doing so to-day. Same old fear of iconoclasm – or just finicky laziness? It even goes so far as a distaste for thinking out the next scene in my play. Feverish incompetence.

10 September 1927

At tea with H.L. I picked a book, containing fragments of Sappho, from the bookcase.* Afterwards brought it home with me. Read some of it at once and was so profoundly stirred that I spent two hours writing an excessively erotic poem addressed to an unknown youth. I hadn't written a poem for six months, and had almost forgotten the intense intellectual excitement of it.

11 September 1927

After breakfast I sat in the sun on the terrace – composing a verse in Sapphics on the margin of my Sunday paper –

> All night long I too the incessant waters
> Hear as seas that break on the coast of Lesbos;
> Calling birds, and voices of lonely passion
> Deeper than Sappho's. –

The remote *sorrow* of the metre fascinates me.

I was quite enjoying myself (in spite of a stomach ache) at old Mr M.'s at tea until I caught sight of myself in a mirror that gave me a perfectly flat top to my head. I was instantly deflated.

---

* The Greek poet Sappho, who lived six centuries before the birth of Christ, wrote of love between women and inspired generations of lesbians.

15 September 1927

To-day I hired for an hour the studio containing the beautiful Bösendorfer piano I usually practise on in London. Not having touched the a piano, save the arts club upright – a more-or-less sort of affair – for two months, I was utterly disappointed in myself – I couldn't get any of the effects I wanted (except in a Scriabin prelude); the superior piano showed up every little smudge, so to speak, in my touch and tone. Most humiliating. Pater says 'the way to perfection is through a series of disgusts'. Smug!

18 September 1927

This afternoon at the British Museum I made a point of gazing – for the hundredth time – on the countenance of Queen Nefertiti – Lovely exquisite thing!* One can almost trace the beautifully formed frame-work of the skull beneath the flesh of the face. Circa 1200 B.C. In some inexplicable way an argument for an elegant paganism. Purposefully avoided going into the room containing the Greek statues of young men. Perfection like that humiliates me, and the physical side of it wakes up a state of sensual libido that tortures me. Last night saw the official film of Battles of Coronel and Falkland Islands. All those men in action, covered with sweat and full of an animal desire to kill their enemies, made me feel I was living a very pale, ineffectual existence indeed. The pen may be mightier than the sword, but it is a damn sight too genteel for a man with decent physical equipment.

19 September 1927

I find the greatest difficulty in not smiling at pretty girls in buses, railway carriages etc. A form of nervousness.

21 September 1927

At a dinner-party last night the table was decorated with great bowls of salmon-coloured antirrhinums (dragon cups) set under yellow-shaded

---

* Egyptian Queen Nefertiti reigned with her husband the Pharoah Akhenaten during the decades either side of 1340 BC.

Courage had friends among Oxford's rowers.

candles. Half-closed my eyes and swam away into a sensuous salmon-coloured sea of light.

The rain poured down all day. D.J. [Dick] and I got sick of the house at 3 o'clock and went off for a walk in the rain. Along a lovely dripping path beneath elms. A few brown leaves in the clay. A toad with its hands over its eyes. A sodden harvest-field with a misty Yorkshire distance. And always *rain*. Trousers sopping. Last night I had a 'levitation' dream. Held my breath, gave a slight jump, and sailed to the ceiling with perfect ease. Roof was thatched, Maori-fashion, with raupo.

22 September 1927

'You're less abnormal than you think,' D. said to me this evening. 'Perhaps,' I replied, knowing perfectly well he was speaking the truth and I was clinging to my 'differences'. By the way, why is it that when D. and I are alone together we do nothing but talk about sex, giving slightly heightened accounts of our own erotic experiences?

24 September 1927

Saw some pomegranates in a shop-window tonight and bought one as an experiment. Took it home and ate it sitting on my bed. Juice! – I began with a piece of paper in my lap, then tried a handkerchief, and ended by wrapping myself up in a bath towel. Fruit disappointing. Coming down in the train from Yorkshire a fair boy of about eight sat opposite me. When he bent down I noticed the most charming little duck's tail of fair hair on the nape of his neck. Wanted to stroke it.

27 September 1927

Yesterday I bought a pair of bath-slippers made of soft scarlet leather, lined with wool. My feet love them. Were I Chekov I would write a story about a man who told his scarlet slippers the little sorrows of his life.*

---

*   Anton Chekov (1860–1904), Russian playwright and short story writer.

29 September 1927

A pouring wet day. Hired a piano for 2 hours and had a rapturous time playing Chopin and Scriabin. I am looking forward so much to having my own piano as a confidant again! In the evening had most disturbing pains in the chest. Rather worried, as the dread of my waking life is to cough one day and find my mouth full of good red blood. Not the slightest foundation for such fear, except such pains.

30 September 1927

In Oxford for four hours on 'business'. Ate an alfresco lunch in St John's Gardens in wonderful sunlight. A small meat-pie, three enormous, alarmingly phallic bananas, and a cigarette. It was so quiet, only faint train-whistles and birds.

1 October 1927

Finished my little sketch about the four children. Called it 'Animal, Vegetable, Mineral'. Quite light and charming, but I can't get what Katherine Mansfield, for instance, had. I'm not *humble* enough.

2 October 1927

I sat in the draughty park and read a paper. Suddenly, with a swirl, a great grey wind, full of cold rain, blew down a crowd of yellowish leaves and turned all the foliage drab-side-out. Some of the leaves were a lovely apricot colour. I turned up my coat-collar and rather enjoyed the fresh rain on my mouth and cheeks.

4 October 1927

St Ives

In my own nest at last! The waves breaking gently on the rocks just below my bedroom balcony – an eternal and as yet irresistible lullaby. So happy I just go round patting things and standing back with half an eye shut.

7 October 1927

Out walking to-day on the hills I smelt burning gorse-bushes. How it brought back old New Zealand days! John [brother] in a light holland coat, very sunburnt, looking a positive little larrikin.

9 October 1927

Late tonight I walked up the hill to post my letters. A bright, bright moon with one superb consort star to the North-East. A clear windy sky with faint films of cloud skimming to the horizon. Tide very low, with acres of pale sand. I stood for a long while watching the house-lights, ashamed before the moon, disappear among the grey roofs. One candle very clear in a high window ... Looked at the faint stars; the eternal silence of those infinite spaces ... God preserve us from smugness and unctuous esoterics.

10 October 1927

Life has done its best to-day be a little difficult. My grand piano arrived but it was found that the stairs were too narrow to allow it to be taken upstairs. In consequence it is at present in my bedroom, while I roost up in the studio. Damnable nuisance. I was so upset that I trembled all over. To make matters worse all my other stuff arrived in large cases and was dumped on the floor while there was no room to move. I have always been terrified of having too many belongings, and to-day the curse seems to have overtaken me. I am thinking of storing the piano again.

12 October 1927

Had a long talk with a young Cornishman I met on the cliffs, sitting in the sun at the old rifle-butt. After a time he produced, a little shyly, a small plain-paper book with some pencil drawings in it – poor amateur things. His intense pride in them really hurt me – a sort of protective pity, like pain. He told me that when they opened the new cemetery in St Ives they had to borrow a corpse from the next parish to make the ceremony valid.

13 October 1927

Congenial surroundings are absolutely necessary to a refined spirit. Not only clean bed-linen, but a polished fork to eat from, sweet pictures to look at, elegant clothes to wear, good music and talk to hear. Without these he is an Ishmael in the wilderness and might, with more profit to himself and rest for his maker, be he a ploughman or a deep-sea fisherman.

The sheer exuberance of the sea breaking round the rocks this evening gave me a feeling of speed – of living ecstatically and intensely. I went inside and crashed away at Chopin's eighteenth prelude.

15 October 1927

A long letter from Leonard. ' ... You cannot think how I look forward to the repetition one day of those little dinners, always in such excellent taste, which one associates with your hospitality.' Dear old pagan Leonard! But he understood or saw through me.

17 October 1927

The anniversary of Chopin's death. I have thought of him constantly all day, and played a dozen of the best mazurkas to his memory. To think that old Queen Victoria had the unbelievable luck to hear him play in London in 1848 makes me exasperated with jealousy. Dear Chopin, how we would have got on together! You, Shelley, Charles Lamb,* Chekhov, and Rupert Brooke I should have enjoyed meeting in the flesh – and I have not forgotten Katherine Mansfield. She also.

20 October 1927

This morning I heard of Archie S.'s death from heart failure 3 weeks ago. It gave me a shock, as for the last six months I had looked forward to seeing him again. His death, also, seemed to destroy one of the most vivid links with my freshman year. – Archie playing the piano; in rowing shorts; stealing

---

*   Charles Lamb (1775–1834), English essayist, poet and antiquarian.

my teapot; the way he said 'Dinkums, Buddy.' Also the way he liked my poem, 'From a Submerged City'. He went about quoting it. He was so easy to like.

21 October 1927

To mechanical men, robots, propagated by machinery, Sappho's poetry would be meaningless (S. as the supreme poet of love).

22 October 1927

This evening while I was listening to a record of César Franck's *A Flat Sonata* the brightest rainbow I have ever seen shone up on the horizon from a hard grey sea, against a sky full of tumultuous storm cloud.* The music and the vision seemed for some moments to correspond so exactly that I wondered in a dazed way why I'd never known this inevitable relation before, why was it not published abroad, so to speak.

25 October 1927

They say that when a man leaves his native country to live elsewhere and, having imbibed the elsewhere-culture, begins to make literature out of what he remembers of his birth-place, he generally gets a false perspective of it. He has lost touch with the soil, the flesh and blood of his old life, and sees it only through the literary eyes of the new. He makes it 'precious', refining from it what was really valuable in it – the colloquial speech, the precise earthy relations between man and potato, the moral twist of its people. If he returned he would at once lose the impulse to write about it – its very circumstances would prevent the detachment necessary for creation – he would be so close to the picture that he could see only the brush-marks. Yet if he had never left the place the impulse to depict it might never have ripened.

28 October 1927

In a state of strange inexplicable excitement and mental unrest all day. Not able to sit still. It began by my getting a letter from grandmother at breakfast

---

* César Franck (1822–1890), Belgian-born composer, pianist and music teacher.

saying how far away I seemed to her in body and spirit. Yes; in a way I am, and it hurts, as all farewells with loved ones hurt. Yet if I could only talk to her again she'd find the distance very little – and I should be the one who lagged, not she.

31 October 1927

Wrote a passionate love-scene in the second act of 'The Rift' which I shall probably have to tear up to-morrow. In the evening began rewriting 'The Shave'. Am taking Chekov's advices and beginning in the middle, with large deletions from my first versions. The [*London*] *Mercury* returned 'A Good Liar' as I knew they would. It is a rotten bit of work.

1 November 1927

E. writes to me about R. 'A completely fictitious person with manufactured emotions, no reaction to life, immense pretentiousness as far as the intelligence is concerned, but with a singularly kind heart.' R. writes about E. 'E. has talent but he's far too centralized to do anything with it at the moment. I wish he had nicer bodily habits, however.' That's what comes of sharing each other's souls and beds!

3 November 1927

When an iconoclast like Wyndham Lewis dissects homosexuality he makes me feel an utter worm.* He calls us 'intellectual snobs' and other pleasant descriptions.

10 November 1927

What a repulsive shock one would get if a school-boy ever said to one: 'my father once slept with Oscar Wilde'.

---

* Wyndham Lewis (1882–1957), avant-garde painter and critic. Some of his work disparaged homosexuals and Jewish people, though he renounced these views later in life.

12 November 1927

What I remember most vividly about people is the way they laughed – the intimacy of a joke between us. Ronnie's half-scandalised chuckle, for instance; Malcolm's sedate laugh; Ronald's face when he smiles; Reggie's giggle; Leonard's quiet roar; Geoff's sudden splash of amusement. When I think of them it makes me long to joke with each of them again.

13 November 1927

Went for a long and invigorating walk with H. Was ridiculously haunted by an idea that I should propose to her if I was not extremely careful. (A susceptible heart needs a doctor just as much as one suffering from disease.) Yet I don't love the girl: I have no great desire for either her body or her mind. Even the idea of having her as a mistress doesn't attract me (naturally!), and my sense of humour refuses to picture her parents sanctioning such a *liaison*. Altogether it is laughable.

14 November 1927

One of the moments in my whole life I remember most brightly and when I seemed to live most intensely was on a certain evening in Athens. I stood alone in the Parthenon, looking through the columns east towards Lycabettus and Pentelikon, and from behind me the light of the setting sun turned the marble to an indescribable, glowing pink. It is easy, perhaps, to rhapsodise over such things, but as I descended the Propylaeum I felt I had seen something I should never forget, and which I should never see again.

26 November 1927

Took my B.A. degree in the Sheldonian [Theatre, Oxford]. A long and boring ceremony. As I had had no lunch owing to a late train, I felt as empty as a drum.

1 December 1927

M. was upset because I said that a Picasso drawing (of some naked Spartan youths on horseback) which he was about to buy for his room, was 'an awful give-away'. He was scared stiff by the suggestion that it might be too outward and visible a sign of his inversion. Good heavens! – as if the very way he spoke to women wasn't a sufficient 'give-away'!

5 December 1927

Passed two sailors to-day in the street. One was young and jaunty and beautiful. He was dressed in a light jersey and a pair of close-fitting washed-blue trousers, showing me (back view) one of the most perfect figures I have ever seen. I devoured the narrow, strong hips and loins with my eyes, so minutely that they fevered my consciousness for hours – Downright lust, of course, mixed up with a horrible, soul-destroying desiderium for something else – ideality perhaps, perhaps an outburst of unrestrained debauchery, to be followed by days of Hell. The expense of spirit ...* It is the duty of the artist to sublimate the desire for prostitution (a cowardly addendum).

9 December 1927

R. writes, saying that he is going to Paris (this June) to complete his service (military). He asks me to go over and take a studio with him, and adds 'would it please you to have all Paris say you were the *bon ami d'un petit poilu?*' [a soldier's boyfriend] What an inexplicable postscript! The trouble is that it's going to be a physical ménage, and I'm not certain I want it. (Though the consciousness of living in sin is certainly a great attraction.)

12 December 1927

I had enough of fame at Oxford to realise what it means. Your true friends don't care whether you're famous or not, and your foes do their best to pick holes in your achievements. As for the rest of the world that hears your name they say, 'Why him, of all people?'

---

* The opening words of Sonnet 129 by Shakespeare: 'Th'expense of spirit in a waste of shame/is lust in action ...'

28 December 1927

I am almost afraid to listen to a Mozart string quartet – it gives me such breathless, almost icy pleasure. Thrills go up and down my spine, saying, 'God, how perfect!'

3 January 1928

Finished a fair copy of 'The Parasite'. [Note in margin dated 28/10/28: I should like to have called this damned play (now lost in oblivion) 'Exile'.] To live in solitude is to possess more of one's self. The object of that possession is to express the whole weight of the self through artistic creation. An existence of constant interdependence between oneself and others is, in part, to dissipate the true essence of being. Love is ecstatic sharing, stretching forth, giving, of self.

5 January 1928

The anus is the sun of a 'sodomite planet'.

1 February 1928

Why three days without an entry? I have been engaged on this first chapter of a novel. I have been going at it too fast – tonight I decided it was no good and would never be. However, the 'melancholy fit' will pass.

10 February 1928

C[arter] says, apropos of my play, etc, that my dialogue is good but that I should keep a mistress and learn how women behave. He's quite right, but if I kept a 'mistress' I should do not work at all.

18 February 1928

Parted with C. to-day and felt sad and a bit hopeless over nothing at all. If I had not slept with him the parting wouldn't have given me a single pang. How damnably sex colours everything.

24 February 1928

Leather, especially belts, has a strong sexual attraction for C. He told me about a boy who had a leather seat to his trousers – to C. the acme of allurement. Some masochist had also wanted him to beat him with a thong of leather.

26 February 1928

Suffered from a *crise de nerfs* [literally, a crisis of the nerves] this morning, chiefly over certain difficulties in my novel, but augmented by a bad attack of inferiority complex about my own future. Got myself back into the right perspective by reading a passage about the Universe, out of George Santayana's essay, 'where there is such infinite and laborious potency there is room for hope'.* Yet the worst of it is, that one can be so conceited about being *nothing*. Later had great fun playing Schumann's *Kinderszenen*.

23 March 1928

It is almost a month since I have written anything in this journal. In a way it has not been a happy time, though outwardly fairly calm. But I am at present suffering from two little private hells, both the result of conflict. The first is that my sexual nature is compounded almost equally of sensuality and of acute fastidiousness. In consequence when I'm in a healthy state I am constantly seeking a sexual satisfaction from an ideal – an impossible state of affairs, productive of a terrible nervous asceticism. The second conflict is in a way the characters of my father and mother fighting in me, their child. My father is intensely practical, resolute and single-minded; my mother has a strain of sensibility and a longing for perfection, for impossible and glorious dreams, which I have inherited tenfold. The two do not agree. The first thirsts after the struggle and the rush of life; the second loves but is *afraid* of life. 'Go out and dirty yourself and fight and make yourself feared of men,' says my father. And my mother – my truer self – says, 'No; stand back and try

---

* Spanish-born philosopher, essayist, poet and novelist George Santayana (1863–1952) spent his life in the United States.

to understand life, give yourself a chance to love it, drink in the loveliness
of music and verse and Nature, and of all arts. That is *your* surer road to
happiness.' At present I stand and argue ceaselessly '*Which?*'

27 March 1928
The back of a well-built young man is one of the most lovely examples of pure
form I know. Were I a sculptor I should enjoy carving young men's backs;
girls' necks; well-shaped hands; the straining thighs of wrestlers; and full,
sensual, disdainful mouths. The Celestial, forming part of the group called
Asia, at the Albert Memorial, has the sort of mouth I mean ...

24 April 1928
A vivid dream last night about a boy I disliked and feared at school. I hadn't
thought about him for five years. How did the unconscious memory come to
preserve him? The boy typified for me a sort of rank earthiness, without the
slightest spiritual quality. I hated him so much that, for a whole week after he
had yelled an insult at me and looked at me with his pig's-eyes, I could think
of nothing but my hatred of him. It was the complete negation of being in
love, but, like love, it affected all my thoughts.

2 May 1928
Sat on the beach in the morning, enjoying the sun. Tried to write but had not
the willpower to concentrate, so lay back and absorbed violet-rays. Watched
a nomadic spider cruising for prey on the hot rocks. Saw it jump a two-inch
chasm with ease ... The smell of some fresh tar made me remember going
to the swimming-baths at my prep school. Though the water used to be
tepid I always shivered and splashed about like an underfed scarecrow. Last
night I dropped in to see Carter. He usually has a mistress floating around
his studio, but I found him laid up with mild dysentery and no mistress
about. He tossed me across a large brown book. 'Have you read that?' It
was *Vol IV: Sex in Relation to Society* by Havelock Ellis. 'No,' I said, 'I haven't,
but of course Ellis – ...' 'Ah,' he muttered, in pangs of dysentery, 'it's a great

book. He knows his subject, that old fellow!' It seems that when C. is ill, and accordingly devoid of gratification *via* mistress, he peruses Havelock Ellis et cetera as a second-best.* Gordon B. came in later and we talked about Spitzbergen. He told me about the sudden glorious spring of six weeks, then the four-month period of gloaming, followed by the long polar night. Finally, the return of the sun, heralded by auroras. I asked him about the period of darkness – didn't they get morbid, on each other's nerves, etc? He said, 'Yes, very badly. The buffer civilization creates between each man broke down quickly under the most trivial circumstances.' His own sense of humour had saved him much, but he could not endure the strain a second time.

3 May 1928
Stopped to stroke a dirty, scraggy cat in the road to-day. It had enormous vacant, soulful eyes – regular pools. But it took not the least notice of me, and said clearly enough: 'Men, like cats, all die. You're just another walking fraud, like the rest who pet me. If you had a mutton-chop about you, it would be a different matter, but meanwhile –.' And it stalked off up the dry, dusty road, the captain of its soul.

4 May 1928
I saw by the papers to-day that it is only 300 years off since [William] Harvey discovered the circulation of the blood. To think that we, who pride ourselves on our intelligence and advance on the ape, should be living a mere flicker like 300 years since the most elementary fact of our bodily structure has been discovered, ought to be enough to take the wind out of the most fanatical believer in an approaching millennium! In another 300 years I suppose we shall have discovered how to control prenatal sex, how to prolong or renovate youth, how to stimulate the senses artificially with no harmful reaction, and the perfect diet! Perhaps.

---

* Havelock Ellis (1859–1939), a liberal English physician and writer, wrote extensively about homosexuality.

6 May 1928

To-day D[ick] has been talking so much about a Russian girl he is in love with that, at last, in exasperation, I told him that I should invent an *inamorata* of my own and do nothing but talk about her. So I have concocted a resplendent virgin called Kathleen Bunbury (first cousin to Wilde),* and now, whenever D. dilates on his *Olga,* I go off into raptures over my *Kathleen.* The device is strangely effective.

12 May 1928

(In London.) D. and I travelled up from Cornwall yesterday. He went straight away to see his Olga, and they have gone off together for the weekend. She attracts him to the point where he loses all sense of direction, and he knows it. The letter he left for me to-day at the hotel is very revealing. –

> My dear Jim,
> I'm going off with Olga. Might as well get it over. Look here, in case I don't see you again the next day or two I'll write as soon as I get back. You were reading the old Wells book (*A Short History of the World*) yesterday so I thought I would leave it in your room for you.† Have it if it's any good. I feel guilty eloping so obscenely, however –
> Love, Dick

I thought to myself in the theatre tonight, as it became later, 'Now they have arrived. Now they are in one another's arms. Now there's the inevitable orgasm, around which all this bother!' Truth is stranger than fiction. D. had been in *my* arms the night before.

---

* To bunbury (or bunburying) in *The Importance of Being Earnest* meant making up an excuse to avoid doing something boring.

† H.G. Wells (1866–1946) wrote widely in many genres. His *A Short History of the World* was published in 1922.

31 May 1928

It often seems to me that only those who are, according to man's laws, perverted, or rather inverted, sexually, ever really understand the full force and the thousand ramifications of sex. They have at once a detached view of women and an intimate view of men – accordingly, since sex resides most plainly in the male (e.g. Phallus worship), they are privileged.

26 June 1928

Life is truly a strange medley. To-day, amongst many other things, I have –

1) Begun reading a book on Japanese colour-prints;
2) Written a letter of deep affection simply because it was expected of me;
3) Seen the film called *Dawn*, founded on the Nurse Cavell incident;*
4) Taken strawberries and tea with a woman who pleases me but is old enough to be my mother;
5) Played through Chopin's *Etude in G flat* slowly ten times;
6) Lusted after at least five total strangers;
7) Read Arthur Hugh Clough's 'Say Not the Struggle Naught Availeth';†
8) Written 300 words of my novel;

– but that is more than enough! It's a day well over.

6 July 1928

D: Don't you find it difficult to sit down every morning and write?
Myself: Yes, damnably. A struggle goes on in me every day. Sometimes I say to myself, 'I should be temperamental this morning and write nothing', but before two hours are past I find myself drawn to read over what I wrote yesterday. Then one more sentence will come, then another. All very cold at first, but gradually warming up to creation-heat.

---

*   British Nurse Edith Cavell achieved heroic status when she was executed by the Germans in October 1915 for helping hundreds of Allied soldiers to escape from German-occupied Belgium.

†   Poet Arthur Hugh Clough (1819–1861) assisted Florence Nightingale in her work. This was one of his most famous poems.

D: Yet, though one hates beginning, there is a constant longing to get oneself back into that created world that was so real yesterday.

Myself: Extraordinarily, intoxicatingly real. I daren't work at night, because I can't stop afterwards. I persist in the surroundings my mind imagined for hours after I have put down my pen. If I work in the morning, I continue to live with my characters all the while I'm having lunch ... of course, strictly speaking, that reluctance to start is a good sign.

D: Yes, all the greatest writers are said to suffer from it, are they not?

Myself: Are they? Perhaps we're putting the cart before the horse, though, in claiming kinship merely through an unnatural form of inertia.

D (laughing): Probably ... I've never come across a good analysis of the process of an author's mind; though one often picks up pregnant hints from stray sentences here and there in a good writer's work.

Myself: There's a good, but partial analysis in a long speech spoken by Trigorin, the novelist in Chekov's play *The Seagull*.

D: And in a (I think) detective story by [A.]P. Herbert, there is an author who explains his irritability when his mind is lying fallow after a great or prolonged creative effort.

Myself: Yes, that must be quite true.

After a pause we began to talk of other matters.

16 July 1928

From Norman Douglas's book *Fountains in the Sand*, (speaking of Tunis):*

> ... It is a land of uncompromising masculinity. The softer element
> – thanks to the Koran – has become non-existent, and you will
> look in vain for the creative-feminine, for those intermediate types
> of ambiguous, submerged sexuality, the constructive poets and
> dreamers, the men of imagination and the women of will, that give
> to good society in the north its sweetness and *chatoyance* [shimmer];

---

*   Norman Douglas (1868–1952), a British writer who had many relationships with young
men. *Fountains in the Sand* was published in 1912.

for those 'sports' and eccentrics who, among our lower classes, are centrifugal – perpetually tending to diverge in this or that direction.

8 August 1928
We are not glad enough of the number of beautiful people in the world.

12 August 1928
Idea: Write a novel, dealing with the writing of a novel, à la André Gide's *Counterfeiters*, but more detailed and luminous.* (Also a homosexual novel, to be called 'The Pariahs'. Discount sodomy, exalt in intellectual subtlety.)

25 April 1929
From Weininger's book: *Sex and Character* – 'The ego of the genius is simply itself universal comprehension, the centre of infinite space; the great man contains the whole universe within himself; genius is the living microcosm' – I came across this, reading to-day.[†]

20 August 1928
The terrible loneliness of the sexual invert! Even those of his own persuasion seem bent on excluding all the higher attributes of friendship by an insistence on sexual indulgence and a frantic forgetfulness of that world that brands them as unnatural. All the nobler faculties of intellect (extraordinarily a part of inversion) are left to grow rank or derided as 'sublimation'. To society at large the individual invert is anathema – an unthinkable anomaly. To himself he is often a collection of half-understood but painful perceptions. More frequently he is aware of his state, and it is then that he understands his loneliness, his seemingly purposeless segregation in Nature. The very longing for a sympathetic vision turns him towards his own kind, however

---

[*] French author André Gide (1869–1951), who wrote more than 50 books, won the 1947 Nobel Prize in Literature. Much of his work refers to homoeroticism.

[†] Otto Weininger, an Austrian who wrote only one book, *Sex and Character*, committed suicide in 1903 at the age of 23.

radically different from himself they may be. He cannot choose his sexual company, beyond small limits: the intellectual comradeship he desires is as rare as a blue moon. He is an Ishmael, verily.

22 August 1928

Listening to music

This evening four of us, quite good friends, were sitting in a room in semi-darkness, listening to music. Some fool saw fit to light the gas, and instantly we were a number of human beings enjoying an intellectual experience (the music) and therefore self-conscious about it. As long as the darkness hid us we were reasonably non-integrate, though following our own dreams; with the light we tidied our minds for inspection.

23 August 1928

If I die without making a will I should like to leave ten pounds annually to Oxford University for a prize for the best sonnet written by an undergraduate. Subject to be given, as for the Newdigate Prize; and entries to be judged by the Professor of Poetry. My own name *not* to be given to the Prize.

1 September 1928

Part of the unrest that *beauty* awakes in the soul is probably the desire to apprehend it through the five senses, instead of, at most, three. – To taste a fine moonlight night, to smell a diamond, to feel a cloud, etc. Hence the longing to make the beauty a permanent element of oneself.

> The sage will go his way, prepared to find himself growing more and more out of sympathy with vulgar trends of opinion, for such is the inevitable development of thoughtful and self-respecting minds. He scorns to make proselytes among his fellows: they are not worth it. He has better things to do … He endeavours to find himself at no matter what cost, and to be true to that self when found – a worthy and ample occupation for a life-time. (*Alone*, Norman Douglas)

It is precisely men who are mentally lonely, philosophers, who should be men of the world if they mean to prevent fatal retrogression in their development. (Hermann von Keyserling)*

10 September 1928

An extremely vivid dream I had two or 3 nights ago has been haunting me: a crowd surging incomprehensibly on a sandy plain. Somebody addressing them; a far voice. Suddenly just by me a man in a mackintosh dissents: his neighbours seize him. At first he thinks they are joking, but they take him to a tall post, bind him to it and begin tearing at him like fiends. He begins to scream. They tear his shirt off, blood runs down his chest. He screams terribly as they set fire to his remaining clothes. His face is distorted with agony. The screams echo in my mind. And I awake, shuddering with horror.

12 September 1928

Went to the National Gallery to look at Leonardo's *Virgin of the Rocks* again ... Was much taken with an adolescent boy of about 15 seen in another gallery, indolently looking at the pictures. Fair hair, round head, brown eyes. Wanted to lie with him at once. Sexual excitement.

12 October 1928

E.W. [Emlyn Williams] got me a ticket for the Arts Club production of Strindberg's play *Easter*, sat just behind Noel Coward. Saw Bernard Shaw (in a black fur-felt hat). Also Edith Sitwell (very acute profile.) ... A strange play, essentially undramatic, yet always interesting.†

---

*   Hermann von Keyserling (1880–1946) was a German philosopher.

†   Emlyn Williams (1927–1985) was a bisexual Welsh writer, dramatist and actor. Swedish playwright August Strindberg (1849–1912) wrote *Easter* in 1900. The plays and songs of Noël Coward (1899–1973) are still widely performed today. Edith Sitwell (1887–1964), one of three famous literary and eccentric siblings, was an English poet and critic.

28 October 1928

A parallel?

Talking tonight to a woman who told me that she, in company with a female friend, were very taken with a couple of ship's officers on the voyage out East. At Tientsin the four went ashore for a gay dinner together, at which repast, it being a sweltering night, the officers removed their tunics and ate in vests (or nude to waist?). Both women experienced intense disillusionment. 'I suppose we were attracted by the glamour of the smart uniforms,' admitted my narrator. 'Because, my word, when they took them off – oh, they seemed such common fellows!' The glamour of the uniforms ... Is that, I wonder, the attraction guardsmen in London have for a certain type of homosexual? It would also account for the remark one such once made to me: 'I've had dozens of them, but, God, they're all the same without a uniform!'

Apropos of guardsmen: The more refined in its far-fetched extravagance, the more abnormal the vice, the more dully & hopelessly unemotional does the practice of it become ... There are many people it is true (& they are generally the most intellectually civilised, refined & sophisticated) who have a hankering after lowness & eagerly pursue their own abasement in the midst of multiple orgies, masochistic prostitutions, casual & almost bestial couplings with strangers, sexual association with gross & uneducated individuals of a lower class. Excessive intellectual & aesthetic refinement is liable to be bought rather dearly at the expense of some strange emotional degeneration, and the civilised Chinaman with his love of art and of cruelty, is suffering from another form of the same disease which gives the modern aesthete his taste for guardsmen & apaches, for humiliating promiscuities & violences. Divorced from all significant emotion, the more sensations of physical excitement & pleasure are insipid. Point counter point.

29 October 1928

Life is a furnace in which one's soul is continually being burnt to keep one's senses warm. Love is a crime in which one cannot do without an accomplice.

30 October 1928

A day of damnable depression. I can't write in this bloody hotel, and see myself wasting my time from day to day instead of *getting down to it*. Consequently I live in a sort of spiritual Glasgow – a cold and murky place; when at my best I exist – or *can* exist – in a world of acute happiness and sensuous pleasure. Once or twice I have thought of going off to the South of France or to Italy, but can't face it *alone*. Solitude demands great fortitude of mind – a fortitude greater than I can provide at the moment.

3 November 1928

Twilight at E.'s [Emlyn's] (helping him red-line his play *Glamour*) met a good-looking young man of twenty-four, of amazing ingenuousness.*

'Nothing,' he said, 'really exciting has ever happened to me' (He is a
   cashier in a bank)
'Perhaps,' I suggested, 'you've never been in love?'
'No,' he said, 'never. I've never been remotely affected in that way yet.'
'Man,' I told him, 'you're not alive! How do you sing (he is a good tenor)
   without knowing the quality of an emotion?'
'I don't know, really. I – don't think I could fall – in love, you know!'
And this from a handsome youth with a peach-like complexion, perfect
   teeth, and a mouth like a sulky, sensual child's!
'You don't understand what you're telling me,' I cried. 'You're exposing
   the lack of something vital in yourself.'
He blushed and looked away. 'Yes,' he whispered after a moment. 'I must
   try to fall in love, mustn't I.'
'Certainly,' I replied softly, 'You must.'

---

* Emlyn Williams appeared as Jack in the 1928 production.

6 November 1928

Went with E. this morning to the Caledonian market. Amidst seas of rubbish, picked out a rather fine photograph reproduction of the head of Leonardo's *Sainte Anne*, which I bought for sixpence, framed! At one stall was displayed an album of snapshots, evidently taken in Egypt by a soldier. Seeing me inspecting the groups, the stall-woman called out 'Only tuppence, them photos. Amuse yer for hours, they would.' E. and I passed on, chuckling.

14 November 1928

Of Charlotte Brontë – 'It was not merely common inadequate art but also common inadequate life also which irritated her imagination with the thought of what might be done, at the same time fevering the nerves because it was not done.' C'est moi!

16 December 1928

R. brought a friend, Eric Z., to see me to-day. Z. took a strong whisky and told us how he had lain with six Chinese boys in one night when last in Singapore. Otherwise he seemed perfectly normal: tall, handsome, with a dark sleek head – the sanguine, equable temperament.

17 December 1928

Spent 1½ hours in the Imperial War Museum, and emerged feeling shattered and sick. War is Hell; it is a crime committed by the human race against its own hopes, ideals and souls ... A vast sense of futility possessed me. What are the dreams of all the artists, poets and thinkers – the most valuable part of mankind – in the face of this bloody chaos? The youth of the world tearing one another to pieces! It is too ghastly and grotesque to contemplate without tears of anger. The picture (by Orpheus) called *The Unknown Warrior*,* with a cross in the background, is a blasphemy, Christ can have had no part in that carnage and horror.

---

*   Courage is almost certainly referring to Irish artist Sir William Orpen's painting, *To the Unknown British Soldier in France.*

5 January 1929

I have been reading Jane Austen's *Emma* with delight, after too many 'modern' novels ... Nevertheless, what snobs, what frigid moralists, most of J.A.'s characters are! Their intellectual interests are restricted to a little music, a little 'elegant' verse, an occasional book or so, with almost complete oblivion of the world of thought or of politics. Yet in their way they are perfect; they are completely their own world, and hence strangely satisfying. The impression is not false: J.A. has sincerely passed her material through her emotional system and set down the resultant integers. In consequence she has produced a work of art. And what occasional humour! – Mr Knightley's 'However, come on a donkey if you prefer it.'*

Journal of my journey back from Greece in 1927

Jan. 6th.

The train left Athens at 9 o'clock this morning. As there is a scarcity of passengers – only four of us on board – we gave each a double-berth compartment – the usual wagon-lit size. My bed seems narrow but is quite comfortable. Next door to me is a Frenchwoman, about fifty years of age, her face somewhat ravaged by time. We share the same 'bathroom' between the compartments.

I stand in the corridor of the train for an hour, watching Athens disappear. The Acropolis towers above the misty smoke of the town: I can see the Parthenon in relief against the early morning sky ... The sun is very hot as we wind slowly up the long gorge below Mount Pentelikon. The trees in the valleys are fine – young fresh Mediterranean pines and a few olives. After the rain yesterday, the soil is a rich volcanic terra-cotta colour, and the shadows on the distant hills very dark blue. Presently, as the train climbs steadily into the mountains, some higher, snow-coloured peaks are visible ahead.

Lunch: at which I sit opposite to a saturnine-visaged Greek officer en route for Salonika. The mountain scenery through the windows very fine,

---

* Courage is close. The quotation is 'Come on a donkey, however, if you prefer it.'

A visit to a Greek temple.

S20-568c, MS-0999/182, Hocken Collections

especially when we come out high above the long flat vale of Marathon, stretching to the sea. The train is going very slowly, wheezing heavily. After lunch we stop at a junction of some sort where the Frenchwoman, speaking good English, tells me that the conductor has told *her* that, owing to the slow progress of the train, we shall probably miss the connection with the Orient Express at Nish, in Serbia.

Presently, with a deal of snorting the train starts again. We now run through high shallow valleys among the mountains. Shepherds in [woollen] frieze-coats by the line, minding the scraggy-looking sheep. It is evidently the lambing-season, as great 'corrals' of reeds, six feet high, have been built to shelter the flocks from the wind. No fences at all: the shepherds are nomads. They apparently live in little Esquimeau-huts of reeds, like beehives. The train is still climbing, twisting upon itself amongst the reddish foothills. It begins to snow very gently – a presage of cold-to-come, though the air is still warm.

The French Lady appears in the corridor in a black tam o'shanter and is amiable to me about the view. I begin to feel sleepy and retire to my bunk. An hour later a train stops with a jerk: I look out the window and see a single soldier standing to attention by the line. Is this a frontier or a hold-up? A long stop while the wheezy Greek locomotive gathers breath, then we proceed. We are supposed to reach Salonika at 8 but are already 4 hours late.

At dinner the French lady sits opposite to me: we talk about Greek history, Bernard Shaw (whom she declares she knows personally), and about English newspapers, which she says are all advertisements. She asks me what the young men of England read of their contemporaries. With hesitation I mention Aldous Huxley, but she doesn't know of him.* After dinner, one of the other passengers (an Englishman), who has seen me talking to the F.L. (French Lady), says I shall doubtless have an entertaining journey. Well …

---

* English writer and philosopher Aldous Huxley (1894–1963) is best remembered for his 1932 novel, *Brave New World*.

Jan. 7th.

Awoken numerous times in the night by foreign gentlemen demanding to
see passports, luggage, money, etc. By daylight we have reached the Yugo-
Slav frontier. The country, under a gray light, looks dull – clusters of small
mud houses and straw shacks. The train is again climbing slowly, across
undulating downs. The French Lady quiet.

About 9 we reach a station with the name of Kymahobo-Kumanovo. Four
to five inches of snow on the ground. Breakfast not until 10.30, as we have
to wait until a dining car is hitched on at some godforsaken spot. During
the meal, F.L. suddenly says, apropos of the landscape: '*Now* I know and
understand the Russians – their characters are velvety like the snow which
covers Russia.'

After lunch we reach Nish, to find that we have hopelessly missed the
connection with the Orient Express, which left five hours ago.

The F.L. tells me, to while away the time, that she is writing a book. She
jumps from that to English aristocracy and says she knows the Asquiths
(Anthony she calls 'the genius').* Thence we switch to the subject of English
food. She admires our roast beef and 'plain bread and butter', but says that
our vegetables are abominable. I say in return that I like French coffee and
omelettes but consider French tea revolting.

At 8 o'clock we reach Belgrade. It is bitterly cold. The F.L. and I go for
a walk along the platform and find an all-night coffee-stall. As there is a
rumour that the train may have no dining-car again until we get to Trieste
– which may not be until to-morrow afternoon – we have a good snack,
and also buy some provisions against possible famine: biscuits and some
chocolate. I change some drachmas into dinars and buy a banana also.

We leave Belgrade at midnight. Snow falling.

Jan. 8th.

Wake with a slight headache, to find us just entering Zagreb. A vast hotel
opposite the station: not a single window open in the place. The station is

---

*   Anthony Asquith (1902–1968) was a noted film director.

crowded with fat peasant-women waiting for a train behind us. One woman carries all her luggage balanced on her head. Another carries a large milk-can in the same position. Zagreb appears a most prosperous place: big buildings of grey concrete with green doors and shutters. Traces of Hungarian rule still?

I say good-morning to the F.L. She says I look as if I had just had a bath: this effect is perhaps due to the influence of a clean shirt. I notice, incidentally, that the F.L. doesn't do much splashing in the bathroom; in fact I doubt if she washes very much at all, except for an occasional dab of rose-water. At lunch I discover that her book is on the love-affairs of Catherine the Great of Russia – a bijou volume which she has contracted to write for the editors of La Vie Amoureuse series.

The train stops for three hours in a pass of the River Sale – a sombre-looking torrent. It is snowing again and is bitingly cold. The conductor says the train has often had to wait here for four or five days when there has been a big snow-storm ahead. Heaven preserve us, I want to get to England.

The F.L. says she is a great friend of Marie Laurencin, the French woman painter, who was interned for six years as a consequence of having rashly married a German on the 2nd of August 1914. The F.L. admits to 'a *snobbisme* for great men'. She regrets not having met Tolstoy or Napoleon. She met Rasputin four times in Russia and has written a book on him. I ask her: 'Was he the dirty old peasant one hears about?' She says: 'No! That is not a bit true. He was taking baths all of the time.' He was, she explains, a rather engaging, simple peasant, very fascinating to women, and vastly different from most of the people at the Russian court. The Czarina, in fact, felt that she was getting to know the Russian people more closely through him. It is not true that he was her lover, though the F.L. had once heard the Czarina referred to in Moscow as 'Mrs Rasputin'.

The F.L. rather baffles me: she seems to have had a wonderful life. I don't even know what her name is. After dinner, as we pass a handsome young Italian Customs officer in the corridor, she says innocently: 'I think one can learn a lot in trains, you know.'

The train is shunted into a siding at Trieste.

Jan. 9th.

Slept very well, save for a pain at dawn. At 7 o'clock the train is hitched on to the Constantinople–Paris Express and we set off at great speed. Fresh coffee and rolls of brownish bread for breakfast. The four of us from Athens are still the only people on the train. We feel we are once more in sight of civilisation, after the interminable Jugo-Slavia. We are now speeding through typical Italian scenery – white houses with tiled roofs, surrounded with cypresses and poplar trees. Snowy alps in the distance to the north – a lovely rosy colour in the early light. Fresh feeling in the air. We are in the land of Mussolini, hush-hush! The two French people in the car do not like him: a national prejudice.

I buy a French paper and read in it the amazing story of the government official who was found dead in Paris hanging by the neck in front of a large mirror: he was dressed in woman's clothes and wearing a blonde wig. Too incredible for fiction, as I tell the F.L. She, however, says she understands, and smiles distantly. She is not in a good temper this morning, being annoyed with the Italian Customs-men for having examined at length the manuscript for her Vie Amoureuse book which she keeps in a green leather bag.

We reach Venice at 11.30 but stay only five minutes. The sea (what one can see of it) is a wonderful opal blue. The town is almost invisible from the railway embankment. I saw only one gondola, moored to a small striped house impudently labelled 'Lido' (the real Lido being the other side of Venice).

At lunch the F.L., at my suggestion, talks of D'Annunzio.* She says: 'His conversation is most wonderful to listen to and is like nobody else's. He makes up words – rich, new words – not Italian, not French, but with a recognisable Latin root, to express states of mind, mood and colour.' Dusé was furious with him for publishing *The Flame of Life* (a novel concerned with

---

* Gabriele D'Annunzio (1863–1938) was an Italian writer in several genres, a military hero and a politician. His famous erotic novel, *The Flame of Life*, was published in 1900.

their personal relations), in which she is called an old woman. There was (the F.L. says) 'A great boost-up about it'.

The train stops at Verona. I am called from my compartment by the F.L. to be shown the tops of the cypress-tress in the 'original' garden of *Romeo and Juliet*. She says that Jean Cocteau, in his French adaptation of Shakespeare's play, cut out all the love-passages.* I say indignantly: 'But they are the essential parts of the play.' The F.L. replies: 'Oh, it was only Cocteau's little joke. He is like that.'

We pass Lake Garda, beautiful, softly gleaming in the sun, with snow-covered Tyrolean Alps on the far side. The soil of the country looks very dark and is marvellously cultivated.

During dinner we pass through the four miles of the Simplon Tunnel. With the dessert, the F.L. and I exchange cards, as to-morrow we are due to reach Paris. Her card, with a deep black border, reads: 'Princesse Marie Murat.'† I blush, suddenly recollecting that she had been seen off from Athens by the French Legation – a lot of top-hats on the platform.

At dinner there enters the dining-car a very tall, chic woman in dark furs, accompanied by a young, frizzy-haired negro. The Princess recognises the lady and rises to talk to her. It is the Marquesa Casati, an Italian Marquise, travelling (so the Princess explains later) from Milan to Paris to collect her monthly alimony, which the Paris Courts refuse to let her transmit through the country. The Princess says she is usually accompanied by a live snake, being absolutely fearless of animals. She says further that the Marquesa appears at all the big balls in Paris, as nearly naked as possible, in order to display a lovely figure. She is the original of Maurice Dekobra's *Madone des Sleepings*.‡ She owns a place in Italy where she has 25 portraits of herself

---

*   Jean Cocteau (1889–1963) was a Renaissance man – poet, playwright, novelist, designer and artist.
†   Marie de Rohan-Chabot (1876–1951), an aristocrat and writer who was born and died in Paris, went by two different pen-names: Princesse Lucien Murat and Marie de Chambrun.
‡   A 1925 novel by this French writer.

painted by as many different painters, all celebrated. She is certainly very lovely, what one can see of her face below her short nose-length veil.

Later, after the two women have had a talk, the Princess confides to me that the negro is (possibly) the lady's chauffeur. She leaves, however, room for another and different conjecture.

The Marquesa says that the Italians are sick and tired of Mussolini: his autocracy has gone too far.

We pass St Moritz and Montreux, going at about 80 miles an hour. A brilliant moonlight night. I sit at the window and catch a glimpse of Chilon Castle as we flash past. The ground is covered with snow.

French Customs officials at midnight at Vallorbes. They do not open anything of mine, but the Princess, next door, is fool enough to declare a Greek vase, hitherto concealed. Much gesticulation. The Princess, in her night-gown, is finally milked of 300 francs. The poor lady, her hair hanging down her face, is highly indignant. 'They think their own nobility are smuggerlers [sic],' she says bitterly.

Jan. 10th.

A fifth day of train-travelling. I'm sick of it.

We reach Paris at 8.30, after a very scampy [skimpy] breakfast which gives me indigestion. I say goodbye to the Princess, who says I am to come and see her whenever I am in Paris, and adds: 'I'm glad I've had such an interesting fellow-passenger' – which is, after all, a charming compliment.

I reach Calais at two p.m. A good crossing on the Channel boat. Two passenger aeroplanes, flying low down, pass the boat: one a German monoplane. At last an English train and an English ham-sandwich (unmistakeable). A quick train to Victoria, thence to the Wigmore Hotel. Feeling tired and dirty, I jump into a hot bath and read my letters there, enveloped in steam.

FINIS

1929–1931

23 January 1929

Began this new volume of my journal. Am wondering what shall have happened when I reach the final page. I find that when I am completely happy I have little or nothing to write down – my soul becomes, in prosperity, like 'a candle in daylight', as Aldous Huxley puts it. Is a journal, then, a record of misfortunes, bad moods, indigestion, and acute attacks of Recording angel? God forbid! However, we'll see.

Just one good resolution ... Be more and more *tolerant* of those people not in sympathy with my own views.

31 January 1929

Had lunch to-day with E. Over the coffee: –

E: You, of course, are the complete *litterateur* – you see life wholly in terms of literature – a good retort is to you merely a good line dramatically.

Myself: Oh, steady on, I'm not quite as bad as that!

E: You are! I believe that when you talk to people you do so purely to absorb them for your future literary ends.

Myself: In other words, I'm a nice, spiritual vampire?

E: Oh, no, but your function is that of a kind of translator. There is little of yourself in what you write.

Myself: Then I suppose I can never write anything good?

E: Not at all! It means that probably you'll do very subtle, shrewd, sympathetic work. But your own ego will never be laid bare: you're too self-conscious, soul-conscious.

Myself: I believe in objectifying myself as much as possible, undoubtedly.

E: But it is *the man who writes* that is interesting, ultimately.

Myself: 'Thou turnest my eyes into my very soul, Hamlet!' (Exeunt.)

18 February 1929

Weininger's theory: – that in a perfect – or at least a satisfactory – marriage the female element in the husband's character complements the male element in the wife's in such a way that the total male elements and the total female elements, when taken from both persons, result in a male and a female norm. But what is this norm? This 100%?

21 March 1929

Talking with E. the other night, we both, after some 'fencing', agreed that there is no real fulfilment of self in passion – physical passion, at least. However greatly one adores the object of desire, his beauty, his being, his apartness, his fascinating uniqueness of body and soul – all those qualities one wants to absorb as though the infusion were necessary to one's very life – the ultimate merging, the repose of a passionate meeting, always escapes like quicksilver from the palm of the hand. Even in the sharpest moments of physical ecstasy one is only cheated into a belief in fulfilment because the body is urgent ~~that~~ one's mind should be occupied ~~only~~ by its physical pleasure, which momentarily depends on another person. The two egos remain apart. ~~This may, I sadly suppose, be part of the revenge sex inversion takes on us. A passion too intellectualised, perhaps.~~

25 April 1929

All my life I shall fight against the unwritten, senseless, cruel law that brands sexual inverts as degenerates and beasts. I have suffered untold agony from the prevalence of this view even amongst normally intellectual people. Sexual intercourse between males – *where both are inverts* – has every scrap of right to be considered as normal as that between men and women. Owing to the nature of inverts, 'love' more often plays a part in it than in those cases considered socially excusable – e.g. habitual copulation between male and female, or unblushing prostitution.

26 April 1929

I think I can trace in myself the following analogy between a creative artist (of any kind) and a woman during pregnancy.

19 May 1929

Portrait of a Bloody Little Fool

'I adore blue,' he cried fervently. 'Do you like green?'

'Some greens,' I admitted.

'We are always supposed to like green, aren't we?' he reflected. (We? Good God, was I of the same species, as this fawning, scented spaniel?)

'I'm afraid I hadn't heard of that distinction,' I replied, double edged.

He tried a new tack. 'You write, don't you? I'm *so* interested in writers. Do you put real people into your books?'

'I happen to have written so few. But I shouldn't "put in" real people, on principle.'

'Oh, but why? They're so *interesting!*'

'In a biography, perhaps; in fiction, they're far too inconsequential to be of any use.'

He gazed round, and adjusted his *green* tie. 'I wish you'd play the piano to me.'

'Certainly.'

'Do play Liszt's *Liebestraum* It always makes me want to throw off all my clothes and dance.'

'I'm afraid I don't play it. If I could, I don't think I would.'

'Why; don't you like it?' He leaned archly over the piano before me.

'No: it's, politely speaking, balls,' I said.

'Oh, is it?' He thought a moment. 'I've got two records of it,' he added. While I began some Brahms he examined my book-shelf and discovered a poem of mine in *Oxford Poetry, 1925.*

'Oh, oh, do you write poems?'

I stopped playing and said in desperation, 'Yes: go and sit down and read it!'

He went, and having finished, breathed: 'Lovely! ... Why did you write it under a chestnut-tree?' (The poem is called 'Sunlight Through a Chestnut-tree'.)

'Why not?'

'Did your inspiration come to you there?'

'Oh, God! ... Naturally.'

'How interesting. But all writing is so *thrilling* to me ... I wish you'd put me into a play or a story, would you?' (Wriggling his posterior on the couch.)

'Would you enjoy that?' I asked.

'Oh, yes. To see myself!' He swept the fair hair from his forehead.

And so on. In fact, half an hour more of so on. Until finally –

'Do you like me?' he asked softly.

By this time I had drugged myself with a good drink and was more equal to him.

'No,' I said. 'I think you're a bloody little fool. You talk utter rot; you stink of disgusting scent; you want every man to make love to you; you've never experienced a sincere emotion in your life; in fact you ought to be shot. I should do it myself if you weren't rather decorative.'

He listened to nothing save the last sentence. 'Do you think I'm nice to look at?'

I gave it up. He had actually enjoyed the castigation.

13 July 1929

To talk of the 'pangs of unrequited love' sounds trite, theatrical, false, yet those very pangs are like the workings of hell in the soul. I have suffered to-day as I never remember suffering before, and (what aggravates the pain) over a person with whom I have, at heart, very little in common and whom I pray to forget in a month. Yet the awful gnawings of unsatisfied desire, of affection derided and made to seem cheap by a single word, the degradation of the whole affair into a mere sensual *liaison* – those are things that hurt like the very devil. The desire for a confidant has brought me to write down this, and I do so not only to ease the pain I am suffering. My thoughts are turning round and round, crying: 'I am hurt, I am hurt', like wounded animals; they torment me, I can't get any rest from them. He will never know; the affair soon passed on my side beyond what he was willing to give to it, on his.

After the first few days he was casual, stupid, thoughtless, finally, to-day, breaking a long-made appointment. 'You didn't come,' I accused him. 'No,' he said, 'I thought you wouldn't turn up. I went to P___ instead.' But he did not apologise, he obviously did not care. I lost my temper. Something about the hard, dreadful sunlight we were standing in and that showed on his cruelly smiling face, infuriated me with anger and despair. I could hardly speak. 'What made you think that?' I cried. 'Oh, I don't know,' he said. 'People don't always turn up.' His eyes despised me. I went away. I don't know where. I just walked about, trying not to think, for a long time. Now the pain has come home and its pangs are giving me no relief. I resort to this womanish journal; storm and stress are written down here; the edge is taken off my knife.

21 July 1929

A week later

Some of that storm and stress still remains if I let myself think. But I can't forget the awful morbid pain that made me write down the above.

What an extraordinary shuttle-cock is this thing called self-esteem! So vain it is, that the admiration of a child or of the biggest fool on earth can make it go jigging upward. This morning when mine had momentarily gone down to zero a letter came from R., in which he expressed, quite incidentally, an admiration for my regular habits of life. And on that ridiculous pretext I found myself thinking myself no end of a fellow – Smiling, Olympian, sailing along on a cloud of regular habits. And as a crowning irony I have the panache to record the reaction in the journal of irregularities! My God!

16 September 1929

Stupid, vain, foolish – whatever it is – I have a horror of being photographed. How I have suffered in the past when, after long cogitation, I have ventured the process. Never does the resulting picture seem to be *me*, but some cruel caricature from which all humanity has been squeezed. I writhe, and tear up the beastly thing. I feel unnecessarily wounded by it, as though I had given myself away badly in a delicate crisis! Have beautiful people nothing to give away, that they enjoy being pictured so constantly for posterity?

13 October 1929

This life I lead is stifling me – I am free and yet hemmed in on every side – by my character, my friends, my very talents themselves. I am fossilizing, becoming intellect-bound, living on my own thoughts and emotions, hopelessly introvert. My very writing, for what it is worth, is a cowardly escape from myself – from the hostility of one part of my mind to the others, which produces in me a constant warfare which, it exhausts me to contemplate, I feel inside me. I do not even write from the heart, but from the head, with the result that my compositions are sterile, cerebral, and do not move me, save in the moment of creation itself. I feel cut off, and have nobody to balance for it but myself. Impossible, insufferable position! I feel that my only hope is to break away, to shed my old self, to be born again as a little child.

16 January 1930

A new lover; and such a gentle, beautiful, affectionate creature! Name Frank; colour, dark; age, 25; height, 6ft 1in; weight (I asked him this) 182lbs:– 13 stone; nationality – father Argentine, mother Cornish. An athlete, and handsome; one of the sweetest creatures I've ever known, with something so touchingly lonely and child-like in him that it makes tears of gentleness start to the eyes. A very passionate lover: he calls me, in soft Spanish: 'Blanco y oro' – 'white and gold' – being amazed at the whiteness of my body, and my general fairness (he asked me, 'Was I a Swede?'). We are both devoted to music; it seems to move us equally. Discussed the love-duet of Tristan and Isolde – which, he said, made him 'shiver with exaltation'.*

3 February 1930
This man has changed my life. For the first time I am willing to surrender my reserve to another. Even my sense of humour 'goes under': and my 'second man' (a sneaking hyper-critical fellow) disappears – which is extremely remarkable. Long may it last!

9 February 1930
My twenty-seventh birthday. I turn back a year in the journal to find that last February I wrote as an aspiration: 'To be famous and to be loved.' Well, I am loved. Now what about the fame?

11 March 1930
I love this man unreservedly. I cannot imagine life without him.

13 March 1930
Paco left. I love him.

3 April 1930
By the way, I finished, some weeks ago, my long-short tale on a homosexual theme – 'Episode in Early Life'. It has quality, but needs re-writing. It begins too slowly, with too much description, which should emerge during the course of the narrative. The insertion of the Freudian dream seems to fall flat with most of those who have read it: perhaps it ought to come out, as being puzzling, and superfluous.

---

* *Tristan and Isolde* (*Iseult*), which dates from the twelfth century, is the story of an adulterous love affair between a Cornish knight and an Irish princess. The love-duet mentioned here is probably a reference to Richard Wagner's opera, *Tristan und Isolde*.

5 April 1930

Le bonheur de saigner sur le coeur d'un ami,
Le besoin de pleurer bien longtemps sur son sein,
Le désir de parler à lui, bas à demi,
Le rêve de rester ensemble sans dessein!

Le malheur d'avoir tant de belles ennemies,
La satiété d'être une machine obscène,
L'horreur des cris impurs de toutes ces lamies.
Le cauchemar d'une incessante mise en scène!

—Verlaine

And South America seven thousand miles distant.

[The good fortune to bleed on the heart of a friend,
The need to weep a very long time on his breast,
The desire to talk to him, half-softly,
The dream of simply staying together!

The misfortune to have so many fair enemies,
The disgust with being an obscene machine,
The horror of all those Lamias' impure cries.
The nightmare of a ceaseless *mise en scène!*]*

28 April 1930

A dream last night about Paco. – A small room with fruit on the table –
Himself in a grey suit. – Atmosphere of jealousy, frustration – Kisses of
paralyzing sweetness. – Sadness. – The overwhelmingly tender embraces of
last farewells. – Kisses salt with tears. – The old anguish, – Adios.

    I awoke longing desperately to see him again.

---

* This poem by Paul Verlaine (1844–1896), titled 'Explication' ('Explanation'), was first
published in 1885 but may date from as early as 1872. This translation is by Dunstan
Ward.

25 May 1930

Paco's aunt came to tea with me. It was the most usual wet London Sunday – I had feared the old lady might not turn up. But she came, in a black dress & hat, and wearing a string of pearls and a little ruff of tulle at her throat.

I found it difficult to hide the suspicion – largely true – from her that I had asked her solely to talk to her about Paco. But I don't think she really guessed, though when she spoke of him as a little boy, then of his adult quietness and charm, it was all I could do to prevent tears of joy and gratitude starting into my eyes. So much did I, and still do I, love her nephew! It was all I could do, too, not to argue rudely with her when she praised his brother, to Paco's disadvantage. Oddly enough, she picked out, to deprecate them, almost exclusively those traits, emotions, manners, in my beloved P., which I know – being one of the fraternity myself – to be the outward visible signs of a deeply rooted Uranian temperament. But I had never before realised the strange, sweet, frustrative pleasure of hearing a loved object spoken of by another person to whom – though for widely different reasons – that same object is just as dear and to be cherished as it is to myself. Yet the result of this stolen pleasure was that, finally, I suffered. For when the old lady had gone she took with her something of the dear ghost she had recreated for me. I felt desperately alone and sad, longing for Paco's presence, – even for those little 'deficiencies' his good aunt had deplored.

27 May 1930

To-day I began writing a sort of fictional autobiography ['The Promising Years'] in the manner of Proust, of my own early childhood. I find that many things that I have stored in memory have now become profoundly interesting & significant to me. I console myself by thinking that, if they are of no account to anybody but myself, at least the writing down of them gives me practice in composition.

> For men like M., mutual love, apart from the difficulties, so great as to be almost insurmountable, which it meets in the ordinary man, adds to these others so exceptional that what is always extremely

rare for everyone becomes in their case well-nigh impossible, and, if there should befall them an encounter which is really fortunate, or which nature makes appear so to them, their good fortune, far more than that of the normal lover, has about it something extraordinary, selective, profoundly necessary.

—Proust, *Sodome & Gomorrhe*[*]

29 May 1930

Writing is to me a sort of drug. When I am unhappy I write.

8 July 1930

In love, how is one to know whether one indeed loves the lover or merely a ghost created by one's own loneliness?

21 July 1930

To-day E[ric] rang me up and asked whether he could come to see me *alone*. He arrived with red eyes: he had been crying. He has been living with B. – who constantly gets drunk. At last E. could stand it no longer and they had a violent quarrel, E. saying that B. must choose between him and *his bottle*. B. said: 'I am a hopeless drunkard, I can't give it up', followed tears, imploring etc. all to no purpose. Yet they are deeply in love with one another. Impasse!

I listened to E.'s story and sympathised, but there was nothing to say except platitudes. After an hour he felt better and had a glass of sherry.

> The elect artist voluntarily purchases a withdrawal from the plane of common life, since only in such isolation can he create. No doubt he takes with him his memories of things observed and things endured, which later may be utilised to lend plausibility & corroborative detail … And sometimes the mind goes of its own accord into this

---

[*] French writer Marcel Proust (1871–1922) is best known for his seven-part novel *À la recherche du temps perdu* (*In Search of Lost Time*). *Sodome et Gomorrhe* (*Sodom and Gomorrah*) is the fourth book.

withdrawal, and reverie abstracts the creative writer from the ties and aspirations of his existence as a taxpayer. Of the pleasure he knows then one may not speak: but it is a noble pleasure.

—Cabell, *Beyond Life**

9 September 1930

And when to such isolation is added the loneliness of the sexual invert, what a crown of thorns is there, indeed!

27 September 1930

A strange reaction to-day – I was walking through Cavendish Square when a smell of rich, rotten wood, wafted from heaven knows where, took me back in a flash to a bush-stream in the mountains of New Zealand. A damp, cool, primeval whiff.

30 September 1930

Took a stroll up Marylebone High St this morning before lunch, inspecting the shop windows and considering the good things of Autumn – principally enormous yellow pears, giant chrysanthemums and rich, mole coloured mushrooms. Having seen a performance of *Richard III* last night, I went to the National Portrait Gallery this afternoon to see the contemporary picture of him.

10 October 1930

F[rank]'s birthday to-day. Was walking in the park, admiring the trees when I suddenly remembered this, all the colour seemed to leave things for a moment because he was not beside me.

---

* American writer James Branch Cabell (1879–1958) was particularly known for his escapist fiction. *Beyond Life* (1919) tells of an imagined conversation between a young author and a successful editor.

15 October 1930

The following note came back to me in lieu of a rejection slip to-day. From the editor of the *London Mercury* –

> Dear Sir,
> You write so extremely well – you are evidently a good novelist *in posse* – that I am sorry you should have expended so much pains on a story that will never be printed by any paper in which a person of your intelligence would wish to appear.
> Yours faithfully,
> J.C. Squire*

I admit frankly that that staggers me! The story in question is the 'Episode in Early Life' which I had hitherto regarded, in spite of its subject, as quite printable. Of course it's the old stigma of homosexuality again but, good God, to a man of Squire's intelligence – to turn his own phrase against himself – I had thought that the subject was above the reproach implied in his letter, whether or not he accepted the story! I feel stung and humiliated, all the more so in that I have only myself to blame.

24 October 1930

Flowers in my room: Scabious and pink roses. The scabious look purple by electric-light but are really sky-blue. The roses are rather frail and have opened too quickly. The scabious look hardy, the roses delicate.

---

* British writer John (later Sir John) Collings Squire (1884–1958) was best known for his editorship of the *London Mercury* but was also a noted anthologist, poet and historian.

26 November 1930

To a private view of Cecil Beaton's photographs and pictures.* A *coup d'oeil*
[glimpse] of an effete and out-played younger aristocracy and of 'the Bright
Young People'. I had the advantage of knowing most of the guest's names
without anyone knowing mine. Osbert Sitwell, Lady Lavery and Nellie
Wallace talking together struck me as the only funny thing of the afternoon:
– a codfish, a henna'ed orchid and a convalescent parrot. All the men sexual
inverts, and the women sterile through anaemia or Lesbianism. What a crew!
William Gerhardi gazed at me as though we'd met before – probably in a
railway W.C.†

2 December 1930

To-day I reserved my passage on the *Alcantara* for Buenos Aires. For once I
am letting my heart rule my head: I pray for the best, but it is impossible for
me to be parted any longer from F. I love him.

14 December 1930

I sail on Thursday (D.V.) for S. America.‡ A cable from Frank last night.
'Cheers. Expecting'.

18 December 1930

Left London 9.15 boat-train. *Alcantara* sailed at noon. Have a cabin to myself,
for which I'm profoundly thankful. We steam slowly down the channel in
a dense white fog. At lunch I am put at a table with a young Englishman
bound for Brazil and a young Argentine in a scarlet tie. The latter surprisingly

---

* Cecil Beaton (1904–1980) was best known as a fashion, portrait and war photographer,
  but was also an award-winning costume and stage designer for film and theatre.
† Writer Oswald Sitwell (1892–1969) was Edith Sitwell's brother; Hazel Lavery (1880–
  1935) a socialite, actor and painter; Nellie Wallace (1870–1948) a famous and much-
  loved music-hall star. William Gerhardi (1895–1977) was an Anglo-Russian novelist and
  playwright.
‡ D.V. is short for 'Deo volente' – God willing.

gives his name as 'Macgalty' and claims Irish descent, which perhaps also explains vivid tie. I try my Spanish (culled from *Brighter Spanish*) on him, and after a joke cry 'Qué risa!' ['How funny!'] He looks at me strangely and sighs. At six o'clock reach Cherbourg and take on some passengers – one of them, a voluble Franco-Turk, does some admirable expectoration in the next cabin to mine. Leave Cherbourg about 9. Evening spent in assessing fellow-passengers, talking to Argentine, Macgalty, about English policemen and drinking gin & tonic in the smoking room. Go to bed early & read *Fortunes of Richard Mahony* until sleepy.* Ship rolling very slightly. Everyone says, somewhat vindictively, 'You wait till to-morrow!' A tiring day.

19 December 1930
Awoken by the steward at unearthly hour of 7.15 with a cup of tea, which he 'thought I might need'. Find ship is rolling worse. No bath, owing to 'water being dirty'. I feel like demanding, 'Who dirtied it?' but bath-steward looks too washed-out, so refrain. Reach breakfast-table feeling groggy, and toy with a few prunes and a cup of china tea. Afterwards walk the deck but, stomach feeling undecided, go to cabin and lie down. Steward says the swell 'goes to the head like'. Ship rolling like a pendulum – the old Bay of Biscay in evidence. Read and ruminate till lunch. Afternoon fine and warm. Play quoits on deck. Decide to try saloon piano after tea, but funk it on seeing the place full of governesses & children; a case of mañana, as I carefully explain to my Argentine friend. In the evening, a cinema performance in the dining room. 3 films of incredibly old and silly slapstick which reduce me to hysterics. One, called *Twenty Legs Under the Sea* a scream! I sit next to my Turkish gentleman who laughs & hawks together – definitely unpleasant. A gin & tonic with the Argentine before bed. Talk of Oxford.

---

*   *The Fortunes of Richard Mahony* is a three-part novel by Australian writer Henry Handel Richardson, the pen name of Ethel Florence Lindesay Richardson (1870–1946).

20 December 1930

Wake at 7.15 to find us at anchor off A Coruña. A long town on a water-front, at the end of a narrow harbour. After breakfast hundreds of Spanish emigrants come aboard and go forward to the 3rd class – a ruffianly-looking collective. Great drama when a well-wisher is left on board: gangway relowered amidst black curses on both sides. I try to remember what part of my schooling had to do with A Coruña and remember Sir John Moore: 'Not a sound was heard, not a funeral note.'* Sun much warmer but still a cold wind as we sail down the coast of Spain – low, arid hills with a few villages. Band plays in the lounge from 10.30–11 ('In a Monastery Garden' & 'Wine Women & Song', ending up with 'Happy Feet!'). After lunch I try the piano, but soon desist: instrument is a Strohmenger that has seen better days. Am implored to play Liszt's *Liebestraum* by a middle-aged woman with orange hair.

Reach Vigo harbour about five, and sail up between purple hills to a most lovely and theatrical-looking city with the lamps just beginning to be lit. Everyone stands entranced at the sight, and it is charming. A tender comes out and some passengers disembark (including the only person I had wanted to talk to in the second class). Dinner while anchored. Later, talk to a young cable engineer (Note: deep sea cable about thick as thumb, but shore cable, where there is friction and tides, about 6–7 inches diameter), and also to an old music-hall actor (John Carnell) who, flattered at my having spotted at once that he was 'of the profession', poured out a flood of autobiography (Vesta Tilley etc).† After 3 brandies & soda, just as he was beginning to act his own 'turn' & others – his own, an impersonation of a young man about to be married, with much face twitching – his wife, excellent woman of ex-barmaid type – enters smoking-room & says; 'Come away to bunk, my love.' They totter off. And so to bed myself.

---

*   Actually 'Not a drum was heard, not a funeral note', from Charles Wolfe's poem, 'The Burial of Sir John Moore after Corunna'.

†   Vesta Tilley (1864–1952), whose real name was Matilda Alice Powles, was a famous male impersonator.

21 December 1930

Reach Lisbon at about 11 o'clock. A glimpse of the *Do-X* in some sort of dry-dock as we go up the wide river-mouth.* Brilliant sun and blue sky. Ship goes along-side quay and is tied up after considerable difficulty – two ropes breaking under the strain. Gangways lowered. The old actor comes to bid farewell to me & says: 'Good-bye, my dear little friend!' After lunch I go ashore, walk along the docks and up into some gardens in the town. See a funeral go by: a bony horse drawing a sort of catafalque, with nodding black plumes: a priest following. Quite ¾ of the Portuguese wear carpet-slippers – or perhaps this is a Sunday habit, to-day being Sunday. Walk back to the ship for tea, then out in the sun on deck – marvellous, warm sun.

We sail punctually at 5 o'clock, the Bright Young People of Lisbon who had come in their best clothes, to look over the ship, hastily disembark at the last moment. I sleep until dinner – 50 minutes late, as clock has been retarded. In the evening read *Some Studies in the Formation of Character*† – found in the ship's library, and am interested in a chapter on Goethe and his book of reminiscences *Dichtung und Wahrheit* [Poetry and Truth]. Find that Goethe read and delighted in *Robinson Crusoe* as a child, as I did. Have a lot of brandy and go to bed. Ship rolling slightly. Warm breeze drifts in the porthole.

22 December 1930

A good night. Warm morning, with breeze. Sing tune of Ravel's *Bolero* in bath, but get hung up after 4 bars. After breakfast (quite a hearty one) walk a mile round the deck, with the Argentine, learning the Spanish numerals under tuition. Visit the luggage-room & arrange that my box to be brought to my cabin to-morrow. Sat in the sun and read *Fortunes of Richard Mahony*. Talk to a fellow-Englishman about railways in the Argentines, & the climate of Yorkshire. Lunch, then sleep 3 hours – extraordinarily soundly – cannot

---

* The *Dornier Do-X*, produced in 1929, was the world's biggest and most powerful flying-boat.

† Written by Charlotte M. Mason, this was published in 1923.

remember where I am or why on awakening. Tea. Write letters to be posted at Madeira to-morrow – Mother, Malcolm, Eric. Weather much warmer. Sea a deep, dark blue under cloudy sky. Play the piano & find myself out of practice already: arrange to practise on piano in dining room, to avoid lounge.

23 December 1930

Steward wakes me at 6.45 & says that breakfast is earlier as we may want to go ashore at Madeira. Look out of porthole and find ship already at anchor. A brilliant morning. After breakfast the ship is surrounded by boats, from which sunburnt youths offer to dive for silver thrown overboard. Throw in a 6^D [sixpence] and see it retrieved. I decide to go ashore, and make up a party of 3 with two Argentinos. We land in a launch & saunter through the town. Houses of white plaster, with red & green shutters, & roofs of Marseilles tiles. Palms and fine-leaved trees and some plane-trees with leaves gone brown but still unfallen (it is mid-winter). We have coffee at a restaurant on the pavement, and I buy some English cigarettes and some flowers – sweet-scented purple violets, & big camellias. Am wholly charmed by Madeira & register now to return one day & visit heights of the island.

At 11 we return to the ship and at noon sail. Sea calm. Cloud-shadows on the summits of the island astern. After lunch read 'Lycidas' to study the adjectives Milton uses, then go to barber's shop for a hair-cut. Barber sleepy & taciturn. After tea play piano in dining-saloon for an hour and enjoy it immensely. Dance in the evening, then discuss modern French painters with Argentino No. 2. See in news-bulletin that there has been the densest fog in London for years, and thank heaven I am out of it. To bed at midnight. Clock retarded eleven minutes.

24 December 1930

Xmas Eve. Bath-steward apologises for calling me late by saying that 'people seem to be soakin' a bit this morning'. A tasty Madeira fresh-herring for breakfast. At 10 o'clock go along to baggage-room & arrange once more that my trunk is to be brought to my cabin. Find the upper tray of trunk given way, but otherwise clothes in order. Listened to music in the lounge at eleven: a somewhat consumptive rendition of the Larghetto from Beethoven 2nd Symphony. At lunch the head-steward comes round with a list and suggests that I should put my name down to be embraced by Father Neptune on Monday. I firmly but gently decline, and make a private note on the willingness of the Englishman to endure self-inflicted horrors.

Sleep after lunch but am awakened by a clump on the door at 3.10 – my trunk arrived from the baggage-room: I rise lethargically & usher it in. After tea find that all the deck awnings are up; also swimming pool. Play piano for 1½ hours. Drink a couple of 'whiskey sours' with young Anglo-Brazilian before dinner. Delicious melon for dessert, cut to look like water-lily flowers. Dance after dinner on starboard deck. Weather warmer, and I sweat like a pig. Drink again – lager beer, iced – with small but hilarious party of ghastly people in smoking room, and sing school songs to assure ourselves that the British Empire and Christmas Day to-morrow are synonymous. And so to bed, in silk pyjamas owing to heat. Private resolution to begin some writing directly the hectivities of Xmas are over. This very material existence produces an empty feeling of aridity in what, perhaps blasphemously, I call the soul.

25 December 1930

Christmas Day. Awoken by a decidedly bleary-eyed steward (up till 4 in the morning 'celebrating'). Breakfast alone. A warm, grey morning – almost like an English Day. Rumour says we are in 'the Doldrums'. Ship begins to roll at lunch-time and continues throughout afternoon. Band plays in the lounge at 11 – a nauseous collection of Xmas melodies: 'A Dream of Christmas' etc – a great deal of 'Good King Wenceslas' with copious infiltrations of 'A Persian Market'. I sit on top deck and read dispiritedly. The children have a Xmas tree in the 1st class, but I arrive too late to see it. Decide I must begin to write again at once to ward off feelings of stagnation. Sleep a little after lunch then get out MS paper and stiffly begin the 3rd part of my book. Feel better immediately. After much labour concoct 2 sentences. After ten a swing on the top-deck. See some flying-fish overside. Ship still rolling & I feel sick but am not. Play piano for ½ hour and am buttonholed by boring colonel with charming Russian wife, and made to talk about English songs.

Xmas dinner in evening – the usual turkey and plum pudding. We drink port and burgundy and make a lot of stupid jokes about females, France, parentage and anatomy. After dinner sit on deck and listen to a band composed of the engine-hands and greasers – a squeaky and amusing affair. Two of the youngest greasers do a waltz à la Russian ballet, with many pirouettes and playful slaps on the hand. Much applause. Later retire to the smoking-room and attempt a lively conversation with a few chosen spirits – not my choice, however. I stay only long enough to imbibe a pint of lager, then retire to bed with the beginnings of a headache.

Am awakened at 2.30 in the morning by a steward rushing in to close the porthole, 'We're changing course, sir; there's a sea running on this beam.' Slams porthole & exits. Hear him give same explanation at door of next cabin, whose occupant, the Turk, hops up in great fright and cries 'Fire' in every known language before being calmed down.

26 December 1930

A grey, muggy morning. I sit on the top deck, write up this journal then carry on with my own writing: do 350 words odd. Have an orangeade and an ice-cream at 11. After lunch find I have a headache and take an aspirin, sleep until 3.15 and awake hot and stupid: feel better after tea and play deck-tennis. Sweat profusely. Heat very oppressive but not as bad as it might be, 800 miles from Equator. Play the piano for an hour – quite well for once. Dinner. Afterwards sit on boat-deck in the breeze, and attempt ineffectually to carry on a conversation in French with a young Portuguese – an undergraduate from Coimbra. He gracefully supplies the compliment (after some thought) that – 'Oxford est le premier université du monde' ['Oxford is the best university in the world'] – a sentiment I tone down by saying: 'De l'Angleterre, peut-être' ['In England, perhaps'], but am secretly gratified. He asks what 'mon ami' means in English: I tell him 'my friend', by which title he then proceeds to address me.

And so to bed. I turn on the fan (experimentally) in my cabin, and release a sort of miniature cyclone which almost blows me out of the porthole, and shakes the ceiling. Turn it off hastily lest the neighbouring Turk should begin tapping on the wall. Finish the 1st part of *Fortunes of Richard Mahony* before sleeping: a fine book, but the authoress cannot disguise that her hero is a patronising prig, deficient in humanity. Nevertheless, am looking forward to the next part. The detail of the book is fine, and the style easy, occasionally urbane. Find, just before dozing off, that I have got over the feeling that the voyage is a dream that may possibly turn out a bad one.

27 December 1930

Am awoken at 7.30 with very strong tea. A hot morning, but a light breeze. Some stewed figs and a boiled egg for breakfast. Afterwards sit on top-deck and write up this journal. Am disturbed by the 7-year-old son of an Anglo-Brazilian clerk, who, after watching me write, says it looks like the weed swaying under the sea – an extraordinarily good image on which my literary mind congratulates him. I write my book for 1½ hours ['The Promising Years'] and get on quite well, though heat becomes stifling. Am told that a silent and sinister-looking passenger in this class, whom we have dubbed The Man of Few Words ('He Doesn't Know Any More') is a novelist, by name Gilbert Parker.* An absolute hermit but that he is writing a screen scenario, the manuscript of which (according to the people at his table in the saloon) is added to, corrected, and considered during meals. Has as yet given nobody a chance to speak to him, and is rumoured (almost certainly falsely) to have told the assistant Purser that he has 'no wish to know anyone on board'. I respect his solitude, and integrity – also envy it sometimes, among these kind but damned inquisitive people.

Lunch, after which I sit on the upper deck in the slight breeze and read. From 3 o'clock until 6 suffer the most appalling fit of black depression it has ever been my fate to experience – probably due to the weather and a slight

---

*   Canadian-born novelist Gilbert Parker (1862–1932) was also for a time a Conservative member of the British House of Commons.

liver. At last in desperation play deck-tennis with Anglo-Brazilian until I can hardly stand. Cool down with an iced lemonade, then play the piano for an hour. Depression lessens, but is liable to descend when am alone. Resort to whiskey to dispel worst moments during the evening. Talk from 10 to midnight with a young 'chap' from Nottingham and his Argentinian wife on merits of London & Buenos Aires. She a handsome and clever creature (magnificent eyes & teeth), a hundred times the better of the North Country husband, who is pleasant but bourgeois to the fingertips. Obviously a case of Anglo-worship on her side. Heat insufferable: 8 degrees from Equator.

28 December 1930

A very hot night, but cooled by rain early in morning. Awoke feeling more cheerful, but am overcome by lethargy; a little dispelled by tea & bath. Morning seems cooler than yesterday: a delicious breeze. I wear my lightest clothes – white duck trousers & shirt – but suffer nevertheless. Sunday morning, and most people go to church in 1st class: I remain on top-deck and try to decide whether Sunday and the heat are sufficient excuses for not working. My irreligion rules out the Sunday, but my body refuses to ignore the heat. At 11 o'clock an absolute cascade of rain descends and temporarily cools atmosphere: whole ship streams water, which must have added 100 tons to her weight in five minutes. Sun comes out again & makes the air muggy.

Decide, finally, to abandon idea of work and reread some old letter from my grandmother instead: her letters perfectly reflect her – humorous, generous, lovely, tolerant. Make resolution to write to her. A short sleep and dream until tea. Later study Hugo's *Spanish Grammar*, in vain hope of eventually speaking the language, though doubtful of my need for asking (as in the Exercises): 'Does your aunt want a cab?' Play piano for 1¼ hours – but it is hot work.

A drink with Argentino No. 2 before dinner: we talk of the attempted English conquest of Buenos Aires at beginning of 19th century, of the anti-English B.A. paper *Critical*. He tells me of scathing comments on British

ignorance made by same journal when, in a beauty contest in England, Miss
Abyssinia was mistaken for Miss Argentina, both beginning with letter A!
Miss Abyssinia being black, indignation not unmerited. I sympathise ...
After dinner sit on top-deck and read *Fortunes of R.M.*, until aroused by wife
of Brazilian clerk who says she has been thinking about me and & decides I
must be an artist. I tell her I am really going to South America to introduce
sanitary plumbing to the Andes. She says she can hardly believe *that*. And so
to bed. Equator crossed during night: my 3rd time.

29 December 1930
Awoken by blaze of sunlight through porthole at 7. Arise, drink tea, and
then, feeling energetic, do physical jerks before bath. Breakfast of melon &
Scotch herring (same as Madeira herring early on in voyage). A stiff breeze
blowing on deck. Preparations, including Proclamation in 'ye olde Englishe',
for King Neptune's arrival on board. At 10.30 ceremonies begin – I watch
for half an hour and come to the conclusion that the Public Schools do this
sort of hollow jollity a good deal better. Neptune and wife, in flax-wigs,
are however, excellent bits of make-up. My Portuguese boy-friend from
Coimbra bursts into tears on being put into the tipping-chair – poor lad,
quite excusably, being terrified out of his life by such an English custom.
Most painful moments for those concerned. I feel all my horror of mass-
habits return with sickening force. However, ceremonies soon over. Just
before lunch ship passes island of Fernando Noronha on port-beam: an arid-
looking place about the size of Madeira, but with two wind-shaped peaks – a
foretaste of Rio. Fernando is a convicts' island – all the villains of Brazil being
there enhoused, apparently to their liking, for I am told that several have
refused to leave at the end of their term. But, since the recent revolution it is
known that the rôles of convicts and warders have been reversed – a typical
little Brazilian joke ... I am glad to see land again – after a week of open sea.
A short sleep in the afternoon, then write until tea-time. Take 25-minute
sunbath which makes me feel giddy – old Sol a bit too genial in this latitude
– 6 degrees from Equator. Play piano badly for an hour. Later sit on top deck

in breeze and read *Fortunes of R.M.*, a book I have come to admire without liking. And so to bed at 10.30, and sound asleep.

30 December 1930

Hot muggy morning, sea like lead. Enjoy my bath & cold shower. Breakfast of grapefruit, boiled egg & iced water. Work from 10–12: fairly satisfactory. Sleep after lunch until 3, then real Galsworthy's *In Chancery* with admiration but not envy. (Holly and Val are as nauseous a pair of Bright Young People as any ever invented by A.A. Milne, Esq.)* Tea. A very sweaty game of deck-tennis, which does me a lot of good. Cool down & play piano for an hour – not very well, accuracy being impaired by fatigue. Lend my *Mercury Story Book* to English wife of Brazilian clerk: She enjoys my story in it and says I 'must have fun thinking out such a plot!' Agree, but with private reservations.

Roast guinea fowl for dinner. Watch sailors dancing together. At 9.15 a cinema show on deck – 3 short films, of which the last, an early Fox Comedy called *Bear Knees* is best, but the sort of thing made up as they go along (butting goats, water-slides, monkeys playing with dynamite, etc.) First two films (American) absolute drivel: I am amazed to hear Spaniards behind me talk of them as 'British tripe'. Turn to say: 'No soy Ingleses – Americanos' but without noticeable effect.

A whiskey & soda and sandwich, & then to bed. Kill a cockroach with my slipper on the cabin wall.

31 December 1930

New Year's Eve. Sun wakes me at 6: take off my pyjama-jacket and have a sunbath. Study Spanish Grammar for ½ hour before my tea arrives. A glorious sunny morning with breeze from coast (not in sight, though not

---

* Novelist and playwright John Galsworthy (1867–1933) is best known for his Forsyte trilogy, of which *In Chancery* is the second book. A.A. Milne (1882–1956) is most famous for his Winnie-the-Pooh books, the success of which overshadowed his seven novels and many plays.

more than 40 miles away). Ship due in Rio soon after midnight to-morrow. Write most of the morning – not badly. Sleep in afternoon & read *In Chancery*.

After tea play deck-games, then attack piano for usual hour. Broach a half-bottle of champagne for dinner and get pleasantly warmed-up, but have to continue drinking to sustain spirits. Somehow get entangled with several engineer officers, drink in their cabins, and at midnight join sticky hands and sing 'Auld Lang Syne' in a corridor smelling of oil & whiskey. Colonel, who has suddenly revealed Scots descent, holds a Hogmanay party and kicks up a hell of a din on 'C' deck. However, things grow calmer towards 2 o'clock in the morning. I put out my light & sleep – by now feeling less drunk.

P.S. Forgot to mention ceremony of haggis, arranged by Colonel at dinner. A great skirling of (Spanish) bagpipes ushers in party of four in various stages of Highland dress, which party threads between the tables (led by my cabin-steward in a glengarry & spats), and exits amid applause. They return in a moment with a salver on which lies semblance of large potato in jacket: it is planted before Colonel, who spears it with knife. Concretion afterwards handed round to those of Highland breeding, who peck at it gingerly. Spanish passengers all gape open-mouthed (which is perhaps not surprising).

1 January 1931

Awake early with doubtful taste in mouth. A very hot morning with hardly a breeze. After breakfast catch sight of Brazilian coast – a distant line of pale blue mountains. Spend morning writing letters (mater, Ronnie, Malcolm, Helen, Ronald & Emlyn). After lunch sleep, then have a haircut. Temperature sinks during afternoon and at dinner-time is quite cool (70). We approach Rio in a full moonlight night. With two others I go up into the bows & watch us come in – an amazing sight – also a slightly anxious experience, as we had watched what was either rockets or gun-fire in the sky, while still at sea, and suspected another revolution. However, all was well. But I pick up a flea in the bows (3rd class)! We sail slowly into the most wonderful and fantastic harbour, lit up by millions of electric-lights, with vague, moon-lit peaks behind. A wonderful sight. Temperatures soars up directly we anchor – and my cabin is like a conservatory. I stay on deck unable to stop gazing at the town & harbour. Eventually retire to a sultry bed at 12.40.

2 January 1931

Awake to find us tying up at a quay. Put on my pale grey suit, ready to go ashore with Anglo-Brazilian youth. Blazing sunlight & mounting heat. We take a taxi for 2 hours and drive out along the sea to Copacabana (a sort of superior Palm Beach, with a cold breeze blowing in from sea) and on for about 10 miles, through the most extravagant scenery I've ever seen and am ever likely to see in this life – towering cliffs of smooth, violety-coloured rock rising out of brilliant green tropical forests into a cloudless blue sky. To my unaccustomed sight it is almost too highly-tinted & theatrical. We finally stop at a small restaurant on a wooded terrace above the sea, and drink a gin-and-tonic (the 'Gordon's Gin' on the bottle was a shock) at an iron table under a tree with bright vermillion flowers. Butterflies and humming-birds flutter about: it is all like an hallucination – and the dream atmosphere persists until we drive back to the city and the concentrated blast of concrete pavements at 95–100° seems to shrivel us up.

Return to ship & am delighted to find 2 letters for me from Buenos Aires (Paco and Billy [Thompson]). After lunch say my farewells to disembarking passengers, and then take a siesta until 3, in my pyjamas. We sail at 5 – out of that marvellous harbour – and in 2 hours reach the open sea. Watch the sun setting on the rocky peaks astern. Send a marconigram [telegram] to Buenos Aires. At dinner I wear a pink Rio orchid as a button-hole. Later, watch Brazilian coast under full moon and enjoy damp, salty breeze on deck. Write up this journal before going to bed, & feel I have given a v. inadequate description of Rio, but its extravagance defeats me – it is only to be described by inspired over-writing. P.S. The vermillion flower reminded me of N.Z. rata (pohutukawa).

3 January 1931

Awoken by intermittency of engines and find us in Santos. After breakfast go up on deck and observe us to be anchored against a modern quay on one side of a tawny-watered, marshy river between high, bluish, wooded hills – tropical Brazil. The town itself looks dull and flat – none of the pseudo-New York skyscrapers of Rio. Learn that this place, which 20 years ago was full of yellow fever and malaria from the swamps, is now the first coffee-producing town of the world. (At present, as is evident from deserted quays, the slump is so great that they can't sell a pound & are burning it as fuel instead.)

As it is stiflingly hot I decide not to go ashore, so sit on the top deck and, read, and watch the brilliant butterflies – gorgeous brutes 5 inches across – orange, sooty, green and white – I remember my *Boy's Own Paper* days and coloured plates of improbable-looking *Lepidoptera*. The ship's upper decks soar above the town, so there is a fresh breeze: I study the Spanish lazily & keep cool in an open shirt. At mid-day the *Alamanzara* sails in, having left B.A. 3 days ago: a big boat, but not so rakish as the *Alcantara*. I sleep for 20 minutes after lunch and am awakened by screams of a French governess in the passage – a rat has somehow found its way from the open hold. Calm her down, curse her noise and try to sleep; in vain. Read again on deck and get sunburnt.

Ship sails at 4 – down the wide river. Banks of reeds, sugar-cane & banana-palms. A charming old Portuguese fort, with *torriones* [towers] near the mouth. A rammed German tramp-steamer in the fairway – a desolate sight – rusty, abandoned, her stern high – result of a collision a year ago. A fresh breeze in the open sea. Later, moonshine and heat-lightning. To bed 11 o'clock.

4 January 1931

The day with least incident since the voyage began. Write most of the morning, but am disturbed too often by people rushing through the smoking-room (where I have taken to working) to concentrate much. Just manage 300 words. Coast of Brazil still in sight 15–20 miles away – high cloudy hills. Weather v. hot & sticky. Sink into deep siesta after lunch, until 4 o'clock. After tea study Spanish Grammar and discuss (with Argentino No. 2) relative merits of English, French & Spanish as a medium for literary expression: agree that Spanish is *el mas sonoro* [the loudest] but too given to exaggeration. French too precise: English the most flexible ... Practise an hour but find heat trying and have a cold salt-water bath before dinner.

Later sit in the moonlight on the top-deck, watch the heat-lightning over the land, and discuss poetry, money and (of course) religion with Nottingham 'chap'. He is deeply shocked to find I am an atheist, but, his own convictions being accepted at 2nd hand, is unable to stump me with any satisfaction himself. Mentally he ceased growing at age of 16: says, for instance, 'Well, God has done a lot for us; you can't deny that.' Argument becoming acrimonious, we eventually agree to go to bed. I am getting as tired of the people on this ship as they probably are of me. Just 2 more days to Buenos Aires.

5 January 1931

Am awoken early by steward stealthily extracting the 'scoop' from my porthole: rain is blowing in. A grey, misty sea. Write letters the whole morning (Uncle A., Roy Jordan). Siesta after lunch, tea, then play piano. As it is the last night on board, we have a *diner d'adieu* [farewell dinner] – roast chicken, asparagus and other dainties. At 9 o'clock the lights of Montevideo appear on horizon & at 11 we anchor off the docks. To bed: a cold night.

6 January 1931

Awoken by steward with letters from Buenos Aires. Find us alongside a quay: go up on deck and inspect the *monte* of Montevideo – a pimple-shaped, sandy hill 200 ft high. We sail at 8.30 – water is now that of the Rio de la Plata & rather muddy. After breakfast medical inspection – Argentine red-tape; then sixth engineer takes 3 of us over the engines: wonderful affairs. A great racket of pistons and valves almost deafens us. The propeller shaft a solid piece of steel 20 inches in diameter, 112 revs a minute – I am obsessed while looking at it with the fear that it may break. Am glad to get up on deck and breathe a bit of noiseless air again. A short siesta after lunch then go up on deck and watch the low shores of Argentina. Finish my packing, do the inevitable tipping etc. At 5.30 sight the skyline of Buenos Aires. Have a last drink on board. Ship berths about 6.30. I spy Frank and Billy on the quay, arrange about my luggage, then go ashore. Rapturous greetings. I am with F. again – Journey's End.

Frank Fleet and James Courage in Buenos Aires. *S20-578f, MS-0999/179, Hocken Collections*

1931–1931

14 February 1931

Buenos Aires

Overheard –

'But do you do any work?'

'Of course not: I have too many other things to do.'

17 February 1931

An Old Story

'I don't understand how I can be the object of so much devotion.'

'No: I don't think you would ever understand … I'm sorry if it embarrasses you.'

'It doesn't embarrass me. But I'm not worthy of it.'

'I sometimes wonder myself, frankly. But one's love is not always chosen by worth. I don't suppose for a moment I could tell you why I love you. I can tell you, however, that you're an infuriating person to be in love *with*.'

'I wouldn't worry about me if I was you, really. You'll have forgotten me in a year.'

'If you believe that, you don't yet know the first thing about my nature. Far more likely that you'll forget me.'

'No: I won't do that.'

'Yes: I will seem like some strange comet or other that hit your world for a time.'

'Causing a few sparks, and a few scars.'

'I don't think so. Scars mean wounds and you haven't loved me enough for me to be able to wound you truly.'

'Well, come and kiss me now, anyway.'

'The last one?'

'Perhaps.'

7 March 1931

The German patrona of this hotel – a white-haired woman of 50 – cherishes the desire to experience once again a European winter. (She has been out here for 26 years.) In her sitting-room she has an oil painting of a village scene under heavy snow, with glowing windows, bare leaves, etc. It is one of her treasures: Her eyes brighten when she looks at it.

10 March 1931

On Leaving Buenos Aires

I will miss – the almost perpetual sunshine; the sight of the smartest women in the world; the sight of men with perfect teeth, hair, and eyes; the taste of S. American peaches; the company of my beloved F; the comfortable, open taxis; the shade of the gardens. I shall look forward to – English tea, English papers; the comparative quietness of London streets; the obligingness of English servants; London theatres; a good circulating library; intellectual conversation; being able to make myself understood in my own language.

There is nothing in us of value save what distinguishes us from others.

—Gide

11 March 1931

Journal of Voyage Home

Almanzora left Buenos Aires at 10 o'clock with me on board. I embarked at midnight last night to save rush. B[illy] came to see me off and I gave him a last note for F[rank]. As we leave the North Basin a royal salute is fired from the Naval Station – not for us but for the British warships (principally the aircraft-carrier *Eagle*) which arrive as we depart. We pass them (with cheers) in the roadstead, then steam down the muddy expanse of the Rio de la Plata towards Montevideo. A beautiful sunny day. The skyline of Buenos Aires slowly disappears to the stern. At lunch am part of the same table as young Englishman named Erdal, returning home after 2½ years with the Argentine railways. Seems pleasant. As an honour we are allotted to the Head Waiter.

Courage and Fleet at Mar del Plata, Argentina. *S10-580a, MS-0999/179, Hocken Collections*

After lunch I sit on the top deck and read Loti's *Roman d'un enfant*, then take a short siesta before tea.* Watch the sunset and feel homesick for Buenos Aires, though God knows why! At eight o'clock reach Montevideo. A few passengers embark. We sail again at 10.30. To bed. Mosquito-bites itch, but am soon asleep.

12 March 1931

At breakfast find a 3rd at our table – a young man with a pitted & pimply face and an appallingly vulgar voice (though he luckily says very little). He turns out to be a professional dirt-track motor-cyclist who has been racing in Montevideo. He has two motor-cycles on board, presumably in the hold. He feels seasick. I read on the top deck most of the morning, and listen to the orchestra – quite good, especially the pianist. Boat-drill at 11.30. I am the sharer of life-boat No. 15 with a thin youth who says lugubriously *'We* won't get far if *we* have to row.' I reply: 'Then we'll drift as well as we can.' ... Erdal is in a boat with two Salvation-Army generals: He says: 'I shall be saved one way or another, anyhow.' I tell him he is 'doomed for Heaven'.

After lunch find Erdal reading a book in French on medieval town-planning. We talk of French books in general: he tells me Loti was a good writer but a hopeless sailor. The conversation verges of course on Proust. Erdal understood that he was a philosopher: I disillusion him and substitute novelist. An excellent & stormy sunset over the Brazilian coast. I have a glass of sherry & go down to dinner. The motor-bicyclist says he feels 'a bit churned-up-like, inside', though why the sea should affect him after the rigours of dirt-track racing I don't know!

To bed at 10.15. Find my port-hole shut tight as there is a 'sea' on this side. Look forward to a stuffy night. Read *The Memoirs of Jacques Casanova* for an hour before turning out the light. And so to dream.

---

* Very few novels by French naval officer Pierre Loti (1850–1923) were translated; Courage would have read *Roman d'un enfant* (*The Story of a Child*) (1890) in French.

13 March 1931

A day almost without incident, except that Erdal told me a good story: at Xmas some Scots lads in B.A. were sent a haggis as a present from home. The package was held up in Argentine customs, as they could not classify the contents by their list of imports. An impasse: the Scots were getting anxious as Xmas approached. At last a compromise was arranged: the unfortunate haggis was given a passport as 'Artificial Manure' …

After tea a passenger best described merely as 'a young female' thumps out *tangos* on the lounge piano in the best 'Come-girls-play-your-piece-now' manner. The piano is – or was – a Broadwood, out of tune and with sticky keys. I try it, but soon give up in despair, although the dirt-track racer says: 'That's fine, give us another tune.' I reply, 'How would you like to ride a motor-bicycle missing on one cylinder? This piano hardly sparks at all!' The metaphor goes home.

After dinner write to F., then have a long talk with a young Brazilian businessman who has a hankering towards self-expression. He speaks English well, but has no idea of what he really wants to say and flounders on interminably: oh, these would-be creators! However, he looks like a poet and is fond of England. Unfortunately, he disembarks to-morrow at Santos.

14 March 1931

A hot, steamy morning. We arrive at Santos about eleven o'clock and leave at 4. All the hills around the town veiled in grey clouds and mist: a light rain falls. I do not go ashore but sit in the lounge & finish reading Casanova's *Memoirs* after fortifying myself with an ice-cream. A siesta: I dream of holding a ridiculous conversation with the Prince of Wales, chiefly on the subject of capricious weather.

15 March 1931

Awake to find us in Rio harbour: a cool cloudy morning. After breakfast I go ashore for half an hour to try to find a shop where I can buy English papers: no success. I am offered an American *Life* but refuse. We sail at mid-day: I mentally bid farewell to the Sugarloaf as it fades amongst the clouds astern. At five o'clock we pass Cape Frio: the lighthouse is set a sheer 500 feet above the sea on a cliff. Later, play a *four* at deck-tennis with Erdal, the dirt-track racer and a female: very hot.

In the evening continue to read *Before the Bombardment*: it is brilliantly amusing but too long* – one has time to see how the fireworks go off. A dance or two to the orchestra's vigorous strains before bed. Change into silk pyjamas as it is so hot.

16 March 1931

Discover a *London Mercury* for last month in the lounge after breakfast – evidently embarked at Rio. Peruse it on the boat-deck until almost drowned by a downpour of Brazilian rain. From 11 o'clock onwards experience a return of my colitis-pains, damn them! Keep off spirits and wine for the day and feel better, but am depressed to think I have not yet got rid of the trouble, after two months.

After tea play with a charming little Brazilian boy of 3, with eyes the colour of mulberries and the size of pennies. Unfortunately, we cannot speak a word of each other's language. His young mother, who is well on the way to presenting him with a sister or brother, spends her time lying down in the lounge.

A cinema on deck in the evening. To bed after an orangeade, carefully non-alcoholic, and a sandwich. Re-read Keats' sonnets before turning out the light.

17 March 1931

We reach Bolivia at about 3 o'clock and anchor in hot and brilliant sunlight – a real tropical afternoon. Ship is at once surrounded by boats selling oranges, limes, monkeys, parrots, pottery and bright orange and black birds in criminally small cages. The monkeys chatter and the parrots scream up at us

---

*   *Before the Bombardment* was a 1926 novel by Osbert Sitwell.

from the water. A large passenger sea-plane, painted red and green, flies low overhead, causing a sensation, particularly to the dirt-track racer.

P.S. The little Brazilian boy and his mother disembarked to-day. He bids me an impassioned farewell, clutching my knees and saying, 'Adiós, adiós.' I shall miss him.

19 March 1931

Awake to find us alongside at Pernambuco. Very hot. Have breakfast and then go up on deck. The town is flat and quivering with heat, but green with palms above the roofs. Portuguese niggers on the quay, selling pine-apples, mangoes, alligator-pears, monkey-cage-birds, and a queer sort of animal – perhaps a raccoon (nobody seems to know) with a long snout, sandy fur and a ringed tail. The sun cruelly hot. We leave at 9 and are out of sight of the coast – the last view of S. America – by lunch-time. A cool breeze at sea. Have a siesta, then play deck-tennis, but find it is too hot to be energetic 400 miles from the Equator.

20 March 1931

A meeting of passengers in the lounge: the usual effusive decisions to organise games and a fancy-dress ball, each motion being explained in atrocious French & Spanish to the foreigners present. After tea play a men's four at tennis but find it very hot. At nine o'clock we cross the Equator, as near as calculations can make it. Dancing on the upper deck to a raucous-voiced gramophone. A particularly tinny tune is called, I find, on enquiry – 'Cooking breakfast for the man I love'.* A good deal of somewhat primitive gaiety in spite of the temperature and a depressing humidity. The dirt-track racer at dinner, discussing the lack of team-spirit amongst the passengers, poor things, says: 'People don't seem to *want* to *muck together* this trip.' Himself having had his teeth temporarily stopped by the doctor is bursting with sociability.

---

* Actually 'Cooking Breakfast for the One I Love' from the 1930 film *Be Yourself*.

21 March 1931

The first rounds of the sports are playing off with incredible ferocity/energy, considering that the temperature is in the vicinity of 90 degrees. Sweet, red-faced English girls stagger about the decks dripping perspiration and keeping up their stockings with one hand: while their fathers reveal purple braces and get to work on the quoits, periodically slapping one another between the shoulders. A gay scene. I play deck-tennis v. the dirt-track racer and am beaten, hence this embittered outlook. After lunch the sea gets rougher (we have just entered the track of the mid-Atlantic N. to S. trade-winds) and the ship pitches a little. I feel a bit sick and lie down: manage however to enjoy a good dinner later. Inspect the 1st class library-list & find that it includes Proust's *Albertine Disparue*, in French. Speculate for some time as to how this separate and highly difficult part of *À la recherche* came to find its way on board ... To bed at 10.30 in a very stuffy cabin.

22 March 1931

Sports continue with unabated vigour. Temperature a trifle less. Dirt-track racer shows signs of winning most of the events, being impervious to exhaustion, and wasting no energy on words. A notice posted up announcing that the fancy-dress ball will take place on the day after to-morrow. I wearily search for the remains of Greek tunic I once wore, and discover it at the bottom of my trunk, somewhat creased. Attempted to construct a fillet or tiara from very prickly artificial laurel leaves: but creation is not a success. Decide to solicit help of young married woman travelling alone. She asks me if I am intending to appear as a nymph: I hastily negative any such suggestion and explain. She promises aid of needle and elastic. Begin to read Somerset Maugham's book *The Gentleman in the Parlour*: it is Maugham trespassing on Tomlinson & not very successfully, but written with ease and urbanity.* To bed at 11 o'clock. Ship rolling very slightly. P.S. Some discussion at dinner as to whether the garments of the Salvation Army constitute fancy-dress. Decision in the affirmative.

23 March 1931

A cool fresh morning. Actually sit in the sun on the top deck. Watch schools of flying fish like crowds of white arrow-heads. After lunch the so-called *comic* sports are played off – potato racing, face-washing, needle & thread etc. Embarrassment caused in the Pig's Eye competition when the youngest passenger – a little boy of six – walks straight up to the pig & chalks the eye in the exact centre, having obviously been able to squint under the handkerchief round his eyes. However, since everyone considers it un-sporting to protest against a child, etc, little Lionel is declared winner, instead of being smacked on the pants.

After tea retire to my cabin and with the help of ribbon, needle & thread, create my fillet of artificial leaves. Prick my fingers, get tangled in the cotton, lose my temper and in general spend an arduous hour before achieving passable result. Before going to bed try on complete costume. Am dismayed anew by the hairiness of human legs and wonder if the Greeks shaved theirs. Am undecided whether bare feet or a pair of rope beach shoes are more Hellenic; in the interests of comfort elect to wear the latter. Further decide that the whole get up is rather a nightmare. St Vincent – one of the Cape Verde isles – was supposed to have been visible this evening. But, though I watched as carefully as the dove in the Ark, I didn't see a spot of land or even a lighthouse. Three more days to Madeira.

---

*   English author and journalist H.M. Tomlinson (1873–1958) was much less famous than Somerset Maugham (1874–1965). Both men wrote of travel through Asia, and Courage is probably referring to Tomlinson's 1924 book *Tidemarks: Some records of a journey to the beaches of the Moluccas and the Forest of Malaya in 1923*. The full title of Maugham's 1935 book was *The Gentleman in the Parlour: A record of a journey from Rangoon to Haiphong*.

24 March 1931

The captain does us the honour of lunching at our table (apparently he descends once every trip). As we had not been warned, I for one was ignorant of his identity, not being able to decipher his shoulder-tabs. A bullet-headed, grey-haired man, with a loud harsh voice and the table-manners of a farm labourer. I perpetrate the day's biggest faux pas by enquiring if he came out (i.e. to Buenos Aires) on this ship. He gazed at me coldly, evidently completely staggered by such impudence. Before evening my little joke has travelled round the boat: the 1st class officers, who dislike the man, being immensely tickled. I shall probably be jettisoned at the next port.

In the evening the great fancy-dress ball: about 20 people dress for it. Dinner enlivened by horse-play on all sides, including the pricking of balloons with forks. My Greek tunic much admired, especially by the women, who keep on asking me what I have on underneath – a quite understandable anxiety, as large stretches of skin are without covering. One damsel takes delight in squirting scent on my bare calves, which may admit of many interpretations, but gives me cold legs. None of the costumes very original, save perhaps Erdal's, who appears as a golfing-girl of 1935 – all tweeds, feet and bandeaux, truly a horrific forecast. The dirt-track racer disguises himself as a wharf-side 'tough'. The young married woman travelling alone comes as a Russian peasant-girl. First prize goes to a gentleman dressed as a policeman – a concession, it is to be feared, to the force of the law. My personal vote goes to the French attaché from Montevideo who appears in his wife's Lido pyjamas, enlarging in all the wrong places. After dinner, dancing between decks. Then to bed, with Greek tunic somewhat creased by gaiety.

26 March 1931

At the end of a chilly afternoon the heights of Madeira become visible above a cloud-bank at about 6 o'clock. We anchor at seven and are at once invaded by an army of hawkers selling basket-work chairs, embroidered tablecloths, imitation amber necklaces and cigarette-holders. Overside, to the light of flares, boys dive for coins in water that looks as cold as ice. I buy some violets, and present a bunch to the Young Married Woman Travelling Alone, who suddenly vouchsafes the interesting information that she was a passenger on the *Highland Hope* when that ship struck a rock & sunk near Lisbon six months ago.* She gives me a long & vivid account of her adventures, which were none too pleasant. She was saved by a Portuguese fishing-smack from a sinking life-boat (the side had been damaged on leaving the ship), and lost all her clothes and even the sable cloak she was wearing over her nightdress – the accident happened at five in the morning. Her jewellery, which she had given to the purser, was salvaged, but otherwise she lost everything. She was on the way to Buenos Aires, however she went back to England and very bravely set off again in a fortnight in this ship, the *Almanzora*. We leave Madeira at 9, and watch the dark shape of the island, as it sinks astern, half hidden by mist.

28 March 1931

Awake to find us in Lisbon harbour. Breakfast, then go ashore for a walk, across the docks and up into the town. Sun warm: very blue sky. Return for lunch. Several new passengers come on board – English women who have been wintering in Lisbon. In their tweeds & 'useful' shoes they look depressingly plain – as indeed do all English people after the Argentinos. Ship sails at 3 o'clock, keeping close to the coast until it is dark. At 7.30 we pass the Farilhões, where the *Highland Hope* struck. It is too dusky to see anything, and believe anyway that only the masts are visible, hull having slipped into deeper water. To bed at 10.15, feeling cold and in bad humour (indigestion).

29 March 1931

Awoken by loud voices in the corridor outside: a Spaniard who had had the next cabin to mine attempts to disembark (we are in Vigo harbour) without tipping the steward – consequently much vituperation, though luckily

---

* The British liner *Highland Hope* ran aground on the Farilhões on 19 November 1930. All but one of the 500 on board were rescued but the ship was a total loss.

neither party understands a word of what the other says. I curse both & turn to resleep.

I breakfast and go up on deck. A heavy Scotch mist over the town, which presently clears off up the hills. It is Sunday morning and we hear the bells ashore ringing for mass. Overside, a woman & daughter displaying Spanish shawls for sale in a rowing-boat – prices: 8, 6, 5 and 3 pounds apiece, colours rather fine. Two are purchased by passengers who declare on inspection of same that they are not hand-made. An indignant dialogue overside on this subject. Spanish woman becomes heated. Think myself that shawls are probably made in Manchester.

Ship sails at ten, and passes the *Asterias* on the way out of the harbour. At five bid farewell to coast of Spain and enter the Bay of Biscay. Sea calm, slight swell. Hear rumours of N.E. gale in the channel & pray it may be over by the time we reach Cherbourg. Play piano for a few minutes before going to bed, and find myself very out of practice. Upset about this.

30 March 1931

Perhaps the dullest day of the voyage, crossing the Bay of Biscay. A calm sea and cold wind. Sun warm. At about four o'clock see the coast of Brittany. We round Cape Ushant and make for Cherbourg. A very cold evening. Do some tentative packing before bed but am half frozen. England to-morrow.

31 March 1931

Spent a bad night, waking every five minutes from the cold, in spite of 3 blankets. We leave Cherbourg at 7.30 and enter the Channel. A bitingly cold wind. Spend most of the morning in packing: despair as usual of getting everything in. Reach Southampton at about 4.30. Endure the customs and then catch the boat-train to London. Arrive at Bentinck St at 6.20.

1 April 1931

Home-sick for Buenos Aires – strange, that its incidence should wait until my return to London.

England Again

Well, here I am in London again. The same old smoky air and smell of soot. I feel acutely unsettled and, for the first time since I left it, suffer an acute, though inverted home-sickness for Buenos Aires. English people all look pale, dowdy, and bloodless after the Argentinos. Six months of winter seems to have drained all the red blood out of them: they all look as if they suffered from a chronic lack of sunlight.

5 May 1931

Statistics

In the past year I have written 110,000 words (and smoked 1000 cigarettes in their composition), not one of which has been published. This should discourage me, but somehow doesn't.

1931–1932

16 May 1931

Finished to-day the writing of my book, provisionally called 'The Promising Years'. It was begun on May 27th last year, and, in manuscript, is about 73,000 words long. I have yet to type and revise the last 10,000 words, which should take me about a fortnight. After that, off the book goes to Jonathan Cape. Excelsior! I feel that the completion of a work which has occupied my mind for almost a year makes a good beginning for this volume of my journal.

14 June 1931

If I could only capture in words the smell of that old haystack that used to be behind the cowshed at home! A scent of dusty clover, gone a little mouldy. The hot sun on it and on the white side of the shed. I used to sit there, read and listen to the cocks crowing. Oh, it ought to be caught, that whole atmosphere!

20 June 1931

Am just beginning to fall out of love again, after three days in which I've hardly been able to sleep or eat. The same old story, but the experience devastates me each time, colouring everything with emotional shades and upsetting me generally. It is difficult to set down the facts without sentimentality – the HMS *Patrol 40* was in St Ives Bay:* the sailors came ashore in the evening. I was returning from C[arter]'s at 11.30, and met a young sailor who had just missed the last launch back to the ship. I offered to let him share my bed for the night in the hotel (*toujours l'audace* [always daring]). He agreed. Drank more than was good for us: I completely lost my heart. He had to leave at six in the morning to get back to the ship. I saw him again the same evening and we talked. The ship left the bay yesterday. Awful heart-ache. All this has happened before and will again. And, each time, it upsets me for days.

---

* HMS *P40* was a 'P class' patrol boat built for the Royal Navy.

21 June 1931

Yes, that Spanish dance by Granados, in a minor key, particularly – that evening when I was suffering, when my heart was aching, when I was in love with him, I couldn't listen to it.* Its sweetness and wildness were too much for my over-sensitized heart. It was a dreadful, subtle torture to listen to the sounds and hear them intensify my passion. An important sadness. His image kept recurring to me. I couldn't sit in the room, listening to music that went through my heart. I felt better outside, in the cold air. Music gives emotion dramatic significance.

22 June 1931

Arrived back in London to find manuscript of 'The Promising Years' returned from Jonathan Cape. Its rejection considerably made less painful by a very charming letter from them, saying that they had been 'considerably interested in reading my book', and that it showed such 'sensitivity and style' that they were encouraged to ask me to send them any other work I might do. They would come to it with 'every prejudice in its favour'. The grounds on which the book was rejected (or rather 'did not justify publication') was the smallness of its appeal. Well, I am not discouraged. All the same I dispute the 'smallness of its appeal'. It seems to me that even if the book didn't sell much at first, there are always being born people who appreciate careful writing and 'the special history of the special soul', and who would enjoy and find something of themselves in the book, and who would buy and recommend it amongst themselves. I am going to send it to other publishers, for their verdict or opinion.

---

*   Enrique Granados (1867–1916) was a Spanish composer and pianist.

25 June 1931

Went last night to see La Argentina, the Spanish dancer, and was greatly impressed and excited.* She has – as a result no doubt of incessant practice and discipline – exalted her body to the dignity of the most sensitive instrument, on which she can produce the most subtle effects of rhythm. And her castanet work is fascinating – at the end of Seguidillas, which she danced without music, she produces a long and perfect decrescendo: a fine pianist could not have done it better. Her dresses were in excellent taste – rich colours of red, lemon, green, and brown: all one imagines as Andalusian.

29 July 1931

A letter this morning from T.S. Eliot, of Faber and Faber, about the MS of 'The Promising Years'.† He says that he and two other directors have read the book with much 'interest and sympathy', but doubt whether it could be published 'in its present form'. However, Eliot asks me to come and talk to them about it to-morrow morning. I have become so immersed in the writing of my new book that I have almost forgotten the mood in which 'The Promising Years' was written, though that mood, constantly recreated, lasted for a year. I don't think I can face re-writing much of it – if that is what they mean by 'a different form'. What they probably mean, I think, is that I will have to split the book's four movements (they are really symphonic movements) into chapters, which I am unwilling to do, though quite realising that a solid block of narrative a hundred pages long – as is the second movement, 'Red Elm' – is tiring to read without intervals. However, to-morrow will see. Meanwhile, I live in an elated world. I am wondering how I shall dress etc, for the interview, so as to look like the man who wrote the autobiographical parts of the book!

---

* La Argentina was the stage name of Argentine-born Spanish dancer Antonia Mercé y Luque (1890–1936).

† T.S. Eliot (1888–1965), poet, playwright, critic and essayist, who would win the 1948 Nobel Prize in Literature, was a director at publisher Faber and Faber.

30 July 1931

My interview with T.S. Eliot over 'The Promising Years' this morning. Unfortunately one of the other directors had taken away the manuscript to read, so that our interview was partly abortive. I am going to see him again next week. Eliot is a tall man with a rather strained, nervous face. Regular features. Horn-rimmed glasses. Quiet manner. He said that he had been impressed by my work, and, to my extreme gratification, remembered details and passages that had struck him as good (the 'realisation of simultaneity' passage after the earthquake in the first part; the boy's noticing that his mother was ageing; the force of the letters quoted in the final part, etc). But what he did not think was so good was the last part, the 'Oxford movement': in fact, after the first 2½ parts the events and emotional memories became too close to me, as narrator, to yield full significance. This was exactly what I had felt myself. We discussed whether the 3 first parts were long enough to make a book, I objecting that I had brought my themes together only in the inferior fourth part. Incidentally, he said that he, being an American, could appreciate those subtle differences between life in and out of England which I had touched on ... He detected the Proustian influences, though he has never read any Proust. He saw no reason why I should not later continue the history I had already begun in 'The Promising Years'.

31 July – 2 August 1931

Ernest stayed here with me. An extraordinary time – half-dream, half-nightmare. I lived his life – we ate and drank more than was good for us, went to the theatres and cinemas in the evenings, visited Madame Tussauds. His easiness of taking life as it comes, his complete lack of spiritual questioning, his physical strength – all have a terrible, heart-aching attraction for me. Yet he tired me out – not as a lover but as a companion whose every wish I tried to anticipate. How can I explain the extraordinary, hysterical feeling I had as we went round the Chamber of Horror at Madame Tussauds? The psychological effect of the place was quite enough, without the consciousness of this youth beside me, bound to me, on my side at least, by an overwhelming physical attraction. I wanted to break the spell by insane laughter, terrible weeping. How to explain, either, the fact that the morning he left I, a cool, controlled person, had to go out of the room in tears when he put a stupid sentimental record ('I'll always be in love with you') on the gramophone? It is his very sexual normality that is so profoundly necessary to me; yet so hopeless, so sad, somehow. I should never have let him come to stay, or sleep with me: it was all a mistake. I am the sufferer, the loser. I remain more lonely in my own self than ever before. He is of another race – in the true path of his life, while I am and always shall be outside of it, fecund in mind only.

16 August 1931
A fortnight has passed, he has not written.

19 August 1931
'Still no word from you. I didn't think you would let me down again. Still, perhaps I should have known better after the first time. I won't trouble you again. Goodbye and good luck. I was fond of you.'

18 August 1931
To lunch with T.S. Eliot and R. de la Mare at the Oxford & Cambridge club.* Talked on many subjects – Henry Williamson, D.H. Lawrence, etc. Eliot brought forward a theory that all poets are either medically- or legally-inclined.† Donne was legal-minded, Bridges a doctor, Keats chemically-minded, Coleridge both, through his interest in metaphysics. Eliot himself legal-minded: de la Mare (the father) medical. Later we spoke of my manuscript, 'The Promising Years'. They want to publish it, but think it

---

* Richard de la Mare, son of poet Walter de la Mare, was also a director at Faber.

† Henry Williamson (1895–1977) was an English novelist best known for his book *Tarka the Otter*. D.H. Lawrence (1885–1930) was a novelist and poet. The other names mentioned here – John Donne, Robert Bridges, John Keats and Samuel Taylor Coleridge – were all poets.

better to wait until I've finished my novel and (if they like it) to publish that first, in order to get a public for a more personal book. After some talk, I agreed. We have also decided to leave 'The P.Y.' as it is, without alteration, as the book hangs together too intimately for cuts. But I may change my mind & alter some of it later. De la Mare thought my characterisation excellent, and picked out the boy's stay with the grandmother as being 'beautifully done'. I also think this bit the high-water-mark of the whole. Meanwhile I am to finish the novel (now called 'The Second Generation') and send it to them. 'The Promising Years' will, anyway, not come out till next year.

30 August 1931
Last night, at twenty minutes to one o'clock, I had a haemorrhage of the lungs. I was laughing with M., when I began to cough, put my handkerchief to my mouth and found blood on it. After that I coughed up about a teaspoonful or more. I rang up the doctor, who came at about 1.30 and went over me with a stethoscope. He diagnoses trouble in the right lung. I am to have an X-ray photograph taken on Monday to decide the extent & nature of infection. The doctor says I shall have to spend 3 months in a sanatorium: he predicts a cure. As to what this may mean I have carefully tried not to think. Of course, I have had presentiments of a like trouble for a long time – somehow knew it was inevitable. Well, I am not afraid of death, but only of suffering. However, I shall get better.

4 September 1931
Read to-day in the *London Mercury*'s 'N.Z. letter' that: 'Critics are still scanning the landscape from the house-tops for *the* N.Z. novel, but there is little to report.' I have more than a good mind to have a shot at that novel myself, if I can think of a fine subject.

7 September 1931

I write this on the last night of my residence at 9 Bentinck Street. To-morrow I go into the sanatorium at Mundesley (Norfolk), where I pray Heaven I may recover from this insidious and weakening disease.* I am sorry to leave my flat. I have been happy here.

9 September 1931

Entered Mundesley Sanatorium. Feeling dreadfully weak.

23 September 1931

Feel much better after a fortnight's rest and pampering. Would feel completely well, but for occasional aches in the right lung. Have lain in bed reading most of the time.

27 September 1931

Last night, hopped out of bed and across the cold San. floor to see the eclipsed moon. A coppery-coloured disk in the lower sky westward. *Remember*: the colossal Miss Wigley who used to go to bed with a pound of boiled sweets on the night-table. Poor Mrs W. died 5 months later in London (of T.B.). Tragic: she had a brave soul.

28 September 1931

This afternoon wrote to Mater, telling her delicately and for the first time of my haemorrhage in London & of my sequestration in this San. As an anti-frightener I enclosed a letter from Dr Pearson saying that I was making good progress. Poor darling Mama, I do hope it is not going to be too much of a shock. For really I am much stronger than I was in town. To-day I was allowed up for dinner, though I felt rather exhausted and went to bed directly

---

*   The large Mundesley Sanatorium, founded in the late 1890s, provided a genial but expensive place to recuperate: it only accepted patients who could pay the fees. Courage's time there inspired *Autumn Flowers*, a low-key and uneventful play, although it is not clear whether this was ever performed.

afterwards. I feel quite well on the whole, except when the devilish little ache begins in my right lung – when this happens I just want to lie in bed and die. However, the pain-periods are getting less frequent. I understand now the *nervous excitability* that tired me so much in London before my haemorrhage. It was obviously a strong sign of tubercular trouble. Well, I know now.

Letter from doctor:

> Dear Mrs Courage,
> Your son J. was admitted here on the 9th on the recommendation of Dr Ledingham. He had Spanish 'flu in S. America, when he had lost much weight. This is to let you know that we consider that he is suffering from Pulmonary Tuberculosis, but at the same time, I am able to reassure you that it is not severe. Furthermore I am pleased to be able to tell you that he is progressing excellently. So the prospects of his making a good cure in a reasonable time are quite good. There is no need therefore for you to worry unduly on the receipt of this note. I can write to you again later, when I hope I shall again be able to send you a satisfactory report.
> Etc.
> S. Vere Pearson.*

30 September 1931
Walked through a stubble-field in the sunshine. An odd poppy, pale red; small daisies; and little tiny blue and geranium-red flowers. Came across a round little nest of straw, like a muff – perhaps a dormouse's or field-mouse's nest?

1 October 1931
A really glorious day: perfect sunshine and a little misty haze on the distance – a day like a ripe peach.

---

*   Sidney Vere Pearson had been the sanatorium's physician since 1905.

16 October 1931

Norfolk

I've known few days better than those of mid-October. Sunny, still with
the slightest of autumnal chill in the air. The trees are still amazingly green
– only the chestnuts and maples are rusty, and the oaks turning brown.
Asters, stocks and dahlias out in the garden. A few peacock butterflies and a
'cabbage white' or two. Thrushes singing well, and robins occasionally piping.
Dew on the lawns until 12. Some fields being ploughed, others in turnips
and beet. Blue mist on the distance. Air sharp in the evenings.

20 October 1931

Afternoon sadness

A roaring north-easterly wind tears the leaves from the trees. Bitterly cold.
I sit with blue hands. Towers and scuds of white and grey cloud, with beams
between. Rooks singing wildly.

9 February 1932

My twenty-ninth birthday. Sobering reflection that I have spent so much
of the last nine years in the company of fools, vagabonds, sex-maniacs and
literary people generally. Well, if I *have* caught T.B. I've at least escaped
syphilis. My great regret is that I have not written, as yet, the really good
book I want to, though 'The PY' has excellent moments. To-day I wrote the
passage about my grandmother and Mr Sherwood.

20 February 1932

A really crushing blow: Faber have returned both the novel and – for some
reason I am too dazed to understand – 'The Promising Years' as well. About
the novel I am not exactly surprised but about the autobiography I am
simply knocked out. *Why* did they first decide to publish it and then let
me down like this? Eliot, who wrote to me, declining the novel, gives no
explanation of the other. It is really as much as I can do to prevent myself

committing suicide. I walk about in a sort of dream, but a dream that aches. I feel that I have to start again right at the beginning of everything.

2 April 1932

Had my tonsils out ten days ago. Local anaesthetic. Very painful. Meanwhile, here I am in bed, recovering. Feel extremely restless, especially as spring is in the air. Sexual desires have begun to manifest themselves in voluptuous lacustrine dreams – a nuisance. In order to sublimate some of this energy, have begun writing a new story – 'Uncle Butterfly'. It ought to be good if I can keep it light enough – a sort of child's vision. A feel of summer tension in the air.

2 April 1932

Details to remember about sanatorium
The unexplained noises on waking up in the morning. Plates in the kitchen chattering together like sparrows. Footsteps on the rubber matting of the corridor. An oblong of sunlight by the corner of the window – reflected again on to the ceiling by the mirror. The half-coconut hung up in the window by a past tenant of the room, to attract tits, robins, etc. The coconut-meat shrivelled inside like white leather. The click of the aluminium sputum mug in the next room as somebody coughs in the night. The night-nurse comes treading along like a hippo in felt slippers. Her little torch as she steals in to shut the windows when a storm comes up and rain beats on the panes – early in the morning, before it's light. The white coats of the doctors – badly-fitting round the neck. Plus fours underneath. The violet-purple tint of some of the bare trees below the windows – naked limbs as beautiful as a young man's.

4 April 1932

T.S., in the room below me, has just thrown a plate out of the window, and shouted 'I'm *furious!*' Another of these temperamental male inverts!

5 April 1932

A letter (such a loving one) from F[rank], just after I had posted off an indignant one to him accusing him of not having written to me for a month and saying he must be 'entangled with a HUSSY'. Oh dear! But I wonder if he really, still, loves me a bit. It's over two years, after all.

1932–1934

13 May 1932

Mundesley Sanatorium

A letter from Mater yesterday (from N.Z.) telling me that seven lads – three of whom I was at school with – have bought a ketch between them and are off to make a tour of the Pacific Islands, starting with Samoa. She thinks they will all be drowned or never heard of again. I must say I admire their *guts*. The ketch is a sixty-footer called *The Water Lily*.

K. opined at lunch to-day that D.H. Lawrence was 'a moral degenerate'. Because K., by token of the *filthy* stories he tells, is far more of a moral degenerate than ever L. was, I lost my temper.

15 May 1932

My happiness

The two months F. and I lived together, two years ago, were the happiest period of my life. The intolerable burden of my loneliness was eased. My need of him and his love for me brought me an extraordinary peace and pride. Everything was, as it were, *vindicated*. The liaisons I have had since have been purely physical and have given me unhappiness and disgust – real anguish of spirit.

17 May 1932

Pear trees in blossom. Apple trees just beginning: a few pink buds – very late. Violets, daisies and a few bluebells out in the hedges – also an occasional clump of primroses, a little battered by the rain these last few nights. Gorse very brilliant on the hillsides. Cabbage butterflies. A chaffinch sitting on four eggs. Wagtails on the lawn. Thrushes singing very loud. Windmill white against a blue sky. For every one who agrees with me my conviction grows tenfold.

19 May 1932

'The P.Y.' returned from the Hogarth Press. They say the MS 'interested' them, but they had decided, after 'careful consideration' not to make an offer for it. Publishers are queer cattle and no mistake. Surely if it 'interested' *them*, it would interest other people too?

30 May 1932

Just back from spending a weekend with the Waters, near Yarmouth. On Sunday we went sailing on the Marshes (Rivers Upton and Yare) in a motor launch belonging to some profiteer friends and filled up with great luxury. The actual 'sailing' I enjoyed immensely: the day was half sun, half cloud, with the light showing up the green marshes well in the distance. Plains of buttercups, with cows grazing or lying down. The windmills (sails like huge Venetian blinds) going round slowly, pumping the water off the low-lying marshes into the river. Yachts with high white sails here and there, as though sailing on land. The clouds very fine. A Constable or a Cotman day.*

10 June 1932

A Red Letter Day. Gollancz writes:

> I should be glad to publish 'One House', which I like immensely (though I am afraid there's little chance of it achieving big sales) on the following terms: a royalty of 10% to 3000, 15% to 10,000 and 20% beyond. If you agree, I will send you a formal contract.
> Victor Gollancz

Well, of course I ought to be delighted and so I am, up to a point. All the same, I'd have preferred Fabers to take it: they've got a 'cachet' which is beyond Gollancz.† Still, it's a beginning, after so many bitter disappointments.

---

* Near-contemporaries John Constable (1776–1837) and John Sell Cotman (1782–1842) were both major English landscape artists.

† Although Victor Gollancz Ltd was founded in 1927, two years before Faber, by a man of strong left-wing political views, Courage clearly regarded it as a less 'literary' imprint.

6 July 1932

Great amusement. In the kitchen are two new kitchen-boys from Cambridge ('Not,' I am assured, 'from *the college*.') At seven o'clock this morning one of them yawned in bed, and dislocated his jaw. Consequently, instead of 'bacon and buttered eggs' (as advertised on the menu), we had boiled eggs – the latter being within the compass of one kitchen-boy to prepare. What the chef, a Swiss, was doing, remains a mystery.

10 July 1932

Pain and depression. My chest hurts: I feel stifled when I cough. A good deal of sputum. Heaven help me.

13 July 1932

Appalling depression – really rock-bottom – everything in the world went black. This culminated in the evening when I burst into tears when Mrs M. came to see me, and wept for an hour and a half. I really think she saved me from suicide. I haven't been so upset since Dec 27th, 1930, on the way to S. America. Completely and absolutely *de profundis*.

16 July 1932

Feeling much stronger: despondency vanished. Mrs M. read *One House* in proof, and liked it – or rather, *admired* it. She envies me my 'easy, flexible English'. I told her it was the result of damned hard work: and so it was.

17 July 1932

The first cherries – fat, black, juicy ones. (Remember the apricot-tree that used to grow on the hot clay bank above the 'calf-pen'.)

10 August 1932

Letter to My Right Lung

Dear R.L.,

You will excuse my addressing you thus familiarly, but our fortunes are rather bound up together. Dr. M. tells me you have been misbehaving yourself lately – a fact of which I was already aware.* In fact, your misdemeanours have brought rather a prolonged blush to my cheeks on more than one occasion. With Dr. M.'s help, as you may remember, we had finally to give you a good 'blow-up' – which you, very rudely, ignored, as though you had never heard of such a thing. However, *understand this*: your undermining of my health cannot go on. I have a career and a future, and it is in the highest degree unkind of you to try to prejudice either. It is not as though you could kill me – thank goodness, your brother Left still remains staunchly at my side. No: you prefer to sulk and refuse me your co-operation. Well, you leave me no alternative but to issue this ultimatum – a ghastly one enough though it is – if I die I will see to it, my dear R.L., that you also do not escape that inevitable mortality.

Meanwhile, partly yours,

J.F.C.

18 August 1932

I see in the paper that the Book Society have chosen, as this month's book, *The Collected Poems of D.H. Lawrence*. I take off my hat to them for their real courage in doing so. To make ten thousand or so people stomach D.H.L. (particularly the essential L. of the poems) is no small experiment. I can't help thinking there will be an almighty fuss about the book in many a good old Puritan home.

---

* Dr M. was probably Dr Andrew John Morland, who joined the sanatorium staff in 1928.

31 August 1932

Exactly a year ago to-night since that ghastly evening in Bentinck St when I had my first haemorrhage. Well, I'm holding the disease at bay, but at present only just. What will the next year show?

1 September 1932

A dream of F[rank], last night. Everything was as it used to be. His beautiful body, and – Le reve de rester ensemble sans dessein.*

20 September 1932

The first frost last night. White rime on the lawn. A bumble-bee flew into my room for warmth, and crept into a corner of the skirting. The last of the sweet-peas in the garden. White chrysanthemums. Red berries. A robin singing. Turnips (astringent scent) in the fields. Blackbirds in the hedges. Ivy in flower. A field of clover gone brown, reading for stripping. Campion in the hedges.

16 November 1932

Awakening by chance at a quarter to four this morning, I remembered that the first display of Leonid meteors was due before dawn, and rose up to see them. The air was very cold and the moon and the sky brilliant. I put on my heavy sweater and dressing gown and walked up to the top of the hill above my chalet, among the pines. Searched the north-east for ten minutes without success. Much impressed by the beauty of the sky, and the pine trees against it. The Little Bear in plain view; also Saturn, gloriously winking to the S.E. The moon almost full and of astonishing brightness. The horizon misty. Saw no meteors; and retired to bed at 4.20, chilled but not displeased.

---

* This, which translates to 'The dream of simply staying together', is a line from the Verlaine poem quoted earlier.

29 November 1932

Stayed the weekend with the B.s at Ormesby. On the whole, and from my point of view, the holiday was not a success. They are kind, but *common*, with that appalling, mutton-tea, colonial commonness which is of the soul and ineradicable. I felt profoundly depressed. Their world is not mine – and never was, even in New Zealand.

2 December 1932

A letter from Gollancz's Publicity Manager, asking for a photograph and a short biography. As I had no photograph and loathe the thought of having one taken, I asked a patient here, Mrs Eliot, to do a sketch of me. The result was the best picture of myself I've ever seen – though the face is far too acutely reminiscent of my dear Uncle Algernon. At any rate, I'm sending the sketch to Gollancz. I don't think the lines are strong enough to reproduce well, but that's their affair, and it can be done. Of course, nobody will believe the biography – or if they do, will have things to say about 'rolling stones', etc.

25 December 1932

Christmas Day. One of the most perfect winter days I remember: brilliant sun and a clear blue sky. Plovers and seagulls on a field of young green corn. Thrushes singing. In the afternoon listened to the Empire Broadcast. The carillon from Wellington brought a lump into my throat. Big dinner in the evening. Champagne.

29 December 1932

Gollancz's spring list arrived, containing the announcement of *One House*. The description of the book reads: – 'The author of this novel is, in the true sense, original. It is like nothing in contemporary literature of which one can think, and for its literary ancestry one would perhaps have to go back to the Brontës. The interplay of character and mood is done with great skill and delicacy and the whole makes a most forcible impression upon

a
first novel
ONE HOUSE
by
JAMES COURAGE

The author of this novel is, in the true sense, original.

It is like nothing in contemporary literature of which one can think, and for its literary ancestry one would perhaps have to go back to the Brontës.

The interplay of character and mood is done with great skill and delicacy, and the whole makes a most forcible impression upon the imagination.

One House, published by Victor Gollancz in 1933. *S20-576a, MS-0999/140, Hocken Collections*

the imagination.' Well, that's that: quite a good puff, and not explosively enthusiastic à la Gollancz. The number of books in the list appals me. What hope has my minnow amongst such a galaxy of whales?

30 December 1932

A Christmas card from Ernest. What a piece of the past. It upset me.

3 January 1933

Left the sanatorium. I thought I should be glad to go, but I wasn't really – in fact, I shall miss the life a good deal, at first. The truth is, a sanatorium life is not at all a bad thing for a writer for a time – and provided he can keep well. It gives him rest, good food, abstraction from the world – just the conditions he needs when he's engaged on a work. Of course, such a life leads ultimately to stagnation, but it does help towards the integral-feeling absolutely necessary for delicate creative work. All the same, a colony of writers, on the Soviet plan, would be ghastly. In a way, each artist hates another artist: the better an artist is the more incompatible with others he becomes.

8 January 1933

St Ives, Cornwall

Went to tea this afternoon with the good D.s, whom I like so much. I hadn't been to see them since June 21st (1931), on that appalling occasion when I was in love with E[rnest] and scarcely knew what I was doing or saying. I could easily recreate the mood, this afternoon. Mrs D. had a tiny vase containing 3 primroses, the first of the year, on her silver tea-tray. It was so pleasant, sitting by the fire, talking to the D.s. I didn't want to leave.

23 January 1933

My six advance-copies of the novel arrived. Extraordinarily enough, I had dreamed last night of Dad coming into my room and throwing down the parcel on the end of my eiderdown. I felt almost a sense of déjà vu when I opened my bedroom door this morning & found the package waiting.

9 February 1933

My 30th birthday. H.L. came to dinner with me, and assured me that I didn't 'look 30'. – That's one blessing.

11 February 1933

A letter from F[rank], telling me that he is *engaged to be married*. I spent a very bad ten minutes on reading this: the news brought back, almost more than I'd have believed possible, the pangs of being in love with F. Remembering that love has meant a lot to me, this past two years. Now I think he is foolish. Not that we were ever likely to have become lovers, in the full sense, again; but marriage will mean the end of his ambition, absolutely. The end of *him*. He says in his letter: 'I don't know how you will feel, J. In most ways you are my dearest friend and I hope you will not want to sever that friendship.' That is hypocrisy. He knows quite well how I feel about it.

11 March 1933

A spring morning to rejoice the heart. Chaffinch and thrush singing: Daffodils and a few primroses out in the woods. Sun warm, with a tempering breeze. Sky blue, a few fleece-clouds. A letter from F.

25 March 1933

To Portreath in the afternoon. Two young men were bathing in the sea. Their lean, beautiful bodies against the blue. *Oh God, the pain, the sweet hell within.*

27 March 1933

Received the following cable this morning from my mother – 'Do not take my criticism of book too much to heart. Have revised it considerably.' Well, I haven't received her letter about it yet, but still – a prophet in his own country, as usual.

(A month later.) The following is my mother's verdict on the book – 'I really don't know how to tackle the subject but I tell you honestly I don't like it. Why write about such nasty people? I am sure English women are not like that, they were all *horrid* & the book has no depth of feeling – well-written but that is all I can say – it really gave me a nasty taste in my mouth. The women were nasty and silly, I am sure you don't know anyone like that ... Don't write about people like that again, I can't bear it.'

And a fortnight later 'I'm afraid I was not very nice to you about your book but I *was* so disappointed about it & don't think you did yourself justice in any way. Don't take any notice of what I say really, but the book didn't appeal to me except the descriptions of the English countryside: it's well written but there's no gleam of humour in the whole book and the love scenes are very crude ... Go on and write, but let the next book be about people with a normal healthy English outlook on life. You must know lots of decent English women ...'

12 May 1933

Back from London yesterday. Caught a hell of a cold in town and had to stay in bed 3 days, at 92 Ebury Street. Eric J. looked after me, rather wintrily – as though it were he who ought to be ill. I went to lunch one day with Emlyn: he was restless and anxious to be off to a rehearsal of his translation of *The Late Christopher Bean* at the St James's.* A few days later he came to tea with me and we got on better, save when he accused me of disliking people who don't speak academic English (a thrust at my style, in *One House*). I objected strongly. While in town I went to Dr Ledingham's and was overhauled, stethoscope, etc. All well, pleurally-speaking. I wish my *mind* felt better – less restless, feverish and lonely in this spring weather.

14 May 1933

To-day I wore my new blue pin-stripe flannel suit for the first time. Not too good a fit across the shoulders, I'm afraid. It is my first new suit since August 1930: almost three years.

---

* *The Late Christopher Bean* was Emlyn Williams' 1933 translation of a French comedy drama called *Prenez garde à la peinture* by René Fauchois.

15 May 1933

In the evening, write to my Grandmother about prospect of going to Mt Somers.

25 May 1933

Looked over cottages with a view to taking one for the summer, here at St Ives. Only one was 'possible', called Gillan Cottage, but that was full of heavy German carved furniture and thick curtains – altogether vaguely depressing. A smell of shut-up-ness. I didn't realise how this place weighed on my spirit until I saw a huge spider in the bath trying to kill with fright a wasp-fly – pouncing on it, then retreating. I rescued the fly and fled from the accursed house. But I think I've found the house I want, if I can get a suitable servant.

29 May 1933

Arranged to take house called 'Bishopsland'.

16 June 1933

A letter from my mother enclosing a cutting about me from a N.Z. paper – the *Auckland Weekly*. I was much amused to read the name of my novel as *'One Horse'*. So typically N.Z. I suppose they argued that *One House* would be much too small to keep up with the N.Z. birth-rate (something like 19 per 1000).

4 August 1933

I had a shock to-day. A young woman came up to me at the Club and announced herself as Frank's sister. A very curious experience.

1 October 1933

I've decided to go out to N.Z. for a trip – get there in time for Xmas. The plan depends, however, on my being able to get an airy, well-ventilated deck-cabin on the ship. Have written to London about this.

5 November 1933

From Malcolm's letter: 'I sometimes dream of N.Z., but they are always rather frightening dreams – strange faces and my people old, and scenes unfamiliar but ghostly and pathetic. But I sometimes think we have been lucky to have had two lives in two different worlds ... the people [of N.Z.] are so kind and yet one felt horribly lonely there sometimes. And the country itself seemed to intensify the loneliness. Mountains and forests of a terrifying beauty ...' I feel frightened. That loneliness, I know it in advance, and feel already a kind of inverted nostalgia for Europe.

13 November 1933

The thirteenth – my unlucky day – and, sure enough, the bad luck came. I had a sputum-test made of a little muco-purulent stuff which I coughed up yesterday morning. The report was 'a moderate amount of Tubercle bacilli'. In other words, I'm still positive, and the lesion in the lung not yet healed. This is *bad*, and has upset me profoundly. I talked about the positive test with J.C., in whose hands I am, medically. He was reassuring – says he can hear *no* crepitations in the lung with a stethoscope, and that the sputum comes probably from the crater of the old cavity in the upper right zone. But I must be careful & keep to my treatment: rest & calm. My God! The inexpressible pain of the death of my baby: my novel. My life at the moment seems empty – empty and bottomless, an annihilation of living.

16 November 1933

Sailed for New Zealand on the S.S. *Rangitata*.

18 November 1933

Started working on the new book (about the boy and his grandmother) and crawled back on to some self-esteem like a wet fly on to solid ground.

19 November 1933

I've been reading *The Life of Katherine Mansfield*.* Her early struggles at self-expression in N.Z. – so exactly like mine – it's positively uncanny. I feel for her almost more than I can bear, when I read.

3 December 1933

A severe fright yesterday when during the afternoon & evening my temperature rushed up to 100.5°. I'd had a mild dysentery, but imagined the fever must undoubtedly be due to tubercle. However, I was normal again tonight, for which Heaven be praised: tubercle would have come down much slower. We crossed the Equator early this morning. The doctor said that the Commander of the ship holds it as a rule that 'those who are going to die on board always die before the Line's crossed. Afterwards, they recover.' I suppose this is a good omen.

10 December 1933

At 11 o'clock this evening the ship called at Pitcairn Island in mid-Pacific. We had received a wireless message that a doctor was needed, so changed our course 150 miles south. Two boats came out of the darkness to meet us – their sudden appearance in the rays of our arc-lights most effective. About 30 men swarmed up the ladder on board selling pineapples, walking-sticks, feathers (of bo'sun bird), dried leaves, avocado pears, little wooden boxes and – a surprise this – honey-suckle and rather dashed-looking little pink roses. The doctor did not go ashore. The invalid's son came out in one of the boats to ask for morphine for his father, who has apparently been ill for many years and has become a perennial excuse for asking ships to call at the island. The ship stayed an hour off the almost invisible island, and sailed again at midnight.

---

* Written by Ruth Elvish Mantz and Mansfield's husband John Middleton Murry, this biography was published in 1933, 10 years after the writer's death.

15 December 1933

The ship's concert tonight. I played two groups of piano pieces – nine items in all. First group was one of 3 Chopin pieces – *Prelude in C major* (*Op. 28, No. 1*), *Waltz in C# minor*, and *Majurka [Mazurka] in C# minor*. As an encore, a Sarabande & minuet by Purcell. Second group – one of Mendelssohn's *Songs Without Words* (F# minor) & Chopin's *Study in F major*. As an encore, two of Schumann's *Carnival* pieces – 'Valse Noble' and 'Chopin'. Quite successful, though I was nervous and played badly.

20 December 1933

Landed in Auckland, New Zealand.

22 December 1933

Home again. A most extraordinary experience after eleven years. Like dream-walking. Feel terribly tired – in fact, nearly collapsed before reaching Seadown [the family property]. Palpitations of the heart.

24 December 1933

A little sputum, but the first for six days, a marvellous respite. I still feel as weak as a kitten, but the good food is helping me to recover.

1 January 1934

New Years Day, and my mother's birthday. In her green, quilted dressing-gown, she brought me in my early morning tea. I shouted 'Many happy returns' to her, but she – being deaf, poor soul – thought I was saying something about the weather. She looked out the window, considered, and said, 'Yes.' Don't feel too well myself this morning. Depressed by a return of sputum. I stay in bed, write up this journal, and do a little of the new novel. Forty pages of this latter finished.

21 January 1934

A lapse in sympathy with Z.F.C. [Zoë, mother] which depressed me. She declared that, since I had come home I had told her *nothing* of my life of the last ten years – in London, Oxford, Cornwall, etc, – nor what kind of people I knew or what houses I'd lived in. I suspect this to be true – in fact, know it to be – and yet I find it impossible to tell her adequately. Facts mean nothing, without an aura of personality, atmosphere ... I felt angry and intensely sad: the real tears of things. Finally, hoping to retrieve my damned amour propre, I followed her (my mother) down to the orchard where she had disappeared with a fruit-basket and a green hat. Almost in silence we picked ripe apricots together: myself on the verge of tears. But I think I'm forgiven. I shall remember this after many years. Sadness, intense sadness.

31 January 1934

To Mount Somers. We pass Anama on the way and I notice a field of thick thistles close to the road.* Poor old place. What happy days and otherwise I've seen there.

5 February 1934

Notes to remember:

The jagged line of the mountains called The Remarkables, standing up under the sky. The bellbird that suddenly sang out in the garden when I was playing the piano. The same bellbird in the fuchsias on the verandah, its long beak sipping the heavy flower-heads. When I was writing up in the garden this morning, lying in my long chair, a leaf fell on me from the white gumtree overhead. An exquisite orange leaf, like a blade, transparently veined. Tiger, the kitten, catching moths and huhus under the verandah light. Bill, the cowboy (freckled arms) said the cold was as intense here in winter as in 'the old country'. I talk to him while I eat raw green peas in the vegetable garden.

---

*   Anama Station was the property belonging to the Peter family.

6 February 1934

A fine drifting rain all day, the mountain quite hidden, even the foothills only dimly visible. The drenched toi-toi hang like wet feathers. The reddish twitch-grass is quite frosted over by the soft, drifting, misty rain. Gran brings me a volume of Tennyson's poems and indication as 'her religion', a poem called 'The Higher Pantheism' which I did not know before. –

The sun, the moon, the stars, the seas, the hills and the plains, –
Are not these, O Soul, the Vision of Him who reigns?

For lunch she has a glass of beer, some slices of cold lamb ('Very good, this lamb, won't you have a bit?'), and a mince-pie. After tea she reads aloud a book on 'Fortune-telling by the Hand', while I play softly the Brahms *Intermezzo Op. 117 No. 2.*

8 February 1934

Pouring wet day, the mountain shrouded in mist. It rains all day & we're reduced to walking quickly up and down the verandah for exercise. I sit on my couch on the verandah: Gran brings me the 'possy' [possum] rug to keep me warm. In the evening Mr & Mrs Frank P. [Peter] come to dinner. Afterwards, Mrs P. tells fortunes with the cards. I suspect her of using other intelligences than the pack in her verdicts i.e. gossip & scandal. She says: 'Everyone likes a little romance in their lives.' Her really magnificent rings of diamonds and emeralds sparkle on her fingers as she deals out the cards in the lamplight.

9 February 1934

My thirty-first birthday. A cold wet morning, with snow halfway down the mountain & cataracts visible in the bush. I have breakfast on the verandah, wrapped in the 'possy' rug. The kitten curls up beside me, purring, and eats a little piece of fish-cake from my plate. Gran gives me, as a birthday present, Wordsworth's *Complete Works* (one volume), Oxford edition. The print is small & she tells me to change it, if I want to.

A Courage family portrait taken when James was back in New Zealand in 1934. He stands second from the left, between sister Patricia and father Frank. Mother Zoë is in the patterned dress second to the right, sister Constance ('Tiny') at the far right and brother John at the front. *S20-568b, MS-0999/177, Hocken Collections*

The rain lifts after lunch and I am able to go for a walk in the wet garden. In the potting shed I find written in pencil on a beam – 'If you can't be good, be as good as you can be.' I eat a few green peas from the pod, also a wet raspberry or two. By the post, I have a press cutting from England. Extract from an article in the *Observer* on 'Novels of 1933' – '*One House* by J.F.C. shows promise despite – or because of – its oddity.' What nonsense. Incidentally, I had a royalty statement from Gollancz yesterday – the book had sold 1014 copies up to Sept. 29th last.*

---

* Copies of *One House* are now extremely rare.

28 February 1934

The last day of a happier month. At home, here at Amberley, it has been a warm, brilliant day – light easterly wind. I've been reading Wordsworth's *Prelude* again: also an odd book on D.H. Lawrence called *Son of Woman*. Middleton Murry nearly lets the cat out of the bag – that Lawrence was a homosexual (hence his appalling struggles to adapt himself to Woman, whom he hated).*

13 March 1934

The thirteenth – my unlucky day, and as usual something happened. In the morning, awoke with a headache, & temperature of 100°. Later in the day the doctor called in: he had a look at me & went over my chest; but says the lung is 'quiescent', save for a dull patch, probably slight pleurisy.

16 March 1934

A return of sputum after a month's freedom from it. Blast and damnation. Am I never to escape from this bloody disease?

17 March 1934

Two boys bathing in a little dirty cold pool in the river here (Goose Bay) –
    1st (on the bank): 'What's it like Stan?'
    2nd (in water): 'Oh, it's a stunner when you get under.'

24 March 1934

Seadown
Acorns falling from the oaks.
    Now here, now there, an acorn from its cup
    Dislodged through sere leaves rustled or at once
    To the bare earth dropped with a startling sound. (Wordsworth)

---

*   *Son of Woman: The story of D.H. Lawrence* by John Middleton Murry was published in 1931.

The Oaro Post Office, not far from the farm where Constance lived.

S14-604e, MS-0999/182, Hocken Collections

31 March 1934

To Hanmer with Dr Birkinshaw.* In the afternoon we both went up in an aeroplane. *My first flight.* The snow on the mountains looked very near and bright: the forests of pine trees very smooth and park-like. Flight occupied about 12 minutes, at 10/- a head.

8 April 1934

Bernard Shaw passed through here (Amberley) yesterday on his way from Kaikoura to Christchurch.† The Mayor had sent him a telegram, asking if he might give him (Shaw) a Town Reception. Shaw, however, did not reply. Nor did he answer an invitation to lunch. Not to be beaten, the Mayor drove up the North Road in his car and at Omihi set it (car) across the road, thus compelling Shaw's chauffeur to stop. A parley followed, and ended by Shaw having lunch at The Crown Hotel – without, however, undergoing any reception. He then drove on to Christchurch, fortified no doubt by much Mayoral talk. P.S. (Later) I hear it was the Mayor of Christchurch, not of Amberley, who caused all the above to-do.

11 April 1934

Saw the Shaw himself in Ch-Ch, at the United Service Hotel. I thought he looked pretty frail but healthy. His eyes a bit tired. He walks, I notice, with a very slight arthritic drag at the knees.

12 April 1934

X-ray exam at the hospital. The report is: 'The stereoscopic radiograms … confirm the presence of adhesions between the diaphragmatic and parietal pleura on the right side … Radiographic appearances in the upper portion of the right lung field are those of fibrotic pulmonary T.B. associated with a

---

*   Frank Thornton Birkinshaw was the father of Fay Berkinshaw, later the author Fay Weldon. The family lived in Christchurch for a time before returning to England.

†   George Bernard Shaw visited New Zealand for a month in 1934.

cavity the size of a hazel nut.' Apparently no active lesions. Yet I still had a little yellowish sputum. My general condition, however good: and weight 10 stone, 7lbs.

18 April 1934

One House

When the book was published (1933) I advised Victor Gollancz (publishers) to send review copies to New Zealand, as it was my native country. The review copies, were sent, however, not to New Zealand but to New South Wales, in Australia. Poor little N.Z., how ignorant even eminent publishers, who ought to know better, are of you in the world! Not one review copy reached New Zealand.

> I think the only way to live as a writer is to draw upon one's real, familiar life – to find the treasure ... And the curious thing is that if we describe this which seems to us so intensely personal, other people take it to themselves and understand it as if it were their own.
>
> From a letter of Katherine Mansfield's.

21 April 1934

I've been re-reading *The Life of Katherine Mansfield*. How is it that one feels sometimes: 'This book was written *for me*'?

1934–1936

29 April 1934

Still in bed. My grandmother brings me a plate of grapes and orange quarters covered with sugar. Outside, a drifting rain. Bellbird singing very sweetly in the rain.

26 April 1934

The Return of the Native
Mount Somers
Snow on the mountain, but a sunny clear day. We sit on the verandah, in the shade of the vine: Gran reads aloud K. Mansfield's story 'Prelude', with many chuckles and mistaken words ('plain' for 'palm'). Aunt F. sews lace on to some undergarment.

9 May 1934

'Wouldn't you like to be a hardy son of the soil?' asks my grandmother, pointing to A.'s farm-boots drying in the sun on the verandah after yesterday's floods. 'Quite frankly, no!' I say, engaged upon writing, and a little resentful of the question. 'Well, I'm not asking you to be,' says my grandmother vaguely and drifts away into the house. But somehow I scent a reproach (that most futile of human expressions) behind the remark. Like the rest of her grandsons, am I to be made a farmer – in retrospective intention?

10 May 1934

Great arguments last night between my grandmother, A., and myself on the theme of 'One loves with one's intellect' (apparently a dictum of Temple Thurston's).* I took a definitely contrary view, in fact became somewhat heated, invoking D.H. Lawrence, Freud et cetera in support of love (or at least its most primitive, the mating-urge) as instinctive, organic, anything but intellectual. A. held that all romantic love must come from the intellect

---

*   E. Temple Thurston (1879–1933) was a British poet, playwright and author.

A scene at Mt Somers, photographed by Whites Aviation in 1960.

WA-53942, Alexander Turnbull Library, Wellington

(and perhaps this is partly true) – later he declared that no novelist knows how to write a love scene.

11 May 1934

Gran speaks – 'When I was a child we lived on the West Coast Road and the guns were always on the hooks by the front door in case of bush-rangers. The coach with the gold used to come past twice a week … My mother hated N.Z. – loathed it, but she never returned to England. She and my father came out in a ship called the *Oriental* in 1860. The colony was only about 10 years old then. When I was first married we used to be so frightened up here (Mt Somers) of the Indians who used to come round selling things. They used to abuse you if you didn't buy … One day I was alone in the house – no men within call – when my cook came to me and said "There's an Indian in the kitchen, Madame, and I can't get rid of him." So out I went to the kitchen, and when I saw him there I said to the cook, "Mary, just run up to the garden and fetch the gardener, will you?" That Indian didn't wait: he was off like a shot, frightened of the police. One night I was sleeping alone at the end of the house in the room off the verandah, when I woke up and saw a man standing at the end of the bed. "What do you want?" I asked. He told me he'd come about some electioneering and had got benighted on the road. He'd come to the wrong door of the house.'

Frank married in Buenos Aires. Rather definitely the end of a chapter.

20 September 1934

Finished the draft of the novel ('Some Other Being'). About 300 pages. Begun about Nov 20th last year ('33). The last section of the book – the journal part – has given me great trouble to write: and, even now, after much work with a rubber, and numerous readjustments of approach, has I'm afraid too scientific a tone for what's after all a kind of 'fiction' – both in the psychological & literary sense. But without any precedent for this kind of psychological unravelling, I found it difficult to keep everything detached enough a focus to work at it, get it into words, so to speak. The next step is to read over and correct the first part (240 pages). I know a good deal of it needs re-modelling, in the light of after-knowledge. The thought of publishing the whole thing makes me shrink a little. Or will it ever be published? 'Tis a very queer fish for any publisher to find in his morning catch. 'Too different from what the public is accustomed to reading, my dear fellow. Might interest a few old maids; but that last part – too neurotic. No, no, it won't do.' – Well, we'll see. Meanwhile, so as to get some sort of a detached view of the book as it stands I'll write an imaginary review of it. –

Review of *Some Other Being*

A year or two ago, Mr C., the author of this book, published a novel called *One House* – a work in which was discernible some psychological perception. In fact, it was a study of what is called an Oedipus complex. In this new book – it is difficult to say whether it is autobiography, biography, or fiction – he is once again given to psychological drama. The story, indeed, purports to have been written by a medical psychologist. And a strange story it is. It is only in the final quarter of the book – written (in contradistinction to the first three-quarters) in the first person – that we learn the true gist of the whole. The story then works, as it were, back to its start.

A young New Zealander, a doctor in London, engrossed in his work, marries a girl with whom he is much in love but who despises his work. After three years she leaves him, taking with her most of his essential confidence in himself. Distracted, he slowly loses his health, and is obliged to enter a sanatorium, where in his despair his life seems to have collapsed about him. As he puts it, he has been sharply wounded in 'the body of adult-love incarnate within him as a man'.

In his need of some anchor, some love-object to cling to, his memory then presents him with the un-erotic and comforting love of his grandmother as it was manifested towards him twenty years before, during a holiday from a school he disliked. His grandmother, he remembers, is still alive. In his hopeless state of melancholia and broken health, he determines to return across the world to her. He sails for New Zealand ...

In his grandmother's home in the country, and fortified spiritually by her care and love, he begins slowly to recover physical health and mental balance. But he does so, he recognises, only by regressing to a pre-adolescent state. He confesses this to the journal which forms the last quarter of the book and which gives a compressed history of the struggle to free himself from what amounts to neurosis (the result of the disruption of his marriage). Partly to objectify this passive regression to an earlier period, and partly to keep the present free from the demons of melancholia, he begins to set down the remembered picture, the chronicle, of his boyhood – or rather of the holiday he spent when twelve years old, with the grandmother.

It is this picture which forms the first three-quarters of the book. It is the slight enough story of a diffident and solitary child among the people of 'Mount Seager', the colonial estate managed by his grandmother, herself a wonderful character, amusing, shrewd, literary, and devoted to her grandson. The boy amuses himself among the estate servants, Irish and Scots people, and senses their relationships to each other and to their 'Madame'. It is a little world in itself, set remotely under the mountains of a far country and surrounded by a clear sharp landscape.

Nothing much 'happens' in the story. Eric, the boy, makes friends with the young son of a neighbour: they ride and shoot together; one of the servants is almost dismissed for drunkenness; a bazaar is given in the mountain village. The virtue of the picture lies rather in its everyday detail, its *genre* quality, and in the depiction of the sympathetic relation between the boy and the grandmother, devoted to each other. The return of the boy Eric to school, fortified by his grandmother's love, brings an end to this, the main section of the book. Indeed, it is complete in itself.

But then, with the beginning of the author's journal, really his own case-book, (kept while writing the main part of the story) we come forward 20 years, to the present time. We learn of his gradual return to health, of the daily writing of his young namesake's story, of the grandmother at the age of 75, of the author's professional activities in London, of the defeat of his disease. We learn also the story of his marriage – the seed, in a sense, of the whole book. Finally, we meet him in a state of recovered sanity and independence, about to set out on a return to his professional life, leaving behind him as a husk outgrown, the 'other being' of his boyhood. In his new knowledge of himself, gained by suffering, he perceives the way to help others through his practice. The journal ends with a post-script, looking forward to his renewed life.

As a whole the book suffers by being broken in two, though this last part adds to the interest of the earlier story – that of the boy. It is by the last part however that many readers will find themselves disturbed, after the detached picture of the earlier. It is difficult, doctor or no doctor, to tell the truth about yourself in this way. It is an interesting experiment, nevertheless.

The style throughout is simple, occasionally marred by an astonishing naivete.*

---

* Even though this manuscript was never published and appears to have been destroyed, the theme of a boy and his grandmother appeared in later writing, including the (also unpublished) manuscript 'Morning Sky' and the successful novel, *The Young Have Secrets* (1954). *The Call Home* (1956) develops the theme of the London doctor returning to New Zealand to recuperate among his family.

30 September 1934

Seadown

Cherry blossom and pear blossom fully out – exquisite against the dark pine-trees. A goldfinch is building in one of the pear trees, and there is a thrush's nest with four eggs across the gully. The last daffodils shrivelled and drooping. The wattle covered with flower just past its prime – brown, like burnt sugar.

18 November 1934

A year since I left England. What a change in outlook, in serenity, in *welfare*, since then.

10 January 1935

Feel myself much at a loose end: nothing to work on, yet a great desire to create something. But it's no good beginning on the little scraps of subjects I have in my head at the moment: they won't extend to a book. Yet I feel lost without a subject: prone to moods of melancholy and aimless sexual desire. Have almost slipped into love for A. on account of the latter. Unfortunately, my ardour not returned, even after that occasion at N.B. one night!

20 January 1935

I am reading William Murdoch's (the pianist) life of Chopin.* A good book, except for a few annoying repetitions. But how wrong-headed all Chopin's biographies are on the question of his relations with George Sand. Why do they all doubt her sincerity? Chopin was never her lover – it is perfectly plain, on psychological grounds alone. Moreover, the woman says that she lived with him for 7 years 'like a virgin' in maternal affection (also that C. never loved any woman but his mother). And Chopin's own recorded remark to her that *certain acts* ruin or debase a friendship – how to reconcile that with a passionate attachment or with physical love? The plain fact is that Chopin

---

* *Chopin: His life* had just been published.

would have been impotent with a woman. His whole character and his every act show him to have been homosexual. His deepest passionate feelings went out to Titus Woyciechowski, in youth.* Chopin loved Titus as a woman loves a man – his letters to him are real love letters. That they were lovers is of course another matter – and highly unlikely. But why has no biographer, with every psychological clue under his hand, never [sic] understood the salience of Chopin's obvious homosexuality? All his love for smart and pretty women is just another sign of it: he could mix with them with heart untouched. Also, T.B., when active, almost anaesthetises sexual performance [and] desire. Chopin, throughout his acquaintance with George Sand, was very much T.B.[†]

2 February 1935
First signs of autumn. Fallen poplar leaves in the gully. First yellow leaves on the willows. Dropping green acorns. Falling apples. Shredding of old birds nest in the trees. Dr Starr rang up to give me the report of the X-ray I had taken a few days ago. The cavity in the lung has apparently closed up, which is excellent.

19 April 1935
Left New Zealand.

5 May 1935
Colombo
Novel ('Some Other Being') refused, but a letter from T.S. Eliot about it.

---

* Titus Woyciechowski (1808–1879) was a Polish political activist, agriculturalist and art patron.

† Composer Frédéric François Chopin (1810–1849), who died of tuberculosis, had a difficult relationship with French writer Amantine Dupin, whose pen name was George Sand.

5 June 1935

Arrived in England. A very cold June day. Landed at Southampton and came up by train to London. The country (Hampshire) looked exquisite. The oaks still with bronze leaves, the fields yellow with buttercups and the hawthorn still white, though a little rusty.

29 July 1935

No entry in this book for almost two months. Have been staying here in Hampstead at the Abbey Court Hotel in Netherhall Gardens (recommended to me by Edna B.), while I look for a flat. After much hunting, have taken (from Sept 20th) the one I first looked at – 109 Hillfield Court, Belsize Park. A perfectly modern flat, as yet undecorated: rent £175 per annum. Two bedrooms, one sitting room, kitchen, bathroom and extra W.C. Flat roof above, on which I can sit. Superb views over London. As for the rest of my life, I suffer from a bad conscience about it. I have written nothing for six months and feel as though I shan't ever write another book. The one I wrote in N.Z. seems to be no good, or 'too slight' – at any rate no publisher wants it. In other words, the last two books I have written ('A Traveller Came By', and this, the N.Z. one) have been failures, having both been rejected. I feel like a mother whose children have a habit of dying at birth. I weep inwardly when I think of them. And at the moment I feel I can't produce another, to end in the same way.

1937–1940

All men are liars, which is not really to their discredit.
One must take the chill off the universe somehow.
—Rebecca West

13 May 1937

I have bought this journal and make my first entry in it in Brighton (Sussex). Am staying at the Old Ship Hotel, having temporarily – and for a very good reason – shut up the flat in Hampstead. I have been here a fortnight to-morrow, staying alone. Solitude by no means as depressing as I had feared, though I miss having somebody to talk to in the evenings. That, I suppose, is the penalty of living out of London – at least for a *soi-disant* [so-called] intellectual. However, for the moment it can't be helped; and at least I've taken to writing letters again, a habit of which the telephone in London had almost robbed me. If I had enough gumption I'd go out and live for a bit somewhere completely away from towns – somewhere in the Weald of Sussex, for instance. But I haven't the gumption, so that's that. I even say to myself, cynically, that there's nothing to do in the country except farm and/ or fornicate. However that may be, I don't feel at the moment that I want to do either. So, at Brighton I stay (where, if the opportunity arises, I can at least fornicate urbanly and in good company – to judge by the mien of most of the couples who populate the hotels). My waiter at the hotel here said yesterday (Coronation Day): 'It ought to have been Teddy (Windsor) they crowned. Then he could have had Mrs Simpson to-night and told England to go to hell!' Evidently Brighton's philosophy is on the pagan side. It must be something to do with that amazing Royal Pavilion of George IV's and Mrs Fitzherbert's.

27 May 1937

London

Am staying at 49 Elizabeth St S.W. while I endeavour to engage a manservant for the flat in Hampstead. So far the Employment Agency have produced little but a procession of haughty little pansies. The odd thing about the said type is that it produces a few extremely good servants and a great many passable ones. The fault of the species are lying, petty dishonesty, general high-horsiness and a lack of initiative. I asked one of the applicants if he ever listened to the wireless. 'Oh, no,' was the reply, 'they never have anything worth listening to.' This seems to me either (1) evidence of incipient cretinism or (2) said in order to impress me (which it didn't.) First night of Emlyn Williams' new play at the Queen's Theatre last night – *He was Born Gay*. Notices in the papers this morning not altogether enthusiastic – complaints of 'costume', dialogue, etc. I sent Emlyn a telegram in the afternoon: 'Best wishes and affection.'

29 May 1937

Have eaten some cherries out of a paper bag, smoked a cigarette, written up this spasmodic journal and am now going to bed.

31 May 1937

The new manservant, Holland by name, arrived this morning ... Weather very hot. After about a week of temperatures between 70–80 one almost forgets what a cold, rheumy place England is for most of the year. Six months of this weather and people would begin to develop Italian or Mediterranean features – olive skins etc. Even Mr Neville Chamberlain, who became Premier two days ago, might develop the potentialities of Il Duce.

1 June 1937

T. rang me up this afternoon and said that he'd been 'pinched by the police' and would I give him 25/- to pay a fine or he'd have to go to prison for 3 months. I said I didn't want anything further to do with him etc, whereupon he answered 'O.K.' Another of his lies, as usual.

2 June 1937

T. rang up again to-day and threatened that if I didn't pay his (so-called) fine he would come up here and beat me up for writing to P.'s father. (In other words from saving P. from further unhappiness.) I told him to go ahead, but promptly rang Scotland Yard and asked them to send a man to see me. In ten minutes two Flying Squad men arrived (having been wirelessed to come here). I told them the facts, they gave me some good advice, and told me to phone WH1: 1212 if I had any further trouble. I heard no more from T. during the day.

In the evening donned a dinner jacket and went to the first night of Elmer Rice's *Judgment Day*.* An effective play but not a moving one. Politics on the stage are to me so much cold fish. Reception enthusiastic.

29 June 1937

Returned from a weekend visit to one of my father's first-cousins, Florence Barthorp, in Suffolk. Interesting because her house, Woodcote, was once the home of the woman whom Constable (the painter) eventually married after much parental opposition. A squarish brick house (in those days the vicarage), about a mile from Flatford Mill, where Constable's father was the miller. I walked over to the mill on Monday morning. Found it still very beautiful but partly spoilt by the usual gangrenous accretion of car-parks, Ye Olde Tea-Shoppes, postcard-stalls, etc.

12 July 1937

Sent a copy of the play I've just finished – 'An Extraordinary Case' – to Norman Marshall at the Gate Theatre.† Received acknowledgement. Also sent a copy to Emlyn Williams.

---

* Elmer Rice (1892–1967) was a prolific American playwright, although *Judgment Day* was far from his best-known or most successful play.

† In 1934 theatre director and producer Norman Marshall bought the lease on the Gate, a private London theatre club.

13 August 1937

News of the play from both Marshall and Emlyn. Emlyn praises the naturalness and restraint but thinks it would have to be performed in a very small theatre to get across. Marshall asks me to meet him and talk about the play. He says it is not strong enough for production in its present form, 'but for many reasons it is so interesting and is so well-written' that he would very much like to produce it if his objections to it can be overcome. I have arranged to have dinner with him on September 2nd, when he will presumably tell me in what ways he would like it to be altered. All this is good news, but I'm counting on nothing until I've seen Marshall.

9 September 1937

Dinner last night with Norman Marshall. The position at the moment is this: he will not produce the play as it stands, but can't really suggest how I can alter it to suit him. All rather difficult. However, he's taken the play, to let a professional play-reader have a look at it and perhaps suggest some constructive alteration. Marshall praised the dialogue and general stage-sense of the play, which, he said (other things being equal) could go slap onto the stage as it stands – without cuts or re-hashing. Encouraging.

6 October 1937

A telephone call yesterday from a play-agent, Humphrey Bradburne, to whom Marshall had given the school-play to read, suggest on, etc. To-day, at 3, I met Bradburne and Marshall at the former's office in Pall Mall. Marshall a bit offhand (seemed to be suffering from a 'liver' and the after-effects of producing *Gladstone* at the Gate). Bradburne, however, did all the talking and suggested a new synopsis for the play. In this new version (which at first seemed to me pretty awful), my play, as it stands, is comprised into about 1½ acts, and a new 1½ are grafted on à la Bradburne. He suggests the homosexual hero of the play should be shown 'on his own ground', four or five years after the events which took place at the school.

11 October 1937

Begin to re-write the play. Easier than I'd thought.

27 October 1937

To see Emlyn W. act in *Measure for Measure* at the Old Vic. A good performance, but Angelo is not strictly his part: he looked too sensual and fleshy, not at all the sex-tormented ascetic.

11 January 1938

Marshall has now verbally agreed to produce the play, in its rewritten version, at the Gate either at the end of this season (i.e. April or May) or the beginning of the next (Sept.) He objects to the title, so I've suggested the alternative of 'Private History'.

3 March 1938

To the Christopher Wood Exhibition at the New Burlington Galleries.* About 450 works, including my own little St Ives Picture (lent for the occasion). The whole exhibition excited me a good deal: I had forgotten what exquisite taste and colour-sense Kit had. I felt proud to have known him and that we had been so fond of one another. Also I suffered a considerable sense of sadness: in 1926–27, when we met, he was at once so poor (in spite of the philanthropic Gandarillas) that I could have helped him (and of course my own cynical self) by buying some of his pictures then. But in those days (I was 23–24) his work rather baffled me and I could see only his surface influences of Pruna, Picasso, Van Gogh etc. I am ashamed to say I bought nothing. In the exhibition, it gave me a sentimental pang to see one of the pictures (Cornish, green fields and white houses) that he painted one day when we went for a picnic (in Gandarillas' car, he being away) together. I sat under the hedge and read 'Eng. Lit' for my Schools, while Kit set up his easel

---

* Painter Christopher (Kit) Wood (1901–1930) died after throwing himself under a train while in a psychotic state. He had a long-term relationship with married Chilean diplomat José Antonio Gandarillas Huici.

down the field and painted. I remember the day well, as I had a slight 'flu and a headache.

7 March 1938

Returned to the Kit Wood Exhibition and, throwing financial prudence to the winds, bought another small picture (*The Archway, Mantes*). Unfortunately it is an early work, but I could not afford any of the later, more individual, ones. Still, the one I've chosen is a pleasant piece of colour and I know it will give me much delight. I wish, nevertheless, that Kit could have had the 20 pounds I'm paying for it: it would have encouraged him.

29 April 1938

Kenneth Marshall, manager of the local bookshop (Wilson's) came to supper. A curious person: had been a friend of 'Lawrence of Arabia' and had stayed at his cottage in Dorset. I asked Marshall point-blank whether Lawrence was – as popularly supposed – homosexual. M. said he thought L. was simply sexually indifferent: in any case not actively homosexual. While on this psychological subject we discussed, inter alia, E.M. Forster.* Marshall told me the interesting fact that the long gap in Forster's fiction-writing (14 years), is due to F.'s unwillingness to publish a couple of novels on homosexual themes written by him in this interval. E.M.F. says they would damage his reputation and enrage his relations. A pity, this, but probably true. I should be interested to see those unpublished novels.

23 May – 21 June 1938

A holiday of 30 days on the Continent. Went straight out to Switzerland first, to stay with the Kesterans (Dad's cousins) for a week. They live in a flat in Vercy, on Lac Leman. View superb, lovely air and Bechstein piano. From Vercy, went back into France and down to Aix-les-Bains for a week, to join

---

* Fiction writer and essayist Edward Morgan Forster (1879–1970) wrote the homoerotic novel *Maurice* in 1913–14, but he did not expect it to be published during his lifetime. It appeared in print in 1971.

Courage's 1938 passport photo, from the year *Private History* was performed at the Gate Theatre. *S20-570a, MS-0999/176, Hocken Collections*

D. who was staying there. A very pleasant, although Platonic, seven days.
Delighted by Aix: a little clean green town, laid out with exquisite taste. From
Aix, travelled south alone to Avignon, where I stayed 4 days. Much impressed
by Provence, especially by the architecture and food (trout from the Rhône;
wood strawberries, & vin rosé). Went also to Nîmes to look at the Roman
remains (Arena, Maison Carrée etc, also the Pont du Gard, nearby). From
Avignon went north again to Geneva, where I stayed a night before travelling
up the lake to Vercy for a long day chez Kesteran again. From Vercy, went
north to Paris, and spent my last week there. C.H. [Chris Huth] came over
to join me from London. Very pleasant (though with some heart-aches)
and *not* Platonic by any means. Returned to London on the hottest day of
the year. All of this is a very sketchy and inadequate summary of one of the
pleasantest holidays I've ever spent. I had meant to keep a daily journal but
quailed before the task, and didn't write even a memo. The days went too
quickly.

30 June 1938

Frank (Paco) rang me up. The first time I'd heard his voice for about seven
years. As we were talking we were accidentally cut off by his little daughter.
Altogether a bit too grimly symbolical, I thought … He is staying in England
for a month or two with wife and nurse before returning to Buenos Aires. To-
morrow I shall see him. A mistake?

1 July 1938

No – not exactly a mistake. The meeting, however, was not easy: we were
both a good deal warier in demonstration than formerly … but it was quite
blissful to sit together again and talk quietly. Le bonheur de rester ensemble
sans dessein – perhaps that was the greatest pleasure of our re-meeting –
quiet and understanding talk, only heightened (like an evening) by a sort of
afterglow of passion.

9 July 1938

F. and I went to Glyndebourne last night to see a performance of Donizetti's *Don Pasquale* (with Stabille [sic], Borghirli and Baccaloni).* The singing was superb, and I don't see how the opera could have been better staged. Unfortunately the weather was foul: rain poured down, and we saw nothing of Glyndebourne's *beaux jardins* [beautiful gardens]. Several details of circumstance could also have been bettered – inaccessibility of men's lavatories, difficulty over booking seats for dinner, necessity for eating the said dinner in a hurry (and being charged half a guinea for doing so), delay in getting away after the performance in the motor-coach to Lewes, etc. I arrived home at 1.15 and am to-day very tired. But the opera itself was unforgettable. I must see a performance of Mozart next year.

27 July 1938

To the Carlton Cinema last night to see two ancient films, now temporarily revived: *The Love Parade* (about 8 years of age) and *The Sheik* (I saw this in, I think, 1922, in N.Z. and wanted to see it again.) Rudolph Valentino as The Sheik himself has a crude and virile sort of attraction that makes the female adulation he enjoyed almost understandable. Good eyes and an expressive mouth.

28 July 1938

Norman Marshall rang me up to tell me the by-no-means-pleasant news that the manuscript of 'An Extraordinary Case' (now re-christened 'Private History') has been irretrievably lost. Damn the man! The MS was lent to Reginald Beckwith (the proposed producer) who swears that he returned it to Marshall, but more probably left it on a bus.† Anyway, I have now to re-type the whole damned thing from my original pencil notes and scraps of authentic dialogue – at least a fortnight's hard labour. To do him justice,

---

*   Baritone Mariano Stabile, tenor Dino Borgioli and bass Salvatore Baccaloni.

†   A playwright and producer in the years before the war, Reginald Beckwith (1908–1965) (often known as Tony) went on to have a prolific career as a television actor.

Marshall did offer me a 'dactyl' [typist], but I'd rather do it myself. The play is apparently to be put on early in the season – in September or October. I shall be glad when the whole thing's over: it has given me so much trouble. And never again shall I type a manuscript without taking at least one carbon copy of every word.

12 August 1938

To-day finished the re-typing of 'Private History'. I have tidied up the play a good deal and re-written certain small scenes (notably the beginning of the Epilogue) but feel depressed about it, all the same. Fear that I've not made, or pointed, the general *motivation* clearly enough. I'm also afraid that some of the speeches are too long and not limpid enough. However if the play *ever* gets into rehearsal I suppose the producer can do a bit of cutting and pointing: the actors can also do a great deal by emphasis. Marshall is going to America on August 30th: presumably he won't see my play. Is he leaving the sinking ship? – I wonder. Frankly, I'm nervous about the play. Can it be put across without seeming maudlin, or morbidly pathological? I doubt it v. much.

15 August 1938

I have just finished reading John Fothergill's *Confessions of an Innkeeper.** How amazingly interesting are other people's diaries, confessions, apologies etc. I have been wondering, in fact, how much of these ten years of journal-keeping on my part might conceivably be of interest to anyone but myself. Very little of them, I fear: they're too gauche, too complaining, too sexually unorthodox (if not repugnant). Private history, in fact.

20 August 1938

D. remarked to me a few days ago that I had 'very nice hands'. I told her that my mother had said to me, in a fit of frankness, when I was about 14–15: 'Jim,

---

* John Fothergill (1876–1957) was an innkeeper and entrepreneur who studied art and ran a gallery before buying and managing hotels from 1922. He was a friend of, among others, Evelyn Waugh. *Confessions of an Innkeeper* was published in 1938.

you are very ugly, you're knock-kneed, you'll be quite bald by the time you're thirty – *but* you *have* got nice hands.' I hasten to add that, though I am still ugly, my knees have ceased to knock and I still have a plentiful supply of hair – or at least, sufficient.

24 August 1938

To dine last night with Norman Marshall at his Chelsea flat, to meet Reginald Beckwith who is going to produce my play at the Gate. Quite a successful evening. After dinner we went through the script of the play and made a few cuts (about half a dozen speeches) and a couple of insertions. We also searched the juvenile leads in the *Spotlight* for actors to play the boys' parts. Certain of my choices made M. and B. laugh. 'Oh,' they told me, 'he's far too old – or two effeminate – or too bumptious – or too difficult – or has an *accent*.' But we finally agreed on two or three – if they're open to engagement. Beckwith, incidentally, I liked, and though sensitive, intelligent and amusing, a good choice. Beckwith told me he thought I'd written a fine play. He also considered that the Censor might pass it for 'general exhibition' as the end was, in essence, 'highly moral'. But I have my doubts.

26–30 August 1938

Stayed with 'Cilla & Tom McKerrell at Kilbarchan in Scotland. I tried to get a seat on the Coronation Scot, going north, but the train had been fully booked for weeks ahead. I had an unsuccessful shot at gate-crashing it but was severely discouraged by the Reserved Seats man at Euston, and so had to travel by the 2 o'clock. Reached Glasgow at 9.55 p.m. Much interested on the train by my neighbour, an American, the manager of a Vaudeville troupe called 'The Stars' Doubles' (i.e. the Hollywood 'stand-ins' for Garbo, Mae West, Robert Taylor, etc – twelve in all) at present playing at the Empire, Glasgow. From him I heard all the scandals of Los Angeles – including the sexual idiosyncrasies of certain stars whom I hadn't suspected of unorthodoxy. As a parting gift he gave me a small photograph of Mae West's double ('You can have it').

'Mac' and 'Cilla met me at Glasgow. The following day (27th) we went to the Empire Exhibition and padded round it in the rain. The Art Gallery I thought poor (the unwanteds of a dozen provincial galleries). I thought the British Government's and the G.P.O.'s two of the best pavilions. In the N.Z. pavilion were two blocks of Mt Somers stone (very smooth fine limestone) that interested me, but the rest of the N.Z. showing was wretched. On Sunday (28th) we took a motor run up Loch Lomond, then across to Arrochar, Rest-and-be-Thankful, etc. Showery weather, but hundreds of hikers and cyclists on the roads. Many laddies in kilts, with fine brown legs. I admired this Scots type and wondered at its numbers (no difficulty, it would seem, about raising a magnificent army from such material).

I returned to London by the Night Scot on Monday (29th) evening. Slept about 3½ hours on the train. My companion in the compartment was a Scotsman from Aberdeen, going up to London on a bust (and staying at the Regent Palace Hotel). He was interested in my name (Courage) and knew quite a bit about the family, confiding to me that an 'Arthur Courage is the greatest authority on love-birds (budgerigars) in Aberdeen.' This is apparently a member of the Courage clan who has remained in the North and did not come south with the brewers, to London. Anyway, I was a good deal amused. He insisted on making up my bed in the train in soldier-fashion, saying that he had been a batman to an officer during the War and knew all about comfort. Result: I crawled into a sort of cocoon of grey blankets and was shut tightly up for the night.

11 September 1938

D. Littledale came to tea having had a Sunday luncheon with Julia Neilson in Primrose Hill. Dickie and I talked of war and the appalling position in Central Europe. I asked him what would happen to the London theatres if war were to break out. 'Oh,' he said *The Fleet's Lit Up* would do double business, and every other show would come off.'*

---

*   He was not quite right: the musical comedy ran for 191 performances from August 1938 to February 1939.

15 September 1938

'Chamberlain flies to Berchtesgaden to see Hitler.' When I read this in the papers this morning the most unexpected and sentimental tears rushed into my eyes. The flight was an extraordinary bold move for a diplomat of the old regime like N.C.

24 September 1938

The play has been in rehearsal for 4 days now. What if war comes suddenly? I feel the immense and angry selfishness of the artist threatened by general disaster.

29 September 1938

After a week of appalling tension – international and otherwise – a great ray of hope has appeared in the news that a 4-Power Conference is fixed for to-day. Pray Heaven it may be successful. Everybody very depressed yesterday at rehearsals (which are otherwise going excellently). I lunched at the Moulin d'Or with Mary Hinton, who according to present plans is playing a part in the play: we tried to talk about theatrical matters but the dreadful shadow of disaster hung over us like a black blanket.* She was afraid that her two sons (seventeen-ish) would go off and join up without letting her know. The relief came at about 5.30 when most of London heard that Chamberlain was again flying to Germany (to-day). Almost hysterical relaxation of horror.

5 October 1938

Rehearsals going well – in fact almost too well. I hope to God the first night won't be a fiasco. But I have tremendous faith in the older actors – Raymond Lovell and Mary Hinton† – and the boys in the first act are just about as good as they could be. I am nervous, however, about the Prologue and Epilogue –

---

*   Mary Hinton (1896–1979) played the mother of Geoffrey Longman, the play's protagonist. She later appeared in many TV shows.

†   Canadian-born actor Raymond Lovell (1900–1953) played the part of Mr Maxton, the headmaster.

the discussion of the 'induced homosexuality'. This is just a little 'faked' in the interests of common opinion – not quite true to itself.

9 October 1938
Saw the play's 3rd Act through for the first time in rehearsal yesterday and was, I confess, a good deal moved by it. It acts, however, much sadder than I imagined in writing it. I consider now that it is the best of the 3 acts, though at first I thought it the worst. It is more *human* than the others. When the boy (Longman) breaks down at the end and sobs, a quite unexpected lump rose in my throat.

12 October 1938
First night of the play to-night. Heaven help me!

14 October 1938
The play is a considerable success. Quite sympathetic notices from all the papers, and a really excellent one from *The Times*. I feel, after all my anxiety, that it is all too good to be quite true.

19 October 1938
The play is, for the Gate, a smash-hit. The bookings have been excellent. Bradburne rang me up to-day to ask for a copy of the play for the Censor (his second-in-command, Mr Geralkin, is going to the play for the second time to-night.) If the Censor will pass the play – or indicate how it can be cut for the public performance – the management of the Apollo Theatre (Reandco) want it for a run there. They would take over the present company from the Gate. Heard in the Gate foyer after the performance last night: One elderly woman to another – 'Oh no, my dear, you're quite mistaken. I know James Courage myself and he's married.' Unfortunately we must lose Basil Coleman (part of Longman) at the end of a month. He's under contract to the Old Vic.*

---

* Basil Coleman (1916–2013) was both a director and an actor, and later had a long career in television.

The cover and (overleaf) interior of the programme of the Gate Theatre's 1938 performance of *Private History*. *S20-542b, S19-601k, MS-0999/005, Hocken Collections*

THE GATE THEATRE STUDIO

under the direction of Norman Marshall

presents

PRIVATE HISTORY

by

JAMES COURAGE

Characters in the order of their appearance:

Geoffrey Longman	Basil Coleman
Kit Brewster	John Kevan
Brian Nuthall	Cecil Winter
Judy Morland	Olga Edwardes
Unwin	Richard Pearson
Melville	David Evans
Garland	Kenneth Morgan
Caroline Nuthall	Vivienne Bennett
Mr. Maxton	Raymond Lovell
Mrs. Longman	Mary Hinton

THE PLAY PRODUCED BY REGINALD BECKWITH

Settings by Hedley Briggs

| PROLOGUE | The Living-room of a small house near Falmouth |
| | August afternoon 1938 |

| ACT I | The House-prefects' Room in Nuthall's House, Bradbourn |
| | Early Summer Evening 1931 |

INTERVAL

| ACT II | Mr. Nuthall's Study | The following afternoon |

INTERVAL

| ACT III | The same as Act II | Five days later |

| EPILOGUE | The same as Prologue | August 1938 |

Telephone kindly lent by the G. P. O.

Stage Director	. . . . . .	A. M. S. Mackenzie
Stage Manager	. . . .	Michael Morice
Assistant Stage Managers	. . . .	Eve Robertson and Muriel Byck
Scenery painted by .	. . . . . .	Joan Knight
Business Manager .	. . . . . .	E. M. Collett
Publicity .	. . . .	P. Laing

20 October 1938

In the audience last night – Beatrice Lillie, Clifford Bax and Phillips Holmes.* Beatrice L., I hear, found the play 'most moving'. My first financial statement of the Gate receipts up to date came from Bradburne this morning. On present calculations I shall make ten to twelve pounds a week out of the limited Gate run. If the play is by any chance transferred I shall of course make a great deal more.

Later: The Censor has refused to give the play a general licence – just as I feared – though he holds out hope of its being passed in a year or two's time. So the present run of the play ends on Nov. 13th. Incidentally I believe that the Censor himself (Lord Clarendon) went to see it.† My agent (Bradburne) assures me, by way of consolation, that I have written a play that is at any rate very successful and is the talk of London. Well!

25 October 1938

Supper last night with Norman Marshall, Tony Beckwith and Cecil Winter.‡ Marshall had just arrived back from New York in the afternoon and had seen my play for the first time last night. He seemed satisfied, but was very much taken up with telling us of the New York production of *Oscar Wilde*,§ which he had directed and which is a great success over there. M. said that Wilde's (Robert Morley's) great speech in Act II on 'the love that dare not speak its name' is rapturously applauded every night by good bourgeois Americans who then go home to comfortable beds with their wives. All very odd.

---

* Canadian-born Beatrice Lillie (1894–1989) was a British actress, singer and comic performer; Phillips Holmes (1907–1942) an American actor; and Clifford Bax (1986–1982) a playwright, journalist, critic, editor and poet.

† The Lord Chamberlain of the Household acted as the censor of plays. In 1938 this role was filled by Lord Clarendon, George Herbert Hyde Villiers, a Conservative politician.

‡ Cecil Winter (1906–1960), who played the part of Brian Nuthall, the sympathetic housemaster in *Private History*, went on to act in a number of other plays.

§ *Oscar Wilde* was a 1936 play written by Leslie and Sewell Stokes.

14 November 1938

Last performance of *Private History* last night. I had a party here at the flat for the cast, and a few others, after the show. It went very well, though I ran a little short with the drinks. I had provided 14 bottles of beer, as well as whisky, gin, vermouth, sherry and lime-juice: and by two o'clock hardly a drop was left. However, everybody seemed quite happy and an excellent spirit of bonhomie prevailed. Everyone felt, moreover, that the play's run has been successful (as it outstandingly has been), and that credit has been gained for manager, producer, actors and author. The audience at the final performance last night was one of the best we've had, and the actors played up magnificently. I hadn't seen either Raymond Lovell or Mary Hinton give such good performances before. All the same, it was sad for me, saying goodbye to my play – though I hope the farewell may be but a temporary one. I kept wishing that I'd had a gramophone-record made of the entire interpretation, to play over to myself in my lonely old age. In saying goodbye to me at the end of the party, Norman Marshall murmured that I must write another play for the Gate. This I shall certainly do – or attempt to do.

2 December 1938

> *For and against* Private History. *Press opinions.*
>
> For:
>
> *Times* 'Very convincing: a well-constructed plot with persistent suspense and sharply defined characters.'
>
> *Evening Standard* 'A real problem, worthily treated ... A powerful play, extremely well-acted.'
>
> *Liverpool Post* 'A very sincere and singularly moving play ... tragic skill.'
>
> *Weekly Scotsman* 'A sincere and at times moving study of adolescent problems.'
>
> *Manchester Ev. News* 'A fine play, with a purpose.'
>
> *New Statesman* 'At least two of its scenes are completely successful ... Excellently written.'
>
> *Time and Tide* 'Oddly moving and admirably acted and produced.'

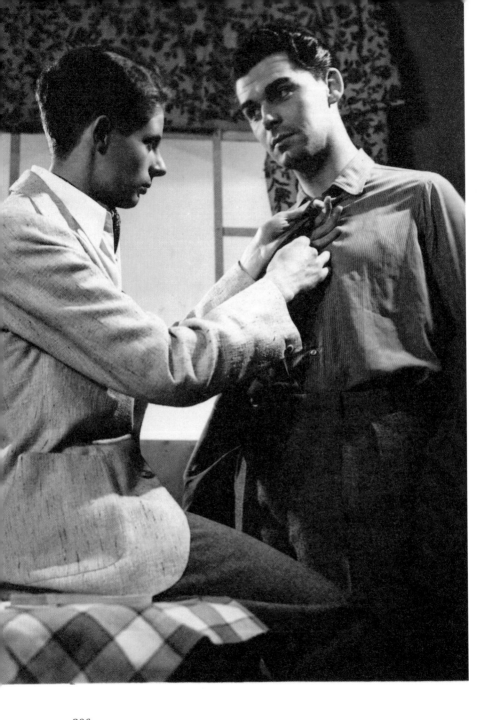

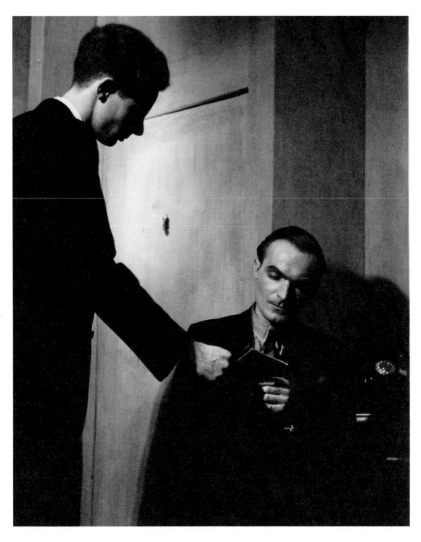

Geoffrey Longman with housemaster Brian Nuthall, played by Cecil Winter. Coleman and Winter were lovers for a time in real life. *S19-601h, MS-0999/005, Hocken Collections*

OPPOSITE: Longman and his partner Kit, played by Basil Coleman and John Kevan. *S19-601i, MS-0999/005, Hocken Collections*

The Stage 'As delicately-written as could be desired.'

Daily Herald 'A problem play … closely knit, finely reasoned and magnificently acted.'

Jewish Chronicle 'A fine play … told with great skill … The characterisation is poignantly truthful and the efficiency with which the author drives home his argument without arguing is extremely well done.'

Against:

Era 'Sickly sentimental play.'

Catholic Herald 'The play suffers as a whole from boggy sentimentality … The author has not the grand manner. His situations are diminutive, unimportant, shrivelled infinitely smaller than his theme. To watch them is like looking at life through the wrong end of a telescope.'

New Statesman 'The play shows some awkwardness in the telescoping of incident.'

Telegraph 'Ominous sentimentality.'

N.Z. poet, D'Arcy Cresswell, turned up here yesterday evening. I had written to him when I was in N.Z. four years ago but had never before met him. My impression is that he is a minor artist and that his talent proceeds, so to speak, almost entirely from a revolt against society due to his homosexuality. This may be unjust but it is my present opinion. After tea, about 6.30, we started out (on my part most unwillingly) on a pub-crawl round the Swiss Cottage district. This ended at 11 o'clock. As far as I am concerned, a dreary and wasted evening. D'Arcy became obstreperous, maudlin and morose by turns. His capacity for hard drinking is, to me at any rate, not endearing. (However, this priggishness may be due to the fact that I have a headache this morning.) He attempted to borrow money from me. Also suggested that we should pick up a sailor or guardsman and spend the night in mutual fornication *à trois*.

31 December 1938

Review of 1938

Perhaps, on the whole, the best and most eventful year of my life thus far. And this despite the fact that I began the year in a Nursing Home, with jaundice, and ended it with chilblains and neuralgia of the face. However, I shall remember the following events with pleasure – my visit to Switzerland, Aix-les-Bains, Avignon and Paris in May and June; my love-affair with K. in Paris and in London (though this involved a good deal of heart-burning also); my visit to Scotland in September; the production of my play in October–November with success; my friendship with the actors in the play; my meeting again with F[rank] after an interval of eight years and our renewed affection (a sop to vanity); lastly, I must not forget my re-meeting with J. ('one returns always to one's first love'). (J.M., that is.) My 35th year, and on the whole a good one.

3 February 1939

D'Arcy Cresswell, speaking about New Zealand to-day on the wireless (National) at 1 o'clock mentioned me twice by name. It was somewhat of a shock to hear myself referred to as 'Jim Courage, our playwright'. He was quoting me as having said that the N.Z. landscape was similar to that of Greece (or vice versa): the same hills, inland mountains and nearness to the sea: also the same clear air.

8 February 1939

I received this morning the following letter from Bradburne's agents in New York:

> Miss Morrison has asked me to tell you that she is most delighted with *Private History*. The theme is handled with such delicacy and taste, and the whole play, dialogue, characterisation and construction is a well-finished, workman-like job. She has already started work on it and hopes very sincerely to be able to get a production for it over here, since, in spite of its very English public school background, the subject should be of universal interest.

5 April 1939

Tony Beckwith told me to-night that he has unearthed a 'certain gentleman' who is willing to put up half the necessary capital for *Private History* to be produced in Paris. The said unknown is at present in Paris himself, having a glance or two at possible suitable theatres. The international situation however – which couldn't well be worse – may interfere with my such exciting plans.

6 July 1939

Saw Chris to-day, as beautiful as I shall ever see him ... Blue eyes, shining black hair, bronzed skin ... Strange it is, the intense sense of privilege I have in loving anyone so personable. – And, at times, of being loved. (A sentimental note, this, one for my old age.)

23 July 1939

Finished reading D'Arcy's *Present Without Leave* and was considerably impressed.* The prose is curious (the *Telegraph* calls it 'archaic'), but is better than any other New Zealander has ever written (from the point of view of absolute respect for the language). Parts of the book, however, I did not care for – the doctrinal parts, which D'Arcy himself sets most store by. The passages I really cared for, on the other hand, are those dealing with concrete events and the evocation of landscape. The curious style gives to these passages a wonderful and fabulous atmosphere (reminiscent of Hakluyt and Froissart).† The quotations from D'Arcy's own poetry, introduced into the book, are not good – full of echoes from Milton and Keats. Paradoxically, he is a poet who writes better prose than verse.

---

* This was a sequel to Cresswell's first volume of autobiography, *The Poet's Progress*, published in 1930.

† Sixteenth-century writer on exploration Richard Hakluyt and medieval historian Jean Froissart.

3 September 1939

Walberswick, Suffolk

War declared between England and Germany. So, after a year of tension, it has come at last. When it will end is another matter and one for most melancholy thought. Meanwhile, millions of young men will be killed, the arts will suffer almost total eclipse, and hatred and brutality will reign everywhere. The September weather, here on the East Coast, is perfect, and like a mocking comment on the foul and filthy skies of international power-politics.

10 September 1939

Walking with Ronald Jeans (dramatist) in his garden here this afternoon, when a ship was torpedoed close to the coast, not more than four miles from us and in plain view.* The ship made a half turn, settled slowly down by the bow and canted her stern high out of the water. An astonishing and somewhat frightening sight in the late-afternoon haze.

11 September 1939

Returned to London with Sam Ainsley (one of Henry Ainsley's sons), who gave me a lift in his car. London a strange city. Sand-bags, barricaded shops, barrage-balloons, tin helmets, gas-masks.† After sundown the streets are in complete darkness. From my windows the whole metropolis looks like a vast dark plain with a few humps here and there. Have spent the whole afternoon attempting to mask my windows with dark-paper, cardboard and double curtains. Not an easy job.

---

* Playwright Ronald Jeans (1887–1973) was known for his adroit social comedies.

† Large air-filled barrage-balloons attached to long strands of wire were designed to deter enemy pilots from flying their bombers too close to the ground and directly attacking the streets, buildings and citizens of London.

Fotos: Kaminski, München (2), Schmälz, Köln (2)

M E L L E R

Willy Meller, 1887 geboren in Köln, Lehr-
zeit als Bildhauer, praktische Tätigkeit als
Steinbildhauer in Ateliers und am Bau, 1911
bis 1914 Akademie der Künste in München.
Seit 1927 Ehrenmale in Neuß, Bochum, Dül-
ken, Lüdenscheid u. a. „Großplastiken für das
Reichssportfeld (Siegesgöttin), für die Or-
densburgen Vogelsang und Krössinsee, für
die Wehrmacht und Industriebauten, 1939
vom Führer zum Professor ernannt. — Im
Atelier (oben) Figuren für die Ordensburg
Krössinsee und ein Relief für die Wehrmacht

Die Bedingungen, sich über das Wesen des Monumentalen klar zu
werden, sind augenblicklich denkbar günstig. Denn auf der einen
Seite haben wir eine Kunst, die sich anschickt, monumentale Aufgaben
zu lösen, und auf der andern eine Kunst, die gerade das Gegenteil dar-
stellt — und der Weg vom Gegenpol zum Ziele ist nicht selten der kür-
zeste — ich meine jene intime Kunst des Stillebens, des Interieurs, der
Landschaft, des Porträts, der Kleinplastik, der wir vornehmlich in unseren
Ausstellungen begegnen und die mit ihrer anspruchslosen Gediegenheit ein
neues Biedermeier (man denke auch an die Mode) wieder heraufbeschwört
oder die Welt der Romantik wachruft mit ihrer innigen Versenkung in
die Natur und das Leben naturverbundener Menschen, ihrem Appell an

23

14 September 1939

Went to the Town Hall (Hampstead) to enquire about taking lessons in first-aid. Was told that no classes are being held at present owing to the lack of a suitably blacked-out hall wherein to hold them. This seems bad management to me. No air raids on London yet, but unfortunately these are bound to come directly Germany has finished her revolting work of 'rectifying frontiers' in Poland and turns to the West. Meanwhile, everybody in London – myself included – goes to bed surrounded by (a) warm clothes (b) gas mask (c) electric torch (d) personal treasures – all ready for instant flight to the cellars and shelters directly the sirens begin to wail. A melancholy and depressing business.

16 September 1939

Have just finished reading *Germany's Revolution of Destruction* by Hermann Rauschning.* This, I consider, is an absolutely masterly book, though very far from easy to read – in English, at any rate (it is translated from the German). Rauschning's analysis of Nazism is so acutely and solidly reasoned that the actual technique of his criticism was almost as thrilling to me as his subject-matter was absorbing and repulsive. And the way in which he delineated the Nazi aims in Europe and the world illuminated – to me at all events – the events of to-day and the last few years of intensified international strain – as sharply as the beam of a searchlight. But God help us all if we fall beneath Hitler's 'dynamic' advance.

---

*   Hermann Rauschning's best-known work was *Gespräche mit Hitler* (*Conversations with Hitler*). Rauschning (1887–1982) had briefly been a member of the Nazi movement.

17 September 1939

Russia invades Poland: the first time a Red Army has crossed a Western frontier. When will the last crossing take place? I'm afraid this is the beginning of the end of our democratic, capitalist Western world: an historic and certainly deeply fateful and pessimistic moment. But then, it can seldom have been amusing to live at any historic moment.

18 September 1939

All the London barrage-balloons gleaming in the light of a clear September evening, with a pale half-moon behind them. The whole sky studded with silver buttons: a curious and even beautiful sight if it were not so suggestive of horror and menace to come. Even the moon, regarding the scene from the south-west, seemed to half-shut a pale and sinister eye-lid.

21 September 1939

Received on Sept 19th the following cablegram from N.Z.: 'Cable if all is well with you – Courage.' Reply prepaid. To this I replied the same day: 'Well but worried. Could you let me have thirty pounds? Love – Courage.' Received to-day the following answer: 'Sending money directly if Government permits – Courage.'

22 September 1939

Went this morning to the N.Z. High Commissioner's office in The Strand and offered my services in my clerical capacity to N.Z. Government, 'for duration'.

5 October 1939

The real war in the West has not yet begun. Hitler speaks to his Reichstag to-morrow. Will the struggle now really begin – or is there even now – with Poland murdered – a way for honourable and justifiable peace in the world? I fear not. This may be the last day of comparative peace this generation may know, for even with Germany beaten there is the incalculable menace of Russia always ahead for Europe – a menace that time will not diminish.

12 December 1939

London

Dinner last night with Norman Marshall. He has read the play I wrote in the summer – 'The Man in the Distance' – and likes it (dialogue, construction, and a partial characterisation). The play has to be 'tampered with' a bit yet, but Marshall holds out hopes of a Gate production of it later on – if the Gate ever does open again.*

22 February 1940

This afternoon, having read lately in Osbert Sitwell's book *Escape with Me*, the fascinating conjecture that Angkor Wat – the immense temple of Cambodian civilisation – was built from the proceeds of selling kingfishers' wings to China, I went to the Zoo to inspect the birds of Indo-China and Malaya. The creatures are incredibly beautiful and strange – particularly one apparently made of deep black velvet with seal-blue azure eyes – but I found their *names* almost as noteworthy: the Scarlet Tarnager, the Red-vented Finch, the Yellow-faced Bulbul, the Blue-headed Weaver, and so on (if these are not correct they are very near it). But, alas, how I loathed seeing such beauties shut up in small cages. In the evening, took a young male prostitute out to dinner. The boy lost his civil job on the outbreak of war and is now unable to get another until he is called up for the Army (being 24, he is due to register next month); accordingly, rather than succumb to complete destitution, and having no home to retire to, he is forced to sell the only commodity left to him … A most likeable lad, I found, and not the insensitive 'pouf' one would imagine. C[hris] had introduced him to me, having himself at present rescued the boy from his Piccadilly haunting by providing him with bed and board. I have promised to do what I can, hence the dinner this evening, for which my protégé was almost embarrassingly grateful.

---

* The Gate was bombed during the Blitz and never reopened.

22 March 1940

Chris came to tea with me. We talked of music, military conscription, sex, Chris's ancestors. While he talked, I watched him ... Am I still in love with him? Yes, but not with that unremitting and murderous passion of two years ago. We are on safer ground: a sort of warm (almost domestic) sympathy envelops us ... Still, on parting, we kissed with real and authentic physical desire. I hadn't forgotten that beautiful mouth, that warm and almost Italian skin ... no, by no means forgotten them ... He goes home to Devon to-morrow, to live for a time with his family. The father is a G.P. with a country practice.

23 March 1940

Went to see young Kenneth Morgan, who is in St Mary's Hospital (Paddington) with meningitis ... His appearance, as he sat propped up in the bed in Greek silk pyjamas, fascinated me: he looked like some little blonde animal such as one can imagine inhabiting the darkest forests of South America. His huge eyes, particularly, gave this effect ... as though they were designed to gather any ray of light that might fall through the immensity of black foliage overhead.

14 April 1940

What can a mere intellectual say about the exterior events of the last week – the invasion of Denmark and Norway. This seems to me worse and more cold-blooded than the invasion of Belgium in the last war. I waited up till midnight last night to hear the final news bulletin on the wireless. The first accounts of the naval battle in Narvik Fjord. Ironically enough, I have almost completed my pacifist play (pacifist by implication, at least) about a conscientious objector. Possible title for it: 'Handicap'.*

---

* No play with this title survives among Courage's papers.

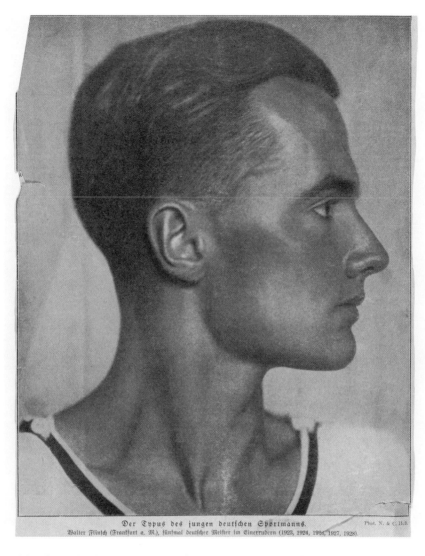

Der Typus des jungen deutschen Sportmanns.
Walter Flinsch (Frankfurt a. M.), fünfmal deutscher Meister im Einerrudern (1923, 1924, 1926, 1927, 1928).

Phot. N. & C. R.S.

A head-and-shoulders photograph of a quintessential young German sportsman.

S20-542f, MS-0999/141, Hocken Collections

29 April – 6 May 1940

The cherry-tree below my window is in bloom. Owing to the hard winter, not so many flowers as usual. Where shall I be when the tree blooms next year? ... At least no longer living in this expensive flat, with a cherry-tree under my windows. In sober fact, if present world monetary and political chaos continues (and this decline seems fated and inevitable), I shall never again be able to afford even a flat with a view. So, cherry-tree, you are the symbol of a past age of plenty, fast disappearing, never to return!

10 May 1940

The War Begins

Heard at 8 a.m. that Germany had invaded Holland and Belgium. Was much depressed in consequence (far from being alone in this, I fear), and spent a pessimistic day, with frequent bowel movements. Attempted to work at the play during the morning, without much success. Was interrupted by Martin (Head Porter of these flats) asking me to assume responsibility for switching off the lift in this section of the Court, in the event of an air-raid. Have agreed to do this. It will mean my haring down to the basement when the sirens sound, and finding a switch in the half-darkness.

Philippe Brossard (French Military Mission) rang me up in the evening. As this evening was Whitsuntide, we had intended going together down to Guildford for a couple of days. This plan is now cancelled, as the Government has discouraged all unnecessary travelling. So in London we remain, hourly expecting an air-raid. I have seldom been so conscious of a feeling of zero hour. Heaven help England. *Same evening 9.20.* Have just heard that Chamberlain has resigned in favour of Winston Churchill. Well, this is certainly a step in the right direction, though a Socialist P.M. would be even better and must come eventually.

16 May 1940

To Hampstead Heath in the afternoon. I never remember a more beautiful spring than this. May-blossom, laburnum, flowering prunus, wisteria, pine-trees – all superb. The air full of fragrance ... At the same time, the Battle of the Meuse* – 'to decide the fate of civilisation for a thousand years' – goes on in France. I felt the thought of this constantly at the back of my mind: impossible to forget ... I find people are at last beginning to ask themselves, with sudden horror, 'can we lose this war?' Myself this afternoon cogitated 'Can an England of such beauty ever cease to inspire people to love her and fight for her?' The may-blossom seemed to answer, firmly enough and with a thousand banners, 'Never!'

20 May 1940

Resolutions

Reading Sir Richard Acland's book *Unser Kampf*.† With all the ardour of the newly-converted, I admit that (as in the matter of D.N. Pritt's two books)‡ the author's case seems to me absolutely incontrovertible ... In fact, my entire social and political outlook has lately profoundly changed. The hideous spectacle and menace of this war has led me to study (for the first serious time in my thirty-seven years of life, God help me) the bases of a society which can permit – or provide the circumstances for – such an appalling catastrophe. And what indeed have I found? That it is my own class and the conditions of monopoly capitalism under which I have unthinkingly

---

* Although it was fought on the west bank of the Meuse River, this action is usually known as the Battle of Sedan.

† Richard Acland (1906–1990), who co-founded the socialist Common Wealth Party in 1942, represented the Liberal and then Labour parties in the British Parliament. His popular 1940 book *Unser Kampf (Our Struggle)* offered a Christian moral perspective on society.

‡ Denis Pritt (1887–1972), a barrister and Labour politician, wrote *The People Speak* and *Forward to a People's Government*. In 1940 he was expelled from the Labour Party for his pro-Soviet sympathies.

lived, that has undoubtedly led us straight to where we now, as a nation, find ourselves. What to do? I fully admit that, as a *rentier*, living almost wholly on unearned income, I am a sinner. Worse than that – a traitor, in my way, to human society ... Well, that settles it! I shall give up this flat just as soon as the conditions of my lease permit (in September), live more humbly, work for others' good and not live for myself so much. Above all, I must seek in my writing to show the coming (not without humour, I hope) of a more equitable and fairer state of human society ... With such a naïve set of resolutions I now for the time being close this confession.

22 May 1940

The war-news graver and graver. Mr Attlee broadcast tonight, announcing the special Government decrees of control over all persons and property.* Also a 100% Excess Profits Tax to be levied. This latter is, I suppose, absolutely necessary in order to take the private profit motive from what amounts to forced labour in the factories, and thus to forestall trouble. The decrees, as announced, are another way of saying that we shall now be under a social and political system as absolute as Nazism; but that has not been stressed. The truth, which such measures amply reveal, is the that we as a country are in great peril.

Since the trivial doings of what may be our last days of relative peace here in London may have some interest in future, I record that this afternoon I walked from Hampstead to the Dominion theatre in Tottenham Court Road, and there saw two films – *Judge Hardy & Son* and *Of Mice and Men*. The latter excellently played: though I had both read the book & seen the stage-play, I enjoyed it again as a film ... *But* this awful war-strain – the thought of young men being killed every minute, every second – is almost unbearable. It gives one a real physical pain in the heart, the chest – like a constant reproach in the blood itself (a reproach that 'civilisation' can permit these things to happen).

---

*   Labour politician Clement Attlee (1883–1967), a member of Winston Churchill's wartime cross-party Cabinet, became prime minister when Labour won the 1945 election.

24 May 1940

To the Gate last night, to see Cocteau's play *Les Parents Terribles*. Fiddling while Rome burns? Perhaps. Certainly I sat with one ear towards the stage, and the other intent on listening for an air-raid siren … The Frenchness of the play, even in its English adaptation, was an aching reminder, toute la soirée [all evening], that France is this moment suffering the most dreadful invasion of her history … I find myself constantly thinking of glimpses of Paris (along the Seine quays, under Nôtre Dame, where Chris and I walked), of the flat northern country with its poplars and reddish tiled roofs, of the rich countryside around Dijon, and particularly of Provence (the white buildings, the hot sun, the flowering broom, the nightingales, the shady plane-trees).

29 May 1940

Gordon Lilburn rang me up.* He leaves for N.Z. the day after to-morrow. I shall be sorry for him to go. One hasn't that many friends that the absence of one makes no odds. Gordon is having some music published over here …

As for this ghastly war: already the awful succession of bad news-bulletins has begun to have a deadening effect. There must be a turning-point, a bottom to this abyss, somewhere … Worked at the N.Z. play (about Mount Somers and my grandmother, etc).† It is, I believe, the best work I've ever done: it seems to have power and freshness.

1 June 1940

Saw Dr J.C. yesterday about the varicose vein in my left leg, and am to wear an elastic stocking for a while. After that, perhaps an injection or two. In any case, depressing. Curse one's damned inefficient, imperfect carcass.

---

*   Born in Whanganui, composer Douglas (Gordon) Lilburn (1915–2001) studied for a time at the Royal College of Music in London before returning to New Zealand in 1940.
†   It is not clear which piece of work Courage is referring to here.

9 June 1940

The Battle for France (and for us) continues near Le Havre, with terrific violence. Oh America, America, why do you hesitate – you will be in it eventually and up to the hilt. Why not at once? Shake yourselves and go for it.

11 June 1940

Italy declared war last night. This depressed me so much that I waited up until 12.15 to hear President Roosevelt's answer (on the wireless), which somewhat restored my balance of mind. *All is not yet lost*. Far from it. But God! Will America be in time? ... As for Mussolini's declaration of war, it can only be described as a dastardly and cowardly act, directed against a France fighting for her life. (It was interesting to hear, on the wireless, the reaction of Roosevelt's audience to his phrase about Italy – 'a stab in the back'. First of all a murmur of approbation, then a furore as the sense sunk in.) Italy, I believe, will suffer badly in the Mediterranean, and before very long. And the Italian people (apart from the young Fascist fools) do not want war.

16 June 1940

To-day ought to be known to history as The Sunday of Awful Rumours. People are saying in London that France is about to capitulate and sue for an Armistice; that the French Navy will remain with us; that England is to be invaded to-morrow; that Hitler is to speak at Versailles on June 28th and offer England peace on his terms; that Congress is to meet in America on Tuesday and declare war forthwith on Germany; that the members of the late British Conservative Cabinet are to be court-martialled – and so on. Meanwhile, as the popular song of the moment has it, 'It's a lovely day tomorrow.'

17–25 June 1940

France's capitulation, culminating in the 'cease-fire' last night – or rather early this morning, 12.35. External events of such magnitude are impossible to fit into the scope of a personal journal like this, and I must revert to the recording of small private matters. Went last evening to a meeting in a private house (2 Keats Grove) to hear a journalist, one Reg Bishop, speak on 'What will Russia Do?'. A gathering of about thirty-five people, whom the chairman addressed as 'Comrades' (a slight shock, I admit, to be addressed as 'Comrade' for the first time). Anyway, Comrade Bishop's words were fluent, consistent and worth hearing. (Himself a man of about thirty-eight, somewhat fleshy, large in frame, going bald.) I found myself agreeing with nine-tenths of his remarks, and violently disagreeing with the remaining tenth (chiefly on the *entire* responsibility of the British Government for its failure to sign an alliance with the Soviets. Surely there was at least *some* pigheadedness and prejudice on Stalin's side also) ... One detail of the meeting interested me, detachedly: at least 95% of the people present seemed good middle-class folk, and the one working-class man who raised his voice (a rather whining, under-dog voice, I admit) was either politely ignored or left in uncomfortable isolation. The comrade-atmosphere froze a bit, and the ineradicable English class-feeling could be felt like ice on the air. But then perhaps the meeting was afraid of giving itself the stamp of a full Communist Party affair.

Reached home at eleven, went to bed, and at one o'clock was awakened by the air-raid sirens. Dressed quickly and went down to the basement, having first performed my A.R.P. [Air Raid Precautions] job of turning off the lift. The basement somewhat stuffy, about thirty people have come down in pyjamas, etc (the women made a much better show of neat dressing than the men). Everybody very calm, save for one poor old chap of about 75, who'd been given a sleeping-draught and then torn from his bed (he complained often and querulously that he liked to stay in his bed o'nights). But no panic. Spread out my rug and cushion and lay on the floor, trying to doze (unsuccessfully). Was much interested and intrigued by a young good-looking man and his wife who likewise bedded themselves and then proceeded to make love – possibly a business interrupted by the raid-warning in some bedroom overhead.

The 'all-clear' did not come till three hours later, 4 a.m., in broad daylight. Back in my own bed I fell heavily asleep, having first smoked a cigarette to calm my nerves. Woke at 8.45, and feel tired and somewhat wilted to-day. I hesitate to think what a week of similar *nuits blanches* [all-nighters] would do to my constitution.

3 July 1940

Two days ago, my father sent me £100 from New Zealand. This reminder of the inescapable fact that I am a parasite – and have been one all my life – afflicted me with an acute attack of conscience. All very well to assure myself that I am an artist and hence by implication exempt from making a living until my own work has found a public capable of supporting me. I know quite well that that is so much bunkum ... The fact is, perhaps, that I am a *bourgeois manqué* – a man without sufficient artistic convictions to regard himself happily as a parasite ... To be truthful, I am a despicable person. Well, so be it. England is waiting for invasion. This extraordinary time is impossible to view in perspective – it is a nightmare, a constant assault on one's soul and spirit. An end or a beginning?

> *The City*
> The walls divide us from water and from light
> Fruits are sold but do not ripen here;
> We cannot tell the time of year
> And lamps and traffic estrange us from the night.
>
> The sparrows are citizens also, and the doves:
> Do they belong here only now, or could
> They live as freely in hedgerows, and in wood
> After generations of town lives?

For we have banished ourselves from the larger world
And grown hearts narrow like alleys: we are afraid
Of quiet, emptiness, the far away.
No one knows what his neighbour is called,
Out-fears him; defences go up; weapons are made
So that the unknown, conquered, shall obey.

6 July 1940

Charles Brasch (New Zealand poet) brought me a batch of his verses to read, of which the above is one. A solitary, metaphysical mind, not always easy for me to understand.

14 July 1940

From a letter from my mother in N.Z. – 'Everything here is in a good old muddle. You can't buy woollen or cotton stockings, for instance, but plenty of silk ones. No sewing cotton and heaps of other things. I have bought two years supply of clothes for myself, which has upset my budget dreadfully. I have been waiting 3 months for a pair of shoes (I have to have mine made, and am nearly down to my present cardboard soles). All this is not so much due to war as to government import restrictions and rise in general wages. (As I am writing this letter by sea-mail, and not by air, it will not be censored, and I can let off steam.)'

14 July 1940

Basil Collier came here to tea and Sunday supper. I had written to him, care of his publishers, after having read a book of his about Provence which had interested me.* A pleasant, somewhat reticent young man wearing blue linen trousers (his Provençal outfit, obviously). We talked until nearly two in the morning, sitting in the window embrasure here, watching the searchlights

---

* Basil Collier (1908–1983) was a military historian. The book Courage refers to was probably *To Meet the Spring: A casual journey through Languedoc, Provence and the Riviera* (1938).

over London (one 'plane came over, lit up like an iridescent mosquito in the beams) ... He has written six books, at the age of 32, and shames me by his industry. As a *person*, however, his temperament is far too akin to my own for anything but a mirror-like (and hence rather sterile) friendship.

26 July 1940

To Cornwall with Nigel Bryant. We have taken Helen Seddon's house (No. 17, The Warren, St Ives) for 3 weeks at a rental of 10/- per week. Nigel is a young artist (he is 19, myself 37: which means that I'm old enough to be his father) who attends an art school in Wimbledon. He wrote to me about a year ago (having been introduced at some tea-party) to ask if he might call on me 'to see my Christopher Woods' (pictures). It subsequently transpired that I was the first frankly overt homosexual whom he had met, and that he regarded me with a mixture of fascination and Puritan horror ... At all events, the friendship has ripened: in fact, it was he himself who suggested this Cornish trip (the equivalent in his young mind, evidently, of sharing a studio in Paris). A nice lad: the idealism and lack of compromise of extreme youth – though, to be frank, I find him a little trying, particularly in the sphere of the emotions. (But, God help me, I was a dozen times more priggish, and frightened, at his age.) The railway journey to Cornwall took over eight hours: a weariness in the spirit.

1 August 1940

The ménage is a qualified success. A few moments of real passion, even ...

10 August 1940

Nigel has suddenly painted four small pictures which seem to me excellent: he has talent of the lyrical, rather Christopher Wood order and of a surprising freshness. One of these pictures – sea, sky, a stretch of sand, a red boat – has been presented to me with a rather touching inscription on the back – 'To James, from Nigel, August 1940'. This is to be hung in my sitting-room in London.

ST IVES HARBOUR   STUDIO ST. IVES LTD. COPYRIGHT

A view of St Ives, where Courage spent time writing over several summers.

S20-542b, MS-0999/042, Hocken Collections

16 August 1940

Returned to London. An air-raid warning on the train: the blinds drawn and everyone attempted to crouch down. Just after leaving Reading a loud *crump* of A.A. [anti-aircraft] fire sounded behind us. Nothing more, and no 'planes seen.

1 September 1940

After a week of air-raids in town, I admit that I feel extremely ill. Mostly from complete derangement of the digestion due to nervous strain. Much looseness of the bowels, abdominal pain, and neuralgic headache: also a few symptoms of jaundice. Am leaving London for a few days to recover my equilibrium in Hertfordshire (chez cousin Pip, who lives in sin with an ex-stage-carpenter and has a small converted farmhouse near Ware).

8 September 1940

Returned to town refreshed, two days ago, and ran bang into appalling air-raids. Last night's, when a number of the East End docks were set on fire, was a horror. The view from my windows here frightening and altogether hellish – like the Burning of Moscow: huge flashes and flames on the horizon, and smoke drifting in huge grey plumes down the Thames Valley. Myself spent from 8.30 til 5 this morn in the basement, attempting without success to sleep amid a chorus of snores, whispers, farts and other indifferently orchestrated delights. If this is to be the communal sleeping habit for the duration, heaven help us! We might be a savage tribe, harbouring our bodies and chattels in a cave ... Hitler's speech in Berlin a few days ago, threatening to 'erase our cities from the earth' is an amazing example of the barbarism of the German mind. It might have been made, gestures and all, by some hirsute chieftain emerging from his forest in the days of Tacitus. The German idea is evidently *Oderint dum metuant* ['Let them hate, so long as they fear', a motto of Roman emperor Caligula].

9 September 1940

Another hellish night last night. Just before 4 o'clock this morning a bomb fell within 200 yards of these flats: a terrific detonation, which at first I thought to be in the building itself. Later in the morning, going out to fetch my paper, I found that all the shops on this side of Haverstock Hill had had their windows blown in. The pavements were as though covered with flakes of ice, which the dustcarts were already collecting. A little news of the havoc of the big raid on the docks the night before begins to circulate by word of mouth. Mrs B. (a young Jewess) told me that she had been in the city to-day and smashed streets had brought her to the verge of hysteria. Particularly bad in the poorest streets of Bow, and further east. In Mrs B.'s own office, the girls had either not turned up to business at all or had arrived in a state of collapse or bitterly weeping (one had lost a sister in the raid). I asked Mrs B. what people were saying in the destroyed areas. Answer: 'Many are unfairly saying that this is a "Jew's war" – that the government provides no efficient air-shelters – that a working class revolt is imminent – that Churchill's cabinet must go, and an administration capable of forming a united Socialist front (to include Russia) is be empowered at once and this war stopped.' Mrs B.'s own opinion (I regard her as an intelligent woman) was that 'the people would not stand for another week's bombing. If it continues, *there will be trouble.*' Myself, I doubt this. The poorer classes are behind Churchill generally and do not think either pro-or anti-Semitically. As to there emerging a Socialist govt. – yes, that does seem possible *in time*, and is probably the only way out of this so-called democratic-anti-fascist war (really a war between divergent capitalist systems).

Felt so tired after a more-or-less sleepless night that I betook myself to Hampstead Heath in the afternoon, lay down in the dry grass under an elm and slept soundly for almost two hours. I find that my nervous dyspepsia, diarrhoea, etc. – symptoms of subconscious fear – are beginning to wear off a little after ten days during which I could hardly call my bowels my own. Appetite slowly returning. Most of the London theatres have closed down or are closing down to-day. Not unexpectedly ... As for one's social life, it simply ceases to exist under these conditions of animal apprehension. One reverts to a kind of feral individualism: a beast in the jungle of a stone city.

11 September 1940

Another pretty bad night last night. Bombs fell nearby at 12.45 and about 3, the last one shaking the building like an earthquake (actually I believe it was a quarter of a mile away). Some incipient panic in the shelter, which Mrs B. very sensibly quelled by repeating in a loud calm voice: 'This building has *not* been hit – this building has *not* been hit – .' Everyone then subsided. Can this go on? The nights are a horror – and if so for us, who are in a comfortable, though stuffy, shelter, what for the unfortunates crouching in Anderson tin-huts in cold gardens?* The patience of the people is incredibly long-suffering,

---

*   The Anderson was a common English model of air-raid shelter, semi-circular in shape, made of corrugated iron and designed to be dug into the garden.

The German bombing destroyed many buildings, as Courage describes. This is
Harrington Square in London, bombed in September 1940. *Wikimedia Commons*

but not inexhaustible. There seems to be a general opinion to-day that these raids are to be the overture of an invasion, to come in a few days. I doubt if, even now, this would succeed. Meanwhile, the morning has been punctuated by the noise of the time-bombs exploding in distant suburbs.

12 September 1940

Another stuffy night: in the shelter for about 9 hours, of which I slept for five. Great noise of anti-aircraft guns. Apparently a new kind of gun, uttering a series of short sharp pug-nosed *barks*, was mounted on a mobile carriage somewhere in Belsize Avenue (150 yards away). These guns, stationed in hundreds all over London, appeared to give the raiding 'planes a fright, for comparatively few bombs were dropped.

Have spent this morning telephoning to furniture removers, seeking for somewhere to store my stuff when my lease for here ends on Sept. 29th. No success, so far: the invariable answers is, 'No Room.' This, I foresee, is going to amount to A Problem. My plan is to store the heavy stuff and my piano, take a furnished room in Hampstead where I could deposit my personal oddments and which I could use as a pied-à-terre, then move about as I wished. If London and Berlin are mutually to bomb one another into annihilation, it seems best to remain in town as little as possible. This is selfish and not admirable, but the world has become so mad.

A letter from my sister Pat in New Zealand, this morning. Her letter is cut about by the N.Z. censor, but one passage reads: 'I wish sometimes I were like John and Betty [Courage's brother and his wife], to whom the war is a myth in a far-off land, and as far from having anything to do with them as if they were fairies. And there are thousands of people out here who think as they do.' Hmm.

17 September 1940

My lease of this flat being up on Sept 29th I have been trying for a week to find a depository for my furniture thereafter, so that I should be free of landlords' obligations and able to move where I wish. There is, however, no room in any depository in London, people having rushed their belongings into storage directly the bombing of the city began. In desperation I have at last reluctantly agreed to resume the tenancy of the flat on a monthly basis, at £150 p.a. This is not at all what I wished, but the disorganisation of life at present makes it impossible to avoid, and I suppose I shall at least have a settled pied-à-terre and a reasonably comfortable air-raid shelter – at any rate, until a bomb lands on it. Heigh-ho. A fragment of German 'plane – 'the one that bombed Buckingham Palace' – was auctioned in the shelter last night and fetched £6 for the 'Hampstead Hurricane Fund'. The German refugees, poor things, who seem to make up half the population of the shelter, were almost the keenest bidders. A present for Goering.

21 September 1940

The night raids on London continue. I have taken to donning my pyjamas every evening at 7.30 in readiness for the nightly descent to the basement. About 40 of us are now sleeping there as a matter of course. From eight o'clock (when the sirens usually sound) until about eleven, people talk to their friends, discuss business and bombs, or play cards. Then at about eleven beds begin to be made up, and the first snores of the night rise into the stuffy air. Lights out at 11.45. The all-clear comes between 5 and 6 in the morning. I rise, fold up my blankets and mattress, and trek upstairs to my own bed, where I sleep for another 3½ hours. A month ago I would have disbelieved anyone who'd told me that I could become used to such an extraordinary routine. Yet these constant raids are upsetting me in other ways: my mind is too jumpy and nervous to continue creative work. I am in the middle of writing the 3rd act of a new play, but have not touched it for over a fortnight, and as a result of my 'laziness' feel discontented, depressed and useless. Despite the fact that to most people I would appear to lead an idle life *at any time*, I find that a strong Puritan conscience afflicts me when, for any reason, I myself consider I am wasting my time.

Those amazing drawings and scribbles (graffiti) on the walls of public lavatories! Cries of unsatisfied lust, physical fantasies, anything-but-lyrical outbursts of desire, masturbation-images, crude solicitations, graphic gratifications! On reading them – and they cannot be resisted – one's first reaction is one of repulsion at such obscenity (the homosexual variety are particularly blatant). Nevertheless, are they not, in absolute frankness, all too like the submerged images and pictures that on occasion rise into one's own mind? Nine out of ten men would deny this vigorously, but that does not make it the less true ... The real shock, the outrage to the conventional mind, comes only in seeing such outbursts of hidden 'libido' written down ... To the Christian soul they are evidences of deadly sin: to the psychologist, on the other hand, they are fragments of an animality shared by every human being, and hence neither sinful, nor, in any absolute sense, obscene. They are common to all of us.

23 September 1940
D'Arcy Cresswell to tea here yesterday. Two of his front teeth had broken off the day before, 'because of the concussion of the A.A. guns'. I laughed at this, but found to my amazement that he was perfectly serious. 'Gunfire does affect one's system, you know.'

23 September 1940
A letter from Nigel Bryant. A bomb fell on his parents' flat in Putney, burying his father and mother in debris, furniture, glass, etc but leaving them, by a miracle, unhurt. Nigel himself was in the shelter below, and though the bomb fell within 20 yards, the outer walls held and save for a great shaking he himself was likewise unhurt. 'The main loss in all this business,' he adds, 'was our eighteenth century glass and crockery, every bit of which is broken.'

2 October 1940
Conditions here in London are unfortunately becoming more and more chaotic as the amenities of civilised life gradually break down under the raids. Yesterday the water was cut off here – and is to remain so, according to authority, for five days. (I luckily had half a bathful in reserve, but I believe

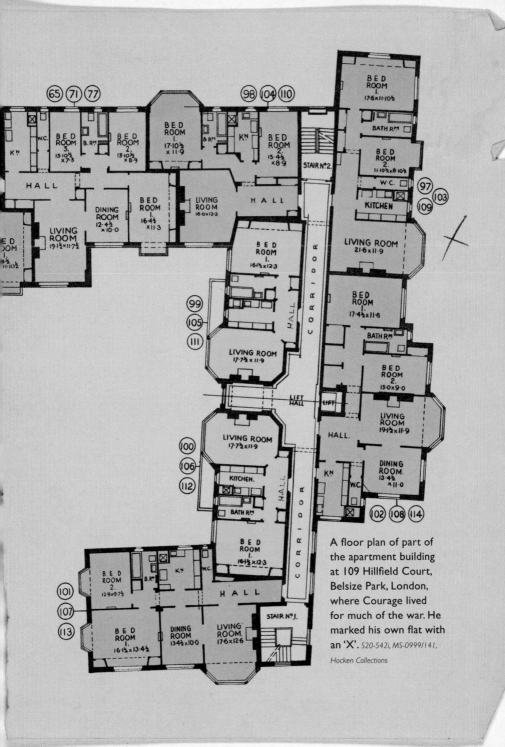

A floor plan of part of the apartment building at 109 Hillfield Court, Belsize Park, London, where Courage lived for much of the war. He marked his own flat with an 'X'. *S20-542i, MS-0999/141, Hocken Collections*

over a million people are without any at all.) The gas supply is reduced to a bubble; the telephone is practically unusable; the local underground railway has ceased running (a bomb landed on Chalk Farm Station). A pretty picture! But Germany will not win *this way*. The people will grin and bear it. And, the more the privations, the less the defeatist talk – or so I find.

6 October 1940

Am still in London. Air-raids continue nightly but have lost much of their terror. Everyone still amazingly cheerful. Walking on the Heath yesterday, I picked up a jagged piece of A.A. shell about 2½ inches long, from the grass. Curious to realise that it would have gone through a man's skull as easily as a pin through butter. I thought of sending the relic to John and Betty in N.Z.: 'A present from London', to gather dust on a peaceful mantelpiece.

7 October 1940

The first night for over a month, last night, during which we endured no air-raids. I woke many times, fitfully, feeling strange to be in my own bed again.

11 October 1940

Have at last arranged for my furniture, piano etc, to be removed and stored. The fell day is to be Oct. 15th. Set to work yesterday to sort out my possessions ready for the move. Old letters, old clothes, old papers, old junk of all sorts, collected over five years, had to be 'gone through'. As usual, on such occasions, I endure one of my periodic 'hates' about owning any property whatsoever. I should like to go through the world with a change of clothes, a dozen books, and the use of a good piano.

15 October 1940

Moved to 5 Cannon Place. The furniture removers' main office was bombed last night, hence their van did not turn up to-day. They have telephoned that they may expect to 'remove' me before the end of the week. Meanwhile, I occupy this pied-à-terre in upper Hampstead: a small top-room, cramped and smelling vaguely of damp and dust. (With rue my heart is laden/For golden friends I had/And many a lightfoot lad.)*

1 December 1940

Harry came on leave and stayed here with me for two nights. Army life has changed him considerably: physically he has put on a stone in weight: spiritually he seems apathetic, withdrawn, less tolerant than five months ago. His army hair-cut, I noticed, brought out a commonness in his face that I had not observed before, but the uniform itself suited him.

4 December 1940

On recommendation of Dr Cyriax, I consulted Harley St (Mr R. Boggon, 40 Harley St,) on the varicose veins in my leg, which, despite the fact that I wear an elastic stocking, have been a nuisance lately.† Boggon's opinion was that I can either spend a fortnight in a nursing-home now and have a series of small operations – involving the sectional sclerosing of the veins – *or* leave them as they are and continue to wear the stocking. In the latter event, they are unlikely to trouble me seriously for another twenty years. I have provisionally chosen the second alternative. B. said the veins would disqualify me for active service in the Army. This opinion, however, did not by any means please me: I dislike feeling a crock, whether it exempts me from military service or not.

20 December 1940

Young Austin Coates here to tea.‡ I accompanied him to the Hampstead Tube Station on his way home, at 6.30 p.m. A none too pleasant air-raid in progress, with planes overhead, guns going off, and searchlights and flashes in the dark sky. On my return walk up Heath St a piece of falling shrapnel hit the pavement ten yards in front of me, throwing off a burst of sparks

---

*   The quote is from 'With Rue My Heart is Laden', a poem from A.E. Housman's *A Shropshire Lad*. Courage has missed out the third line: 'For many a rose-lipt maiden'.

†   James Cyriax (1905–1984) was a pioneer in the field of orthopaedic medicine.

‡   A civil servant and traveller, Austin Coates (1922–1997) worked in air force intelligence during the war. He was the only son of famous British composer Eric Coates.

and ricocheting with terrific force against a house opposite. I can see that I shall have to sport a tin hat after dark, or else remain in the house for the evening ... Austin, having inspected the photographs of some of my past (and present) loves, stigmatised 'my type' as 'dark and tough'. The crystallisation of a truth I had not fully realised before. And a truth indeed, hélas.

24 December 1940

To the Mitre Hotel at Oxford for Xmas, as the guest of Dick and Mrs Spiers ... In the afternoon walked round the town with D. Visited St John's but found my erstwhile rooms – in the New Quad – occupied by Ministry of Agriculture officials and hence closed to the inspection of such ghosts of the past as myself. The rest of the college so much – so extraordinarily much – the same as fifteen – no, seventeen – years ago, when I first saw it, fresh from New Zealand: the same even to the wintry smell of damp plaster and football boots in the passages and cloisters. And St John's gardens, the same too: tranquil as ever, with an almond-tree just beginning to open a pink bud or two in the rockery – old Bidder's rockery (I just faintly remember old B., in my freshman year, a small, bent, ancient man in black and a flattish black hat. He died in 1923.) And the long, wonderfully green lawn where, as members of the Archery Club, we used to shoot a desultory arrow or two on hot summer afternoons ... the same – the same. Did I feel sad? No, not exactly: peaceful, rather, as though in a dream of the old place –
    'With her fair and floral air, and the love that lingers there,
    And the streets where the great men go.' (James Elroy Flecker)
Funny, that I should dislike my old school in N.Z. so much that it gave me the horrors to revisit it, yet feel only love and warmth for Oxford. Or perhaps not so funny ... I was violently unhappy at school, and at Oxford (on the whole) quite the opposite.

26 December 1940

Before returning to London, took a solitary stroll round St John's again. Went into Derek Schofield's old room – where our freshman's club – the

Coffee Club – once presented me on my 21st birthday with a couple of books – Squire's *Anthology of Modern Verse* and Mackenzie's *Sinister Street* ...* The room was deserted – a film of dust on tables and chairs; and in the 'bedder' a piece of hard, cracked soap on the marble-topped washstand ... What has become of the twenty-odd young men who gathered there on the evening of Feb. 9th, 1924 and made that warm-hearted presentation to me? I can't even remember more than half a dozen of their names – Allen, Schofield, Raby, Edwards, Lord, Strange – the rest have gone (save that wasn't there an Indian we used to call 'Hassan'?). Well, the sixteen years since have gone also: a mere flea-bite in the age of Oxford herself ... Or is she already dying – of old age, the decline of her civilising tradition, economic sclerosis? This filthy war may well be the end of her.

30 December 1940

A bad air-raid again last night. The warning went about six o'clock, and at once a fiendish row of anti-aircraft fire broke out (one gun is obviously very close to this house, for the doors and windows rattle like skeletons). I did not go down to the Basement, having been in bed for two days with one of my most stubborn winter colds. Instead, lay in bed and read J.G. Cozzens' new novel *Ask Me To-morrow* – an extremely well-written, amusing and depressing piece of work.† Finished soon after eleven. Before turning out the light – or rather, after, owing to black-out restrictions – drew back the curtains and opened the windows. The whole sky one glow of reflected light from fires burning somewhere in the city. People talking in the dark street below (snatches of observation about the fires) and a man obviously vomiting quietly under the trees on the pavement ... This evening, learnt that the Guildhall was destroyed in one of the blazes ... God, how senseless.

- This is J.C. Squire of the *London Mercury. Sinister Street*, by Compton Mackenzie (1883– 1972), was a 1913–14 novel about growing up, partially set in Oxford.
† Pulitzer Prize-winning American author James Gould Cozzens (1903–1978) once described the main theme of his 16 novels as an exploration of the harsh realities of life.

31 December 1940

A letter-card from Chris, who has been ill at home in Devon with synovitis. For the past six months he has been training for a (Signallers?) commission in the Navy, and has been stationed first at Skegness, then at Chatham.

> 13 Prospect Row
> Old Brompton
> Chatham, Kent
>
> My Dearest,
> Such a bother. Here I am, back in Chatham and our routine quite upset by most of the population being on leave. Weekends start again on Jan 14th. So I cannot be coming to town *before* that. We *do* get alternate nights ashore. So maybe you could come down here one evening? ... Am feeling v. well and rested. Came back yesterday and am glad to say I've not missed a draft or anything important in the way of instructions.
> Much love, C.

Letters are no reliable guide to the emotions. Nevertheless, on reading the above, I suffered the most sudden and violent physical craving for C. Isn't there something in the 'Song of Solomon' about the belly being like a head of white wheat and the legs like pillars of ivory with the gate between? 'Had, having, and in quest to have, extreme.'*

Wrote a letter to Dora. An extract:

> What kind of an Xmas had you? You'll be surprised to hear that I spent mine in Oxford, at the Mitre Hotel ... Such food, drink and dancing and gaiety – I haven't experienced the like for years. No wonder I had an awful hang-over, and a bad chill into the bargain: revenges of the Gods, the mean old twerps ... The hotel was packed with people and the food incredibly good: nobody would suspect for a

---

* A quotation from Sonnet 129 by Shakespeare.

moment that a war was in progress, save for the presence of uniforms at the dances in the dining-room on Xmas Eve and Xmas night ... By the way – and this'll amuse you – on Xmas night three New Zealand officers turned up after dinner, and stood just inside the dining-room door. As they looked a trifle lost, my hostess (Mrs Spiers) suggested I should go across and ask one of them if he'd care to join our party. This I did, whereupon he called to his two companions "Come along, boys!", and *all* of them trooped to our table! And – my saints! – could those lads drink! By eleven o'clock they were singing unison songs in Maori (very well, two) – love songs to Mrs Spiers. By midnight they were all three appallingly tight and were chasing the waitresses and kissing them under the mistletoe, and generally kicking up a shindy. In fact, they had definitely become A Problem ... The next thing was that one of them (called Jim too, save the mark) disappeared: we had to spend until 2 o'clock trying to find him. He was discovered in some hysterical girl's bedroom, where he declared he was staying the night. It took the entire night staff of the hotel, aided by the girl in question, and ourselves, to get him down to the lounge, where at last his two companions – now a trifle sobered – bundled him together and out into the night ... I will say that all three came and apologised quite charmingly, next day, but perhaps – for Puritans - the best motto is – let sober New Zealanders alone.

Purely Personal Remarks on 1940
Financial

(1) I spent about £480. This includes £35 due under the dilapidation-clause of my lease at Hillfield Court, and another £20 incidental to my removing from my flat there (tips, cartage, taxis, removal of piano, etc).

(2) Dentist's bills: £2.10.0. Doctor's bills £6.

(3) Amount in hand on Dec. 31st, including £18.15.0 in National Savings Certificates (which I prefer to treat as cash): £110.

(4) Spent on clothes during the year: about £30; but bought many things in advance, to escape Purchase Tax.

(5) Dad sent me £100 in June.

Health

(1) Three bad colds (about annual average).

(2) Slight trouble with varicose vein in left leg, above knee and below ankle. Am wearing an elastic stocking.

(3) Not much dental trouble. Two small stoppings, and two porcelain fillings replaced.

(4) Slight attack, in January, of 'married man's clap' (streptococcal infection of anterior urethra): this as a result of an extremely enjoyable romp with A. in December last. Was relieved that the trouble was not gonorrhoea. *MORAL: wash more carefully after pleasure.*

(5) Slight return of jaundice in October, due to chill on the liver and general anxiety during air-raids.

(6) Had my eyes tested in May, but was told: 'No deterioration.'

(7) No increase in baldness – or none to notice. Shampoo once a month, at least.

(8) Bowel-motions generally excellent.

(9) Slight thinning of flesh below chin and consequent accentuation of neck-sinews. This a natural result of ageing of tissues.

(10) Weight fairly constant at about ten stone (in clothes). No accumulation of abdominal fat.

(11) No boils – have never had one yet – and only about four pimples. Small acne – due to possible anaemia? – on chin in January. Also 'ridging' and redness of fingernails.

(12) No rheumatism.

On the whole: a fairly healthy year. Am not growing old too rapidly (even Cousin Aileen remarked on my youthful figure).

Love Affairs

Constant – in thought, at least – to my good Chris. Two and a half years of it now.

Temporary fixations (mostly sexual, in all frankness) on H[arry], N[igel], and D. The most satisfactory of these was H., though even that could admit of improvement.

Suffered, generally, from loneliness.

Writing

Wrote two plays: 'Of Military Age' and 'The Turning Point'. The second, much the better.*

The War. (But this does not come into purely personal remarks and is evident enough in the journal entries themselves.)

Final Word. Not a vintage year.

---

* Neither manuscript has survived.

1941–1946

2 January 1941

Distant sounds during the morning, of dynamiting in the city – the necessary demolition of buildings after the bad incendiary bomb raid of two nights ago, when Guildhall, among others, was damaged. Very cold weather here. Cold water tap frozen in my bedroom. Mrs Ridewood, meeting me before breakfast in the obscurity of the hall, asks abruptly 'How are your pipes?' For the moment, was completely taken aback, imagining she was inquiring about my chest-cough.

14 January 1941

Bought the first daffodils of the year (2/-).

17 January 1941

Returned from a visit to Chatham, to see Chris. It was ten months since we had met. I found him well and happier than I think I've ever known him. The sailor's uniform – he is an Ord. Seaman training for a Commission – suited him, making him more handsome, and certainly more desirable, than I'd remembered. The evening a great success. Was unable to get a room in Chatham, so stayed the night at the famous 'Bull' in Rochester. Chris dined with me (an indifferent meal in itself, but helped by an extravagant bottle of excellent Rüdesheim) after which we talked and embraced until 11.45, when – all buses having stopped running – he was obliged to walk back to his digs in Chatham. Came back to town this morning, after a cold night (the 'Bull's' sheets were thin and smelt slightly of anchovy paste) and a long and boring train journey (1¾ hrs) through a frozen countryside. But the trip had done me good, nevertheless, and seeing my beloved Chris again has greatly alleviated my loneliness. There is an extraordinary peace and understanding between us – and this not only as a result of sexual desire and union.

21 January 1941

I have two pictures of my own, here in this boarding-house room. A small, early Christopher Wood, and the small sea-scape Nigel painted for me last August at St Ives. I found I couldn't bring myself to store them with the rest of my stuff, last October, so brought them along as part of my voluminous luggage. Lying in bed to-day, I have more than once lain back and gazed at them in pleasure.

22 January 1941

The first thing that caught my eye in this morning's paper was an account of the suppression of the *Daily Worker*.* This act of the Home Office seems to me madness, outright. England apparently is to follow the same path as France, by suppressing her socialist opposition in favour of pro-fascist big business … By a coincidence (or is it?), in the same paper is Berlin's latest decree that no employee in industry is allowed to change his job. This, again, is a fascist (Nazi) symptom. But the *Daily Worker* case strikes me as being extremely serious. There are certain to be damaging repercussions in factories and ship-yards – discontent, strikes, even sabotage. In fact, just exactly what Hitler and Goebbels could ask for in the way of internal division. These things make one despair of England – and of democracy. God knows, I've never held much of a brief for the *D. Worker* (which is a whining, sore-arsed concoction often enough), but at least it should not be suppressed – in the interests of free speech alone. (*Later.* No doubt a hint from America – which is scared stiff that England may veer too far to the Left – is responsible for the suppression. How sickening it all is.)

24 January 1941

This blacked-out, bourgeois, boarding-house life – God in Heaven, how I really loathe it! The smell of evening cooking in the passages, the businessmen's faces, the church clock chiming, the police quarters down the street – the whole cauchemar d'une incessante mise en scène. Pfui! Am I alive

---

* A left-wing newspaper founded in 1930 by the Communist Party of Great Britain.

or dead? What I want is to get drunk, to lie in the hot and generous sun, to sleep with wild boys – yes, that is more like it.

25 January 1941

Charles Brasch came to see me in the morning. He had with him the proofs (and proof-photographs) of an article on N.Z. he's just written for the *Geographical Magazine*. The photographs all grandiosely scenic and looking like a sort of shingly Switzerland ... Charles brought a N.Z. book for me to read: Frank Sargeson's *A Man and His Wife* (published by the Caxton Press in Christchurch). Read some of these stories after C. had gone, and was very considerably impressed. Here is the real voice of N.Z. *at last* – twang and all. A million times more expressive of the country than those shiny photographs which are going to illustrate Charles's article ... Sargeson, as far as he goes, is the real thing.

26 January 1941

Chris here to lunch (Sunday) in his Ord. Seaman's uniform. As I had nothing here to drink I sent him off to the local for beer, etc ... Looked out of my window ten minutes later, to see him returning down the street, his arms full of bottles, his sailor's cap on the back of his head, a real nautical roll in his walk – a Chris I'd never seen before: a real lad of the Lower Deck. – And don't forget the wave of black hair on the forehead, supporting the backward-tilted cap with H.M.S. on it. An authentic bit of naval panache, that forelock.

29 January 1941

Royal Proclamation, including men of 37 to 40, announced in the evening papers. This means *me*.

2 February 1941

First lesson in fire-fighting (use of stirrup-pump, etc.) ... Is this to be the first real crack in the ivory tower?

11 February 1941

Nigel came to see me.

16 March 1941

Harry left yesterday, after spending a week of his Army-leave here (5 Cannon Place) with me. It was pleasant to have somebody to alleviate my loneliness (sexually and otherwise), though the conversation wore a trifle thin towards the end. We have such different natures, the two of us. He is mentally a child in many ways, and I have always to make an effort (though God knows, I am childish and naïf in some respects myself) to accommodate myself to his level. Everything in me of the artist – if I must call it that – is quite foreign and quite un-understandable to him (art of any sort that appeals to him is what I mentally call *Kitsch*). – Which is far from meaning that, from my side, he is either to be despised or is without attraction. His simplicity and very lack of sophistication appeal to me, *at moments*, enormously: they are what attract me in all ordinary people as distinct from those bitten with the humiliating detachment of the artistic life. But – to live with indefinitely? – no, I am afraid not. I could not continue to act my part: the pretence would become intolerable.

17 March 1941

To-day came a letter from Harry, thanking me for my hospitality and saying that, on returning to his unit, he had felt homesick, and that it had been 'a wrench' to leave me. Which means, I suppose, that I played my part – that of a mere 'good fellow' on his own level – sufficiently successfully to deceive him. Hypocrite and coward that I am. A letter also from Harry's sister, thanking me for my kindness to H. Does she realise that we were lovers or doesn't she? I wonder. H. had told me that she is a nurse in the hospital and was 'curious about me'.

20 March 1941

A land-mine fell last night on Jack Straw's Castle, 300 yards up the hill from here. This house shook like an earthquake, and in an upstairs room which had its windows open the carpets were blown against the inner side of the doors. This morning I went to see the damage. The mine fell in the garden: about five surrounding houses are now in rags and tatters. An apple-tree had been blown on to the roof of one house, a bath was hanging out of another.

23 March 1941

Down to the city to-day (Sunday) to see the damage about St Paul's. More extensive and awe-inspiring than I had expected. On one side of Cheapside, only the facades of the buildings remain: behind is a mass of reddishly-burnt stone and masonry and a tangle of iron girders, wires, pipes and plumbing. Likewise in St Paul's Churchyard. Amazing that St Paul's itself has yet escaped serious damage.

25 March 1941

Announced in the paper to-day that my age-group (Jan. 1903 – Dec. 1903) must register under the Armed Forces Act on April 12th next. If I must, then I must. At least I have a choice of some Civil Defence Service – providing that the medical board passes me as fit, which is unlikely. Began tentatively on a new novel a few days ago. This call-up business makes a difference, though I suppose I ought to go ahead with the book if I can. But the subject is *not* a popular one, to say the least, in other words, I am attempting a novel which shall accept homosexuality as a natural phenomenon like any other (which to me it is). But the clear creative focus on such a taboo-subject is, I am finding, far from easy to hold: all too easily a moral squint creeps in, so to speak! But it is time the subject was properly tackled – and without the usual English fury or giggle against it, either.

12 April 1941

Registered to-day, at the Labour Exchange in Kentish Town. Was lucky to find myself near the head of the queue, so the ordeal was over in ten minutes. The clerk rather resembled myself, but with less hair (the top of his head bald, with a sort of quiff brushed across it). When, in answer to his question 'What is your occupation?', I replied 'Writer', he said 'What sort of writer? Thrillers?' Hopefully I ventured 'Dramatist', which he wrote down with a flourish. So that was that. Asked for Civil Defence. In the afternoon went to an L.P.O. [London Philharmonic Orchestra] concert at Queen's Hall. *Leonore No. 3*, Brahms *No. 2*, some Delius and the Elgar *Enigma Variations*. Felt lonely, restive, and not very attentive.

15 April 1941

Was asked by a woman in the street to-day, 'Are you our coalman?' Just managed to summon up the presence of mind to reply, 'Not yet.' But, God help me, I wondered afterwards if I really did look like a coalman.

17 April 1941

Bad air-raid last night: the worst I remember. Went to bed at eleven but found myself unable to sleep for the terrific noise of the barrage. At about 2 o'clock a couple of bombs came down nearby and landed in the Hospital grounds, three hundred yards away, with a whistle and bump. Couldn't stick it out in bed any longer, so got up, put on dressing-gown and went down to the basement, where I found everybody else busy drinking brandy provided by the landlady. Stayed in the basement, talking and smoking till three, then went up to bed again but did not sleep properly till the all-clear sounded at five. Feel very tired to-day – 'burning with a very feeble wick'. All the streets near here are white with fine plaster and cement dust from the Hospital bombs. Even the pink almond-blossom in the gardens has gone quite colourless and grey with dust, as though sprinkled with pepper. Before lunch went to the Horse and Groom for a glass of sherry to revive my spirits. Found the publican exhibiting a 6x4 inch slab of iron, which he said was part of a bomb-casing that had hit his windows last night. Actually, it was a piece of a boiler, sent flying when the bombs fell on the Hospital outhouses. It weight about four pounds, was grey and jagged. Basil Coleman came here to tea. Though a conscientious objector he had spent last night putting out incendiaries in Chelsea, as calmly as the best of 'em.

18 April 1941

Into central London to-day, prompted by a ghoulish desire to see the damage. Piccadilly has come off worst: three bomb craters in the roadway between the Circus and the Ritz. A bad smash in Leicester Square too. All that's left of one corner is a tall crag of brick wall with, climbing up one side, several enormous, greenish ventilating-shafts leading to a square black mouth stuck into the air. The shafts exactly like huge entrails. In fact the whole scene had a surrealist look. Glass everywhere in the streets. Dust and 'Diversion' notices. Water flowing along gutters from cracked mains. Charred window-frames. Bricks.

19 April 1941

Chris's birthday. I had written to him yesterday, but two letters from him arrived by first post this morning, both written five days ago when his ship called at some port unspecified (the letters were franked by the Censor's office only). Very depressed about the war. It looks as though at any moment there may be another Dunkirk – this time from Greece. And this death of a second Greek P.M. in a few months is not cheering. It begins to look horribly as though God is a Nazi, after all. I have often suspected it.

20 April 1941

New Zealand

From E.H. McCormick's book on *Letters and Art in New Zealand* (Centennial Survey):*

---

* The 11 volumes of the Centennial Surveys were published between 1939 and 1942 to mark a century since the 1840 signing of the Treaty of Waitangi.

p. 130. The situation behind this drift to Europe (in the years after 1918) was a complex one. There were cogent economic reasons why writers with ambitions beyond journalism should seek publishing facilities lacking in N.Z. ... Again, writers sought in the old world more sympathetic and stimulating surroundings than those of N.Z. They migrated to London for the same reasons that Americans of the "lost generation" migrated to Paris ... Education, reading, prevailing sentiment – all turned the New Zealand writer's thoughts and ambitions towards England; and, given the opportunity, it was to England he migrated ... A few of N.Z.'s literary émigrés were to learn in the condition of exile a new understanding of their country. But the greater number quickly discarded all traces of their colonial origin ... Neither their country's literature nor the world's has been greatly enriched by their self-imposed exile. With only two notable exceptions, the single ticket to England ... has proved itself the entrance to a blind alley. It was, however, in the old world that New Zealand's greatest imaginative writer (Katherine Mansfield) found the conditions she needed for self-expression.

Yes! That puts my own dilemma very well, and explains a great deal of my own thoughts lately. I mean, have I failed as a writer because I fell between two stools – the New Zealand and the English? In other words, I didn't know the English scene well enough, although I knew how to treat it, and the New Zealand scene I knew all too well but had no idea of how to tackle it properly. I think that expresses the difficulty, and my own disappointment at my scanty achievement. Like Wordsworth in his early days, I have often 'felt the dejection of one conscious of high powers, but everywhere baffled in the attempt to use them.' (Herford).* Consider this also, from McCormick's book, apropos of the early nineteen-twenties when I wanted to become, and thought of myself as, a N.Z. poet:

---

* Courage appears to be quoting from *The Age of Wordsworth* (1897) by English literary scholar and critic C.H. Herford (1853–1931).

p. 161. New Zealand poets were [then] in one degree or another spiritual exiles ... They found it more natural to use the traditional language of English poets than the very different idiom of their own country ... Physically they remained in N.Z.; as poets they dwelt twelve thousand miles away ... So they turned either to the trite exaltation of natural beauty or inward to the examination of feelings which, in the absence of literary distinction, could have little more than a personal reference ... A final stage in the exhaustion of the Romantic [English] tradition ... The work of Rupert Brooke, not without its virtues in expressing a phrase of early-Georgian England, [was] wholly disastrous to its colonial imitators.

This is excellently true: an exact picture of the position in which I then found myself and couldn't surmount. Queer, that I should only understand it now, after twenty years, and through McCormick's book. Alas, the knowledge comes too late. I have lost the lyrical feeling of those years, when I might have written something memorable *and something purely of my beloved New Zealand.*

21 April 1941

Following on the above: I have to-day been working on the book about my own childhood in N.Z. Like Katherine Mansfield, whom I idolize, I want to make my 'undiscovered country leap into the eyes of the Old World'.*

23 April 1941

I feel only sorrow and anger – sorrow for the N.Z. boys who are being killed and anger against the Germans for overrunning a country that has fought as Greece has fought.

---

* This autobiographical manuscript is titled 'Present for K'.

14 July 1941

Medical exam. 3½ hours in a kind of disused shop in Holloway. Four doctors. Have been sent to the T.O. [territorial officer] for Hampstead, for his report on my T.B. lung. X-ray, etc.

22 July 1941

T.O. has told me that he will recommend me to the medical board for 'non-combatant duties' only.

23 July 1941

Am hopeful that the authorities may give me some intelligent war-work to do. At least it would alleviate the constant pain I suffer from loneliness, lack of love (sexual and otherwise) and consequent introspection. This has been *unbearable* lately. I cannot continue like this and keep sane. Everything turns to morbidity, somehow. Yet I know quite well that there is no *organic* flaw: I wake up in the morning fresh and happy. Only gradually, during the day, do the shades of everything turn darker and bleaker until I am lost.

6 September 1941

Began work in Wilson's bookshop, here in Hampstead. Enjoying it enormously. Salary: £2.10.0 per wk.

9 October 1941

Half-day (Thursday) at the shop. Went into town this afternoon to have a haircut and to buy some new clothes at Simpsons: four white linen handkerchiefs, one tie and one pair woollen socks. Total: six coupons. Cash: £1. And all this while the biggest battle ever known in the world goes on in Russia. Have thought of this, guiltily, at intervals during the day. Overheard two 'bus conductors talking in the 'bus on the way into town.

> *A*: I see by the placards Russia's asking us to invade this side, Bill.
> *Bill*: (*despondently*) Yes.

A: 'Spose we'll be too late, just as in Poland ... Seems kind of funny, doesn't it.

(Silence. Profound silence and deep cogitation.)

My God, *can* we lose this war? It seems impossible and not-be-thought-of, and yet ... there's so much in England that looks like a reflection of poor Jain's impotence ... If Russia falls we're just about dished.

15 October 1941

Heard the enemy 'mystery voice' butting in on the nine o'clock evening news (Forces Programme). A high indignant tone, shouting vehemently 'That's a Lie!' after an announcement that German troops which had landed by parachute behind the Russian lines defending Moscow had all been wiped out.*

16 October 1941

A furious argument at dinner here tonight in the boarding house: the Pros and Cons of England invading the Continent. The old men all Against, arguing on the example of the last war (Gallipoli, etc), as usual. Lost my own temper and said that at least an 'honest attempt' might be made to lighten the pressure on Moscow.

Christmas Day 1941

Alone.

16 January 1942

Met Eric Coates this afternoon, both of us on our way into central London in the tube.† Talk, for some reason I can't remember, about happiness. E.C. said he was glad he was over forty and past the terrors and abysses of youth! As Mrs Coates had met me in the street a week ago and subsequently remarked

---

*   Courage is probably referring to the German propaganda broadcasts made on British radio during the war, most famously by William Joyce, known as Lord Haw-Haw.

†   Eric Coates (1886–1957) was a prolific and popular British composer of light music.

to Austin that I looked 'amazingly young' and 'did I cling to youth?' – E.C.'s remarks to me to-day may have had a personal bearing.

25 May 1942

Whit Monday evening, a holiday, and perhaps a moment to take stock. I am happy in my bookshop job, but even now do not like being alone for too long. For in solitude I am haunted by the unfulfilment of the dreams and aspirations of earlier years – the hopes of fame, of personal happiness in love, and the giving-forth of what nobleness and feeling I possess in my own soul. These fulfilments have largely passed me by, and to remember them in moments of self-communion is bitterness indeed. My discomforture is measured only by the ardour of the self-belief which for so many years kept me going. At the same time I am not unhappy enough to write. A state of betwixt and between ... And it is only in solitude that the real ghosts haunt me.

16 October 1942

Reasons for my failure as a writer.

(1) My deepest, instinctive, childhood memories – the memories on which every writer bases so much of his best work – are of New Zealand, where I was born and lived until I was twenty. I have tried to use these early experiences, in literary form, in various ways, but have almost invariably been told by publishers that they are not of sufficient general interest. No one is interested in New Zealand apparently, despite Katherine Mansfield's success. At any rate, I have given up trying to utilize my early background.

(2) The fact that I am profoundly homosexual in temperament. I cannot write with absolute sincerity – or indeed with absolute knowledge – of love between man and woman, and have a dislike of faking what I cannot instinctively feel. On the occasion when I have attempted to use homosexual love as a theme for literature or fiction I have again

been rebuffed by being told that the subject is not of general enough interest (I must except here my play *Private History*). Consequently, I have in this (as in (1) above) been reduced to silence.

(3) Lack of inventive powers which might have obviated (1) and (2), and which would have produced, in any case, writings or fictions lacking what Galsworthy called 'power of author' – the only kind of writing which really interests or concerns me.

(4) Laziness, undue sensitiveness and lack of ambition.

13 November 1942

Using a hand-mirror this morning while I was dressing, I noticed how thin my hair is getting on top of my head. Felt depressed for a couple of hours in consequence. Yet, considering that my hair has always been extremely fine in texture and never abundant, and, moreover, that I shall be forty years of age in February next, I still look at least eight to ten years younger than my age (my barber, though possibly wishing to flatter me in view of an extra tip, put my age the other afternoon at 'thirty-one or thirty-two – but then you have a very fresh complexion, sir, and that *counts*'). Well, there it is. Time passes, middle-age approaches. Nevertheless, save for occasional moments, such as that I have mentioned this morning, when the failure or decay of some *physical* attribute or function suddenly pricks at me, I don't feel depressed at getting older. I am well aware, however, that I am lucky in *one thing* (and I write this here in all frankness, since I have given some thought to it and it seems important) – I have as 'mistress' a young man of twenty-two (I.A.) [Ivan Alderson] whom I care for and who in turn cares for and cherishes me ... whatever the world may say about this, it makes an immense difference to my life. Without sex – and I speak for myself – sex itself becomes an obsession, feverish, distracting, morbid. On the other hand, with sex satisfied, what I might call sensuality or the powerful phallic element in life as such, takes its natural place in existence and the mind is freed to go off on its own ways

– seraphically free in fact … As I get older all this becomes clearer, even though sex ceases to nag at me as much. Had I not the pleasure of I.A.'s body and his comforting presence, to be frank, I should feel not forty, but a misanthropic fifty.

15 November 1942

To dinner with Charles Brasch, a few nights ago, to meet Denis Glover – the man who founded the only decent printing-press in New Zealand, the Caxton Press in Christchurch.* Glover was wearing naval rating's outfit, with *New Zealand* on the shoulder. A youngish man, rather stout, with hair plastered down in front and untidy behind, like a school-boy's. He talked – v. interestingly – of book distribution in N.Z. Later the conversation turned to N.Z. slang. I recalled the poetic expression used among tramps (or *swaggers*) for spending the night in the open: 'To sleep with Mrs Green'. Denis capped this with an even better way of saying the same thing: 'To sleep in the star hotel'. He then went on to give some slang terms he had heard on shipboard, but these unfortunately now escape my memory – except that they were one and all crapulously obscene.

8 February 1943

Ivan spent the weekend with me here (67, Greenhill). Owing to rather too much to drink (or rather, mixing whiskey and gin) on Saturday night, he had a bad hangover on Sunday and stayed in bed until four. Hugo B. came round in the evening but left about 10.30, when Ivan and I went to bed. When we had been together about ¾ hr, Ivan – who, in consequence of his malaise – had eaten little during the day – suddenly said he remembered seeing a cold sausage in the refrigerator after supper – and could he eat it. He brought in the cold sausage on a plate and ate it on the bedroom floor in my checkered dressing-gown, while I lay naked in bed and watched him with laughter. He

---

* Denis Glover (1912–1980), one of New Zealand's leading poets, served with distinction in the Royal Navy during World War II, earning a DSC for his bravery on D-Day.

left this morning to return to work (he is in the Air Ministry).* I wished he could have stayed longer, but he has promised to come for a further weekend in the future.

9 February 1943

My fortieth birthday. For over two years I have dreaded the passing of this milestone – yet when I reached it to-day I felt very little emotion: less than I did on my thirtieth birthday, if I remember rightly. Jimmie Cyriax sent me a book as a present, and Leslie Hurry sent me a telegram.† Leslie came to dine here in the evening (it is his own birthday to-morrow). For dinner – a good curry and an apple-pie.

13 February 1943

I shall remember this day all my life for the sad news it brought me. – When I reached home at 5.30 in the evening I found an envelope from the Returned Letter Office containing two of my letters (written in Dec. last) to my much- and long-loved Christopher. On each of my envelopes was pasted a typed notice telling me that the addressee had died on active service. For about an hour I hardly felt the shock. I even played the piano and read. Then when Mrs Timmons (who remembered Chris) arrived to cook my dinner I told her the news. Directly she said 'Oh, how terrible', the tears rushed into my eyes and I wept. Later in the evening I rang up Joan V. who knew Chris well. She told me that he died of wounds 'due to shell or bomb blast' on Dec. 11th last (two months ago) somewhere in the Mediterranean. The announcement had been in the papers but I had not seen it. Chris was 27. Before going to bed I wrote to his mother, though I found this difficult.

---

* The Air Ministry was the government department that oversaw the Royal Air Force.

† British artist Leslie Hurry (1909–1978) designed sets for ballet, theatre and opera. He drew his inspiration from surrealism.

14 February 1943

A sad day. Have thought of Chris every hour – almost every minute. I find it difficult to believe that he is dead, and tell myself, 'This is a joke. Chris and I will meet in due course and have a good laugh about it.' But alas, it is no joke. I remember writing to him once, in a letter, 'If anything happened to you I don't think I could go on without you in the world.' Now I know that the tragedy is that I *shall* go on – getting older and sadder. I have decided to write down in a note-book everything I can recollect about Chris while I can still remember it. *Somebody* – and why not I? – should try to save from oblivion something of what his mother (in a letter to Joan) calls 'his rare and radiant spirit'. And I suppose I knew him better than any other living person – probably better *in certain ways* than his own parents.

15 February 1943

Tried to busy myself all day, but have thought constantly of Chris. Why did I not know he had died? Have found myself at odd moments during the day murmuring to myself the words of Alice Meynell's sentimental sonnet –

> I must not think of thee, and proud yet strong,
> I shun the thought that lurks in all delight –*

21 March 1943

A little of the ache of loss has gone. But the shock remains. When I hold even the most beautiful body in my arms I cannot forget the skeleton beneath the flesh.

10 April 1943

Ivan here staying with me. Much sweetness in our love.

---

* The quotation is from 'Renouncement' by poet, critic and former suffragist Alice Meynell (1847–1922). The first line is actually 'tired yet strong'.

20 May 1943

A day of perfect May sunshine and heat, but to me dark and cold. There is something much amiss with my life. Outwardly – that is, to other people – I am calm and cheerful: inwardly – to myself – I suffer from fits of melancholy, bitterness and extreme loneliness: in a word, moods of introspection. After all, I am forty, no longer young, and what have I done with my life and gifts? Precious little. Like Byron, who confessed as much to his own journal, I 'shall never be anything, or rather always be nothing'. Byron wrote that sentence when he was 26. I am fourteen years past that age. A melancholy business.

10 October 1943

Ivan has killed himself – my boy, my child, my love – he was 23. It happened on Friday night, two days ago; I knew only this evening. He must have died in a mental anguish I cannot contemplate. A difficult time. I cannot write about it.

10 December 1943

Two months since Ivan died. The evidence given at the inquest and printed in the papers was to the effect that he was unhappy owing to the war and its enforced interruption of the true bent of his life, which was creation, not destruction (he had been the youngest qualified landscape gardener in England). This is only partly true, I know, and in itself is certainly not the major cause of the tragedy. The boy was fundamentally melancholic and suffered terribly and cruelly from his own *inward* nature. Even I, whom I am convinced he loved as much as he loved anyone, could only partially alleviate his immense loneliness. He had clung to me so often, asking for help, for advice, for all the love I could give him (and there *was* love between us as well as passion) ... Yet not even all this fully explains a desperate act. I do not *know* – circumstantially – the exact reason for his death; yet I know enough to guess at it. Poor child, poor Ivan.

20 December 1943

I cannot get this unhappy business out of my mind. Two things that I keep on returning to, often when lying awake at night: His father, at the funeral, so most pathetically anxious to assure Ivan's Air Force associates that the boy had never been a coward – had never feared war – was not afraid of any death in action; My own last sight of the smallish coffin, in that hideous church, as it slid slowly into the wall of the crematorium: in that coffin was what had been a most beautiful body – a body I had admired and embraced: now I should never see it again, in an hour or so it would be nothing, ashes, an unrecognisable crumbled ... Why should I hypocritical about this? My physical love for the boy was as valid to me as the love I had for his ways and his companionship. All the same, in that coffin, in that hideous cold brick church ...

25 December 1943

Xmas Day: To Leslie Hurry's in the evening. John Simons played Liszt.

31 December 1943

The end of a not too happy year. Chris and Ivan have gone. Once again I am alone. Sadly? No – I am learning to face it, to stare Loneliness in the eyes and defeat the bitch.

14 January 1944

Leslie Hurry rang up and came round to see me after dinner. He'd just finished his designs (stage) for *Hamlet* and was in a more than Hamlet-like despondency. Talked of his melancholia – his terror of criticism as an attack on his inmost ego – and said he envied those who, like Ivan, could find the guts to take their own lives. Later he cheered up and we had a good talk. But I can sympathise with his black moods, having had all too many of them myself. He is at present living alone in his Vale of Health house: not good for him: only a black cat, called Billy, for company.

WIGMORE HALL
WIGMORE STREET, W.1.

Thursday Evening
FEBRUARY 10th
at 8.30

JOHN SIMONS

𝔓ianoforte 𝔯ecital

BLÜTHNER GRAND PIANOFORTE

TICKETS (inc Tax) res : 9/- and 6/-   unres : 3/-
From Box Office, Wigmore Hall ; usual Ticket Offices ; and

IMPERIAL CONCERT AGENCY   *Telephone :*
Empire House, 175 Piccadilly, W.1   *REGENT 4441-2*

A stamped addressed envelope should accompany all applications for Tickets by post.

P.T.O.

Courage's friend John Simons performed in public as well as privately during
the 1940s. *S20-542g, MS-0999/141, Hocken Collections*

12 February 1944

To the first night of Helpmann's *Hamlet* last night. Leslie's designs, sets and costumes all very rich, sombre, and Rembrandt-esque ...* An air-raid warning (? The first ever to be sounded during a production of *Hamlet*) came at the most exciting moment of the play – the scene with the players and King and Queen. Some restiveness in the audience, with a continual distant rumble of guns outside and a few startlingly near detonations. The All-clear came after the second interval.

3 March 1944

A great noise of our bombers going over here to-night at about eight o'clock, all bound for Germany. A continual high drone-like hum, similar to the distant noise of a cream-separator in action, for nearly twenty minutes. I drew back the curtains and looked out, but nothing was visible except a cold clear moonlight and the thin beam of a searchlight to the south. The planes were all flying high and fast. A strange time to live in – this lull before our invasion of the Continent begins. We are undoubtedly in for a tough time ahead and may look back on this present as the last comparatively peaceful, unanguished interval for many a long year to come. At least I trust we may never hear German bombers over London in such thousands as ours are humming across tonight.

9 March 1944

I have always been a solitary person and have always felt and been most at ease and happiest when alone. It is only the sexual instinct that has time and again wrenched me out of line, so to speak. The effort to make parallel lines meet – mine and some other's – has caused me a vast amount of unhappiness. The marriage of true minds, whatever other people's experience of it may have been (and, viewing most marriages I have seen, it

---

* Australian-born Robert Helpmann (1909–1986) was a ballet dancer, actor (especially in Shakespeare), director and choreographer.

comes extremely seldom, if ever), has certainly not come my way. Loneliness, in fact, is inevitable – or rather, I should say 'alone-ness' is inevitable. Only youth and the delusions of sex would make it appear otherwise and necessary.

11 March 1944

This terrific bombing of Berlin by the Americans and the R.A.F. [Royal Air Force] ... what are the reactions to it of the ordinary people I meet, to say nothing of my own? Uneasiness, I think, a vague feeling of shame. Whatever the Germans did to London in 1940, this catastrophic battering of Berlin has something cold, prodigiously purposeful and even inhuman about it. Most people, I find, are slightly conscience-stricken – as though accused of a personal revenge. And revenge, as a valid motive, has come to seem medieval, outgrown, something that only happens 'in history'. At the same time it *is* recognised that the Berlin bombings are necessary to shorten the war. But as to the human suffering involved – that is perhaps better unthought-of.

12 March 1944

Before Leslie left London a fortnight ago he gave me a small bowl of tannin-like earth containing the bulbs of three snowdrops. In the last ten days these have come up: I've had a really enormous delight in watching them – first the pale-green nipple pushing out of the brown bulb-case, then the division of the leaves, then the small whitish green transparent petal-head (?spathe) of the flower held upright and protected by the spears of the growing leaves ... I feel I had a real bit of Spring in the room – a bit of circumstantial evidence, so to speak.

27 March 1944

Bought some ochre face-powder for my forehead. Too pale.

18 April 1944

Tiny [sister] sent me a large match-box full of small paua shells from New Zealand. Mother of pearl insides, very pretty. I had written, last year, asking her for them, as an inexpensive present.

19 April 1944

A large box of primroses arrived from Devon, sent by Mrs Huth. I had forgotten that to-day is Primrose Day and would have been Christopher's birthday. It is almost eighteen months since he was killed ... Touching of Mrs H. to remember that I used to send C. a birthday present.

21 April 1944

The pear-trees in the old garden behind the bookshop are in full blossom – a superb sight. The scent of the flowers a little over-rich, honeyish, even a bit repulsive. The petals of each flower curved-in slightly, like the fingers of a hand, protecting the red-pepper stamens – or are they pistils. (Am more ignorant about botany than I ought to be.)

4 May 1944

Had my hair cut.

'You have such a small head,' said the barber, 'that if I cut your hair too short it makes you look duppy.'

'Look what?' I asked.

'DUPPY.'

'Oh.'

He's quite right, of course. Duppy's the word.

9 May 1944

A tin parcel of food from Mother, who imagines wartime England is a desert island, to be provisioned out of mercy, bless her. Two packets of raspberry jelly-crystals, and old tobacco-tin full of sultanas, a tin of Nestle's Malted Milk Powder, a tin of Sweetened Condensed Milk, and a (slightly rusty) tin of clover honey. The last is the most welcome, since bought honey seems at the moment to consist of cellulose, artificially coloured. I am lucky, surely, at the age of 41, to have both parents alive and still in a present-sending state of mind.

14 May 1944

Walking on the Heath, I stopped to look at that view of Kenwood House, seen between the boles of two huge elms, which Christopher was so fond of. It is just over two years since I saw him for the last time. Now, dead these eighteen months, killed when his ship was torpedoed, he lies in a cemetery in Algiers.* I loved him very greatly – all the more perhaps because he loved me intermittently in return. He was the most physically beautiful person I've ever known. Life being as it is, a mess of might-have-beens, I am of course grateful that we were ever lovers at all. Still, the view to-day would have been finer with him beside me to enjoy it.

28 May 1944

A vase of peonies (red) in my room: my favourite flowers.

Edward came here for the first time.

'Do you like me a little?'

(Vibrato) 'I never stop at a little.'

4 June 1944

To tea with Elizabeth Jenkins. Those present: hostess and her younger brother, Elizabeth Bowen, Theodora Benson, Stella Gibbons (*Cold Comfort*

---

* Sub-Lieutenant Christopher Raymond Huth of the Royal Naval Volunteer Reserve, son of Sydney and Ruby Huth, was serving on HMS *Marigold* when he was killed. He is buried in Dely Ibrahim War Cemetery, Algeria.

Farm) and myself.* A gaggle, as one might say, of female novelists ... I talked to Elizabeth Bowen about driving (in wartime) in traps, gigs and other horse-conveyances, about E.B.'s house in Ireland (Bowen's Court) and about Jane Austen. Later, the conversation became general – mostly about a new book (*Face Without a Frown*) on Georgiana, Duchess of Devonshire, which I had not read.† Everyone else seemed to be an authority on the period. Left the party at 6.30 and came back here to meet Edward. The behaviour and events of the rest of the evening would no doubt have startled the fictionists of the afternoon ... Edward is 20, I am 41; yet he has rung me up twice a day every day of this past week. I confess I am flattered – and touched – by this.

6 June 1944

Invasion day. Was awoken very early – about five o'clock – by 'planes flying over Hampstead in large formations. At breakfast Mrs Timmons said she had heard on the eight o'clock wireless news that the Germans had announced our landings in Normandy. Great excitement and restlessness in the bookshop, among the staff, during the morning. As everyone says – 'Well, it had to come, sooner or later.' But several of the staff with sons or husbands likely to be involved were on the verge of tears, poor things. I thought frequently of Nigel and Harry, both of whom are likely to be 'in it'. A windy, rather cold day, with rain in the evening. Having no wireless I did not hear the King's speech: only such fragments as drifted in from the open windows of other flats. I could also hear snatches of the religious services broadcast later. The usual appeals to the God of Battles. Childish. Better to trust Montgomery and Eisenhower.‡ Before going to bed read Freud's study

---

*   Elizabeth Jenkins (1905–2010) was a novelist and biographer. Irish-British novelist Elizabeth Bowen (1899–1973) was particularly well known for her evocations of life in wartime London. Theodora Benson (1906–1968) wrote experimental novels about a cynical social world. Author, journalist and poet Stella Gibbons (1902–1989) is most associated with her first novel *Cold Comfort Farm* (1932), a parody of rural life.

†   By Iris Leveson Gower.

‡   Bernard Montgomery and Dwight D. Eisenhower were the British and American military leaders who oversaw the D-Day landings in France.

of Leonardo da Vinci, which I have been trying to get hold of for years. An amazingly penetrative piece of deductive psychoanalytical reasoning. As I write this – at ten o'clock at night – formations of 'planes are still flying over London ... There's no doubt about it – I have a feeling of shame – I ought to be fighting too.

7 June 1944

I see in the paper that a female child christened yesterday in Texas was baptized with the name Invasia. People in a more sober mind to-day about the Normandy operations. I had expected that London would have air-raids last night, but none came.

11 June 1944

The extraordinary experience of being made passionate love to by a boy young enough to be my own son.

13 June 1944

A curry at dinner which I thought was made of either crab or lobster. It turned out that it was made of *Toheroas*, Mrs Timmons having opened my one and only tin of this rare New Zealand shellfish. A wonderfully rich flavour, best tasted in soup: in fact, Toheroa soup is one of the world's delicacies. Currying rather confuses the fine fishy relish on the tongue. A dull day. Very little business in the bookshop. Rain in the morning, and a high wind. I kept on thinking of young Harry Morgan, who rang me up last night and who was crossing to Normandy, as a unit of his Scots brigade, to-day. He himself seemed cheerful and said he was 'as brown as a berry' from battle-training (manoeuvres).

14 June 1944

A party at the C.'s little house last night. As we drank our coffee out of glasses, everyone told his bomb story. The small hostess, Mrs C., said, 'I was sleeping in the cellar with my mother. A land-mine fell, and all the sand-bags burst and blew in the doorway … Our faces were sore and just like *sandpaper*.' Then an alert sounded and a real flying-bomb came over. We all huddled into a cupboard under the stairs which smelled of mint and boot-polish. All-clear half an hour later. But the bomb stories had meanwhile lost their flavour: we spoke of other things.

I have asked Mrs Timmons to try to renovate an old blue flannel suit of mine which is falling to pieces. 'Well, sir, I'll try, but it's in a terrible state: no suit for a *gentleman* to wear: I don't know what your mother would say.'

16 June 1944

A disturbed night last night: air-raid sirens, guns and horrible *swooshings* in the lower heavens, culminating in a terrific bang, somewhere near here at half past seven this morning. The Germans are at last using their secret weapon – winged bombs, radio-directed.* Much excitement and discussion about this, all day. A pretty devilish and inhuman device, is the general verdict: like being shot at from Mars. After dinner I went to inspect the crater made on the Heath by the bomb (or plane or what-one-may-call-it) which caused the 7.30 explosion this morning. A deep hole, in clay soil, on the slope near Highgate Ponds. Fragments of clay had been flung for a radius of 200–300 yards round. An oak tree, ten yards from the crater, completely blasted: not a single leaf remaining, and only the stronger boughs. Crowds peering into the crater.

23 June 1944

Attacks on London by flying-bombs continue. Everyone slightly fractious from apprehension and lack of sleep – everyone, that is, except Mrs Wrayman (one of our madder customers at the bookshop) who swears that she's 'been up in one' and there's 'nothing to fear'. Awoken at 2.45 this morning by one of the *things* flying directly over the top of the building in a loud, brazen, stuttering flight, appallingly close overhead. It exploded somewhere towards Highgate, two minutes later.

---

*   The V-1 flying bomb was also known as the buzz bomb or doodlebug.

25 June 1944

Edward stayed here last night (Saturday), having a mattress on the floor in my room. The night noisy with flying-bombs falling in the near distance. I fell into a sound sleep about 2.30, to be awakened at 6.45 by Edward nuzzling into my bed, where he stayed – both of us dozing – until nearly 10 o'clock, when we arose and ate a large breakfast of coffee and kippers.

26 June 1944

A misty muggy day. Flying-bombs falling bumpily across London during the latter part of the morning and early afternoon. This, truly, is being 'under fire'. I find myself thinking (probably inaccurately) of life in Paris under the Commune: wasn't the city shelled by long-range artillery?

28 June 1944

As far as flying-bombs are concerned, the worst day yet. Dozens coming over, seemingly low overhead. In the bookshop, we all threw ourselves down at least three times during the day, and at lunch, a bomb coming over, somebody called 'Duck', and everyone got under the tables. Overheard a man in the post-office say 'These bombs make me feel as though I'd eaten too many gooseberries.'

31 July 1944

Last night was the first occasion when I have been really frightened by these flying-bombs. At about 3.30 a.m., two, in rapid succession, came straight over the top of this block of flats. I had been awakened by their far-away coming, and, jumping out of bed, grabbed my dressing-gown, torch, spectacles, money and latex stocking and ran into my small hallway. The noise of the bombs overhead was similar to that of a heavy and furious express-train, supposing one to be flying under the railway-track in a tunnel while the engine passed above one's head: a thunderous drumming. When they had passed over (they flew on as far as Barnet, I hear, and exploded there), my knees were trembling so that I had to lean against the wall for support. Talk about 'bats from hell ...!'

12 August 1944

Was asked to-night to have a drink at Sir Kenneth Clark's house, here in Hampstead.* A superb establishment (perhaps a trifle too like a Hollywood film setting for an English mansion – also perhaps a little too resembling a museum). While I drank gin in the drawing-room my eyes nearly stretched from my head as they took in the pictures – three or four Renoirs, at least half a dozen Cézannes (one large one, over the mantelpiece, of some French houses on a high tree-covered bluff: green, blue and restrained browns and reds), a couple of Pissaros, a Henry Moore, and what seemed like several hundred artists lesser ('There are more upstairs,' said Sir K.). Our host left the room for a moment, to return carrying a small Rodin bronze – 'I always think R. was at his best when his work came within the circle of his thumb: the bigger statuary seems partly to have been hacked out for him by a stone-mason.'

13 August 1944

A feeling abroad that this may be one of the decisive to-days of the war: [Field Marshal Günther] Von Kluge's armies being trapped between Orne and Seine. Everyone optimistic and hanging on the wireless news bulletins. In myself, again the familiar feeling of inadequacy I have when great events are in train. A noisy night last night: many flying-bombs over. My good Mrs T. says she is 'sleeping in her Anderson' these nights, and has 'a crook in her back' in consequence.

---

* Kenneth Clark (1903–1983), knighted when he was only 35, was a British art historian, museum director and broadcaster.

23–31 August 1944

On holiday in Cornwall, at St Ives. Three nights of rain during the week, but brilliant days. I returned to London with a face like a harvest-moon, also with an inflamed left eye due to the intensity of the Cornish light. Wonderful war-news almost throughout the week: the liberation of Paris, the change-over in Bulgaria, the sweeping advances in France. I bought two papers every day in order to keep up with it. Nearly five years of war and at last we're getting somewhere. Incidentally, after the same five years of war, it was strange and distasteful to see the Tregenna Castle Hotel in St Ives full of men in dinner-jackets in the evenings, also women in long full evening dress. A colonial (to say nothing of being a Socialist), I can never quite get used to this English keeping-up-of-appearances, even now when I've been over here twenty years. I confuse it, or associate it, with callousness, which is probably wrong. The trains, both to and from Cornwall, packed to the doors. To get to the lavatory it was necessary to fight along the corridors, over people, suitcases, dogs and children.

3 September 1944

Fifth anniversary of the outbreak of war. The news to-day consistently good, with rumours that the American forces have crossed the German frontiers at Aachen. Paris has, apparently, been suffering from flying-bombs. A three-day lull, here in London: in fact I haven't heard an Alert sounded since I came back from Cornwall, thought I still wake frequently in the night, mistaking car-noises and planes flying over for authentic doodle-bugs.

10 September 1944

The bombing and gunfire of Le Havre (in France) astonishingly audible here in Hampstead at about seven o'clock this evening. I was resting on my bed and could hear the continuous faint drumming, coming from the South, quite clearly: so much so that I imagined at first that the noise was being made in the adjoining flat by somebody using a typewriter supported on a heavy felt 'shock-absorber' ... The gunfire died away – as the wind changed? –

after about half an hour but could be heard again just before midnight. Leslie Hurry and John Simons (pianist, on leave from the Army) came here to supper. Afterwards, J.S. played Chopin, Schubert and Liszt: a technically fine performer, lacking in subtlety of tone and touch. While he and I discussed music and played records on the gramophone, Leslie half-mockingly read the day's *Observer*.

12 September 1944

Awoken at 6.15 a.m. by a whiplash-like explosion somewhere towards the west of London: a similar bang happening the other evening just before dinner. Has V2 arrived?[*] Everyone seems to think so and that we are deliberately not being told about it by Mr Herbert Morrison.[†] I heard to-day that the other evening's explosion was at Chiswick (given out, I believe, as a 'burst gas main') and this morning's at Kew. Referring to the Chiswick 'bomb', Mrs H. told me at work this morning that a friend of hers had seen the fire-service official report on the incident: this stated that fragments of the weapon were found which were 'coated with ice'. The assumption is that the projectile is a rocket-bomb, ice-coated during its passage through the stratosphere, and fired, possibly, from Norway. Other rockets are rumoured to have come down in or near Epping forest. Myself the detail of the jacket of *ice* strikes as fabulous, devilish and out-Verneing Jules Verne. A rocket from Norway, hitting London! The idea is incredible, but, alas, at the moment also confoundingly possible.

17 September 1944

The first 'dim-out' night of the war. Edward here and me in bed when the hour to half-draw the curtains came: I hopped out and did them. Half an hour later, the sirens sounded and the familiar sound of a flying-bomb approached. We put our heads under the pillow until the thing dropped –

---

[*] The V-2 was the world's first long-range guided ballistic missile.

[†] Labour politician Herbert Morrison (1888–1965) was minister of supply and then home secretary in Churchill's wartime Cabinet.

somewhere over central London. An All-clear five minutes later ended this typical German thumb-to-the-nose of our first 'dim-out'.

21 September 1944

Very nearly a quarrel with Edward last evening. 'Jimmy, if *you* don't understand me – then who does? – who in the whole world?' To my shame I was silent. Before going to bed, wrote him an affectionate and consoling letter. Went out in the dark to post it in the corner pillar-box.

26 September 1944

The Government White paper on Social Insurance published: a great event, truly, in this old Tory country. New Zealand has formerly led the world in these social schemes: now England has, at a bound, caught her up.

28 September 1944

My day off work. Met Edward at 6.15 at Victoria. We went into the Station restaurant and had tea and spam sandwiches. A commotion caused at a nearby table by some girls who had seen a rat running along a beam or moulding near the roof. 'That's nothing,' said our good-natured waitress with slight scorn – 'they ought to be here in the early morning, to see rats. Scurrying everywhere … ' Edward and I walked slowly up past Buckingham Palace and into St James's Park – no, Green Park – where we sat in the dim light under the trees. Whitish September mist over the grass, caught in the lights of the cars in Piccadilly. Later, as darkness fell, we walked together up Constitution Hill towards Admiralty Arch. Rose and ivy foliage form a shelter on the public side of the gardens of St James' Palace: we paused here in shadow and kissed passionately. Further along the Hill (which is no hill), where the basements (? old stables) of Carlton House Terrace stretch along under the trees, we kissed again, many times – once surrounded by big blocks of bomb-fallen stone that gleamed white like neo-Pompeian ruins. We both enjoyed the walk and the embraces in the September evening.

29 September 1944

So much for kisses given on Constitution Hill – I am in bed to-day with a bronchial cold and am almost speechless. Have spent the day drowsing, reading the Government White paper and dipping into Kilvert's Diary (a new edition, just out).* What a *good* man – old Kilvert! No night-excursions along Constitution Hill, kissing boys, for him. Well, I am what I am – a human being as much as he. In the evening Leslie Hurry came in for half an hour's talk. He sat in the armchair in my bed-room and we spoke of current ballet and theatre and artistic matters. He was wearing a black suit, dark tie and white collar: a slightly clerical ensemble that suits him.

30 September 1944

Rather more than usual of my hair came out at its first brushing this morning. This depressed me, though I have been losing hair for over fifteen years and have still a reasonable crop left. My mother, now I come to think of it, once told me (a child) that the family doctor, seeing my hair so fair and fine in texture, had prophesied complete baldness for me at the age of thirty. Well, I am nearly forty-two and am not by any means unthatched yet. Edward has just rung me up: he roared with unfeeling laughter on hearing I was laid up: young wretch. I told him he must ring me again to-morrow before coming over to supper, as I might not be feeling well enough to cope with him. He promised but with a bad grace – 'Don't you want me to come and rub your chest for you?'

10 November 1944

After two months the news that we are being bombarded by V2 (rockets) has at last been made public by Churchill. Well, the silence couldn't go on much longer: everyone felt it was becoming farcical to attempt not to notice

---

* Clergyman Frank Kilvert (1840–1879) wrote a series of diaries about English rural life that became instantly popular when they were published just before and during World War II.

the 'Mystery Explosions' (and some of them, notably last Sunday's, have been terrific); the long startling reverberations; the 'ghost' bumps and bangs during the night. Now they are, officially, V2. The nearest one, so far, to Hampstead fell in Highgate, at Archway, a week ago. I was sitting by the fire, reading, and imagined the noise to be a great explosion of thunder (rain was falling heavily at the time). Windows rattle, dogs barked, shutters clattered. I believe about 80 people were killed or wounded. Life becomes more uncertain than ever. One carries on as usual and tries not to think of, or imagine, V2.

6 December 1944
I am miserable when I have nobody to love. Yet, when I do have somebody, I am often detached, rude, scornful, satiated, beastly, bored or merely uninterested.

6 February 1945
Mrs T. managed to get me a bottle of whisky. In consequence, drunk.

9 February 1945
My forty-second birthday. Edward, bless his heart, sent me a card. A busy day until the evening. When I got home in the late afternoon, I played the piano for an hour – the first Mozart Sonata, some Brahms (2 Intermezzi) and some Chopin (Mazurka and Waltz). After dinner played the gramophone: Fauré's *Barcarolle No. 2* and the Chopin *Scherzo No. 4*. Edward is having dinner here with me to-morrow evening.

12 March 1945
'You desire me. That's obvious. But do you really love me?'
   'What do you think?'
   'I think you *think* you do, but there's such a thing as deceiving oneself.'
   'Perhaps you'd rather I loved you completely but didn't desire you in the least?'
   'Such a situation would be impossible between two people like us.'

'Very well, then.'

But is it very well? Such conversations are liable to go on indefinitely with no comfortable Q.E.D. to finish them off.

17 March 1945

After being in bed for four days with an attack of violent influenza, I was awakened at 5.30 a.m. this morning by a terrific crash and whang as one of Hitler's rockets (V2) landed less than half a mile away (actually at Arkwright Road, N.W.3). None of the windows of this flat were broken, but I could hear a tinkling cascade of glass out in the street. Surely enough, half an hour later the police rang me up to say that the windows of our bookshop (across the way from here) were shattered and to ask what I intended to do about it. I replied: 'Nothing – I'm in bed with influenza.' However, I gave them the number of Mr Reif, the assistant manager (whose wife, poor man, had given birth to a daughter yesterday), and later rang him up myself. Thinking that half the books from the shop-windows might be strewn over the pavements, I also rang up two others of the staff and asked them to hurry along as soon as they could (it was still only about 6.30). This they did, finding, however, when they arrived, that the glass windows had broken almost apologetically and that nothing was missing or unduly exposed. I hear tonight that the whole staff had a harassing day trying to get in touch with the Managing Director, to ask for his instructions. Mr W., however, was 'out gardening' or 'having a day off' (this being a Saturday) according to a wifely voice on the telephone. Nevertheless, he did turn up, I believe, just before closing time and helped Reif fix chicken-netting – the only available *stop-gap* – over the gaping windows. From all reports the rocket fell on fairly open ground and caused only three casualties, none of them fatal.

31 March 1945

The war-news is so extraordinary, with Montgomery said to be over 50 miles beyond the Rhine, that it really dawned on me this morning that the European war may be almost finished. At present the greatest relief, here in London, is that the constant menace of flying-bombs and rockets is lessened and is possibly over (no disturbances for the past 3 nights). This is a real lightening of the mind, as to one of my nervous disposition the constant realisation that one may be blown-up or crushed has been a considerable strain for a long while now. It is possible that the V2 that fell on Hampstead a fortnight ago may be the final one of its species – like the last dinosaur or mammoth? As far the further effects of an early end of the war on me personally – h'm, that's not so easy to determine. Life will seem so different that, in a way, I actually fear it – as a prisoner may actually fear freedom outside his cage. I say this frankly, as I am perfectly well aware that, compared with others, the war has touched me lightly and glancingly (though I have lost two of the people I most cared for in life, Chris and Ivan, through its direct or indirect action). Nevertheless, peace is going to bring its own quite considerable problems for everyone, not excluding myself.

3 April 1945
Five (or is it six) quiet nights without V-Bombs. One wonders whether this horror can possibly be really over.

4 April 1945
Signs of the approach of middle age – slight dullness of hearing in one ear (and sometimes both), varicose veins on both legs, slowly thinning hair (though this has been going on for 20 years) on the temples and crown, occasional slight rheumatism in the knees, a more stubborn beard (bristly at the end of the day, despite a close morning shave), slight fleshy thickening of the knuckles on both hands, a noticeable deviation towards long-sightedness in the eyes (already, however, short-sighted). Finally, absolute necessity of at least eight hours full sleep a night. A melancholy enough catalogue. Perhaps the one blessing is that I have not yet an increasing belly.

5 April 1945

Heard to-day that [the magazine] *English Story* have accepted a short story of mine called 'Uncle Adam Shot a Stag'. As the 'Uncle A.' in question is partly a picture of my Uncle Robert (immured in an asylum these many years), I expect family repercussions if and when the story reaches N.Z.

23 April 1945

End of compulsory dim-out in London. I have been sitting at my desk here, writing a short story, for the past two hours, while the evening darkened outside. I have the curtains undrawn (and the windows open) for the first time in over five years, after official black-out time.

Later. Have just returned from a short walk up to Jack Straw's Castle. Remarkably few fully-lit windows in the main streets: I suppose that people have become so used to curtain-pulling that it's second nature. Yet this evening should be a great occasion (I *did* notice, by the way, a larger number of happy people turning out of the pubs as they closed), and the end of a trying tyranny – the half-ventilated evening room.

6 May 1945

What a week ends to-day. Hitler and Mussolini gone, and Germany as good as done-for. Yet no official V-day yet,* though I hear that crowds rejoiced in the West End last night (Saturday). Maybe they were wise to rejoice – to have their exaltation now – before the interminable post-war wrangles begin (they seem to have begun already, with the Russians and ourselves quarrelling in San Francisco over Poland).† I feel like the captured Italian who's reported to have said that he wanted to go to sleep for five years and wake up in a reconstituted world. The merely personal seems pretty small against last week's events, and I haven't much notion of what to put down – save that we spent a cold week in the bookshop, where our windows, blown in by

---

*   The V stood for victory. The official name was VE Day, for Victory in Europe.

†   Fifty Allied nations took part in the United Nations Conference on International Organisation, aka the San Francisco Conference, from 25 April to 26 June 1945.

one of the last rockets to land in London, are still un-replaced. Meanwhile, of course, there can hardly be a window left in the majority of Germany's towns. Have I any sympathy for the Germans? No – none at all. The swine are even now trying to provide their alibi for defeat, by saying that their efforts to force Europe from Bolshevization led them to neglect their defences in the West and hence allowed us to beat them. What is to be done with such a people, short of a cold-blooded extermination? They will go on giving us trouble, even yet.

7 May 1945

Rumours all day that V-day may be declared at any moment. No particular elation on any one's part: a few women carrying Union Jacks in shopping-baskets. At dinner this evening I looked into the courtyard of the flats here and saw several large (and a few small) British flags hanging from windows. One woman was trying to anchor a small one to her windowsill but the wind kept blowing it away and she gave up in despair. I fancy that most of the flats sporting flags are those belonging to German refugees (the Germans at home have been hanging out white ones).

Later: I have no wireless, and have just (10 p.m.) heard the news that to-morrow is to count as V-day and a holiday, that Churchill is to speak at three, and that peace (or surrender) of some sort is being signed at Rheims in France (why Rheims, one asks). Well, so it has come at last, and one begins to wake from a five and a half year's nightmare. Can I really have come through it (and in London), I ask myself? It seems extraordinary, incredible. For some reason – I can't decide why – I feel afraid and apprehensive.

8 May 1945

VE-day

The day, at last. And ushered in by an extraordinary night – a violent thunderstorm lasted from 12 till 3 this morning. I hardly slept at all. And then – of all things – a cuckoo started calling at 6 from the trees near here and went on till nearly 8 (I've never heard one so persistent). Such portents and omens! Anyway, I felt tired this morning and a bit fractious. The weather sunny but close and thundery. Went out in the morning for a short walk only. Hampstead is much beflagged and this block of flats looks like the League of Nations building (British, French, Greek, Polish, American, S. African flags and big V-signs in white cardboard).

After lunch I went into central London. First in the Embankment at Charing Cross to have a look at the dear old Thames and the dome of St Paul's down-river; then up to Trafalgar Square. The crowds enormous, all singing, dancing and shouting. Churchill's speech at 3 o'clock was broadcast from loudspeakers, but nobody could hear more than the opening words, and most gave up trying to listen. A sailor climbed to the top of a flagstaff, his trousers splitting with the effort, and the crowd roared and clapped. The Trafalgar Square pigeons flew round dementedly overhead and planes came down low (taking pictures). Then everyone sang God Save the King, a bit feebly and self-consciously, and the dancing began again. The air was stifling, and everyone sweaty. One thing I noticed – how well-nourished most people look after nearly six years of war, particularly the younger people! Very few thin and peaky faces. I was standing near a group of youngish girls who had formed a picnic-party on some stone steps and were eating and laughing and doing a few dance-steps. All were well-built and a few might be called whoppers. The soldiers too looked well and had sun-browned faces. The ordinary citizens were quieter. I spoke to one man (about 40, hatless, in a blue suit, with wife and young daughter). 'I can't believe it's all over – I just can't' – he repeated this again and again, and was very angry when somebody let off a small bomb or grenade near the National Gallery building: 'We've had enough of those sort of noises.'

Later I pushed my way (literally pushed) up through Leicester Square and Piccadilly Circus. Dancing soldiers and girls, all wearing small flags or streamers or cardboard hats. Not much out and out drunkenness (save for one little blonde A.T.S. [Auxiliary Territorial Service] girl with a scarlet face, who was hopelessly tight and being riotously propped-up by companions). In the evening I went up on the roof here to see the searchlight display at midnight. The sky was cloudy and smoky (from bonfires) and the lights not very clear – like a subdued Aurora Borealis display. To bed at 12.45, exhausted.

P.S. I have forgotten to add that, as a symbolical gesture, I took down all my black curtains in the flat.

10 January 1946

Opening meeting of the United Nations Council. I should write something profound about this. Instead I'll record that to-day – for the first time in at least five years – oranges were to be bought *off the ration*. Everyone is going about with a glazed and slightly yellowish look, having guzzled a few too many. The world is at least free again to eat its oranges.

1945–1950

12 July 1945

The Warden of St C.'s Hostel for Boys – an Anglo-Catholic affair – asked me to dinner there tonight at six. So I found my way thither – i.e. in Halton Garden – by 5.45. Dinner was in the boys' dining room and was good & plentiful – meat soup, cold sausage & salad and mince pies. Nine or ten boys are at present inmates of the place – all of them orphans, 'lost boys' or delinquents. Seeing one small lad of about 14 – as innocent-looking as a robin (which he rather resembled) – sitting silently at the end of the table, I whispered to my friend the Warden: 'I suppose that child is an orphan?' 'No,' was the reply, 'he was one of a family of seven whose father married again. The boy is under our care because he broke into a house with another youngster, did £50 worth of damage, and tried to set an old woman on fire.'

15 July 1945

Called on Leslie in the morning and found him working on an oil painting. John Simons was at home (they share the flat) and played me Ravel's *Ondine* on the piano – technically a splendid performance but not delicate enough in tone (too much mezzoforte). John is setting off next week with an Army concert party to play to the troops in Germany. In the evening the street lights were on again, wonderfully bright and exciting after nearly six years of utter darkness.

26 July 1945

Returned from a week's holiday at St Ives, Cornwall. Arrived back at the flat at 6.15 and went almost straight out to buy an evening paper to see the Election results. Was amazed and delighted with the huge Labour majority (I had voted Labour here in Hampstead, but as usual the Conservative candidate was returned, though with a much-reduced majority). Well, now for a new era in British politics – or will it be? – or will the Conservatives stage a counter-revolution on the Franco model directly Socialist legislation gets going?

Reverting to my holiday in Cornwall – I enjoyed this only partially. Felt disoriented and vaguely melancholy – as though I were getting too old for St Ives, the place I've been to for so many years. The small-town scandal and artists' back-biting bored me after a couple of days, though the actual *beauty* of the harbour and bay pleased me as much as ever.

15 August 1945

*VJ-day**

While I was dozing off to sleep at about ten minutes after midnight last night, Hugo B. rang me up to tell me that V-J day had just been declared over the 12 o'clock wireless, and that to-day and to-morrow were consequently holidays.

Woke up at seven, having slept badly, and got up to fetch the newspaper from the doorstep to see if it confirmed the news. It did. Went back to bed and had breakfast there at 9.30. Weather, showery and dank. Stayed at home in the morning. At 2 o'clock set off for St Paul's, with the idea of having a look at the old building again and seeing what bomb damage had been done. Large crowds on the steps and larger ones inside, mostly sight-seeing. I pushed my way down toward the temporary altar under the central dome. Sat down to rest in the 'front of the stalls' and, while looking about, noticed that candles were being lit on the altar in preparation for a service. I asked a verger about this: he said 'yes, there was to have been a 3 o'clock service but we've had to postpone it till 3.15 owing to difficulty in collecting the choir'. At 3.15 the choir were led forth to their seats, looking, I must say, as if they'd been collected in a van from nearby hot-houses: red-faced, elderly and middle-aged men, most of them chewing their teeth. I sat in my front seat and hence had a good view of the whole service, while at the same time I was able to look up at the dome and round me at the transepts, etc. It was so long since I had attended a service in a church that I had almost a pagan's view-point – and it all struck me as highly extraordinary. Those

---

* Victory over Japan, after the dropping of atomic bombs on Hiroshima and Nagasaki.

references to the God of Battles (Jahweh) and well-tuned cymbals – all repeated by the huge congregation in full earnestness and as though reciting a magic formula – I found this most curious as a form of thanks-giving for a mid-20th-century people after a ghastly war of rockets and Atomic bombs. Nor did I care for the sight of the Canons and Minor Canons winking, whispering and smiling amongst themselves during the service. As I say, extraordinary.

After the service I walked down Ludgate Hill and up the Strand, looking at Wren's churches. The sun was out and high white clouds in the sky. The air full of floating fluffy seeds of the willow-herb which has taken root in the dozens of bombed and derelict sites. The Strand's pavements almost ankle-deep in torn up paper and tickertape showered down from windows of offices. Two sailors, surrounded by a crowd, were playing strip-poker on the kerb, benevolently watched by a policeman. One matelot had already lost his shoes and socks to the other: he was kneeling on the pavement complaining to the amused sightseers of housemaid's knee and chilly heels. Stopped at a lunch-counter and had a glass of iced coffee and a sandwich, both served by a good-looking, sly-eyed Cockney youth wearing a paper hat with 'Get Up Them Stairs' printed on the peak. And so to Trafalgar Square, where a band was playing on top of an air-raid shelter. The crowd were dancing and letting off fireworks. A youth and girl, half-dressed, waltzed drunkenly in the basin of one of the fountains, in the dirty water.

19 August 1945
The first Sunday of the peace
After lunch I went down to St Paul's again, intending to see the Royal drive to the three o'clock service. But the police would not allow the crowds, including myself, into the approaches (side-streets) of Ludgate Hill, where I had meant to go. I was angry about this, as were many others (one man shouted 'You can't stop us – the streets belong to the people' to the police, unavailingly). Eventually, walking along alleys, I got to Ludgate Circus and into a pushing, struggling crowd. By now, of course, I had missed the Royal

drive to the Cathedral, but I wedged myself forward on a slightly raised traffic-island and waited here for over an hour, so as to get a view of the return drive up the Strand and Fleet St. It seemed a long wait. Luckily the grey sky did not rain on us. The mounted police rather officiously pushing the crowd back (one police-horse reared and threw its rider on the freshly-gravelled road: an interesting and – it must be admitted – most welcome diversion), kept everyone restive and on their toes.

The service, which began at 3, was supposed to last half an hour but St Paul's bells did not start ringing for the end of it until just after four o'clock. I could just catch a glimpse, up Ludgate Hill, of the cathedral doors in the distance. Eventually I saw the postillions' red coats and then the grey horses, behind a troop of Household Cavalry, coming down the hill with the open carriage, containing K. and Q. and 2 Princesses. The Q's. blue halo hat was the first sign I saw of Royalty (in fact, this was the first time I'd ever seen a single member of the family). A woman behind me said – 'There she is – but I wish she wouldn't always wear those hats.' Then the carriage was crossing the Circus, more-or-less in front of me. I couldn't see much of the Q., except for the blue hat and shoulder fur, and the K., on the far side, was only a back (he was bowing on that side): but I had a good view of the 2 Princesses, particularly of P. Elizabeth, who was wearing a grey and royal blue hat and a grey coat or coat and skirt. A very peach-like complexion and a vivid red mouth (evidently lipstick has Now Been Allowed). The future Queen – if there is ever to be one – looked, I thought, a bit stiff and haughty, but maybe she was only anxious to get home to tea and was a trifle sick of crowds, understandably. A couple of minutes after the regal outfit had passed came a closed car containing – I think – Attlee and [Ernest] Bevin and others. The crowd was not certain of this, but gave a subdued cheer, on the safe side. Then, after a pause and a few more cars, came a blue closed limousine, going rather fast: inside this, at the back, was indubitably Churchill with Mrs C. beside him. I saw Churchill's chubby profile for perhaps a third of a second, then he was gone, much too rapidly. After him the procession tailed off and people started to move away from the back of the crowd – whose interest, at

least in my immediate vicinity, had for a minute or so been captured less by
the minor figures of the passing ceremony than by a girl with vivid red hair
and wearing trousers who was now crying loudly that somebody had opened
her bag and stolen all her money and belongings. Blubbering and collapsing,
she was led off by a stout and rather embarrassed bobby towards the local
police station.

25 November 1947

To Constable's, the publishers, this afternoon to see Michael Sadleir about
my book 'The Farmer's Family', which I had sent them two months ago.*
Sadleir received me on the dark stairs (the whole building is bomb-damaged)
and drew me up into a comfortable room on the first floor. Here he
introduced me to another partner, a woman in black with grey hair, whose
name I didn't catch. I was given some strong tea, the time being 4 o'clock.
Then Sadleir said:

'We've been impressed by your book, but we thought it was written by a
woman. You *did* write it, didn't you?'

'I most certainly did,' said I.

'I was only judging by the way you handled your central character's [Mrs
Warner's] feelings.'

'It's only a matter of intuition, I assure you,' I said. 'As a novelist yourself,
that must be evident to you.'

'Oh yes, yes – but not to such an extent as you have carried your
sympathy – intuition rather.'

'Well, there it is, I wrote the book – I give you my word on that!'

After this exchange of incredulities, the interview went smoothly,
the female partner putting in a word now and again. Sadleir said that the
compressed style of the writing reminded him of Maugham – a compliment

---

* Michael Sadleir (1888–1957) was a novelist in his own right as well as a publisher,
bibliographer and book collector. Courage's manuscript would be published under the
title *The Fifth Child*.

I didn't entirely relish (Maugham being too 'dry' in the vinous sense, for me – and too arid in human sympathy). Anyway, Sadleir wants to publish the book – and without my cutting or changing it in any way – which I'm glad about. The title may have to be changed, either to 'A Winter in the Town' or 'Mrs Warner' or to an alternative of my own choosing; but this is not vastly important. The important thing is that I have regained my confidence in myself as a writer – and as a good writer.

This evening I rang up Pat: she was glad to hear about the book's acceptance but had some sisterly fears as to how it will be received in New Zealand and especially by my own family, who will take the book's characters as amusing but malicious caricatures of themselves. This may be so, of course, though, as in all fiction, no portrait – or so-called portrait – of a living person is in the least bit accurate in my book. Novel-characterisation just doesn't work out in that way, whether one wishes it to or not … I am a little concerned, it is true, about my mother's reactions to 'Mrs Warner' – but I cannot cancel the book on that account. In any case, publication cannot take place for another year – next autumn at the earliest, Sadleir says.

25 January 1948

A Sunday morning walk. And the creative process begins again, after many months of blankness and restiveness. I think out the outlines (plots & characters) of two novels; one with a N.Z. setting and one with an English. Now remains only the distasteful and miserable task of writing the books: in each case a probable pregnancy of two years (like an elephant).

6 May 1948

Almost half-way through the novel about Mrs Kendal & her son. I haven't yet given it a title. Things are already happening in the book that I didn't mean to happen or foresee would happen. The earlier chapters may have to be recast. As for the second novel (see above) – the main character is to be a pianist – a fine artist but in private life 'queer' and a complete and absolute swine. I have some things to say on the relation between artistic ability and sexual aberration. And I shall have no mercy whatsoever on the inverted character; seedy, shifty, opportunist ... Yes, I know it, and it shall not escape.

13 September 1948

The first six copies of my novel *The Fifth Child* came from Constable to-day. Almost exactly 2½ years since I wrote its first words.

4 October 1949

Finished typing the new novel – 'The End of a Golden String' – which I began January 1948.

6 October 1949

Read through the typescript of the novel in one sitting of about six hours (5 to 11pm). It turns out to be a good deal better than I'd anticipated, and is much better-written than I'd hoped. I must have laboured at least seven hours over each of the 280 pages, and yet the whole thing (except for an occasional over-punctuation due to anxiety) reads as easily as a casual letter. I was particularly pleased, in re-reading, to find that the 12-page introduction, 'Persons and Events', came across so effortlessly.

28 October 1949

A letter from Michael Sadleir about the novel – 'Your new book is quite beautifully done. There is no doubt whatever that as a piece of writing it more than fulfils the promise of *The Fifth Child*. My partners shall read the book in turn and I shall report on their reactions later.' My relief is comparable to that following the extraction of a furiously aching tooth. But does the letter mean that Constable will publish the book? I assume so. Or at any rate, I know that *somebody* will publish it, sooner or later.

James Courage's theme is the crisis in the life of Mrs. Warner, and the effect of this crisis on her own character and on the lives of those for whom she is the centre of existence.

She has spent nearly twenty years of a busy life in bearing children, nursing children, planning for children, dreading the pain and terror of having more children. And now, at the age of forty-six, she faces her fifth pregnancy.

She is spending the winter in a rented town-house, waiting for the unwanted child, separated from her husband who is on his farm in the country. Having for the first time in her married life opportunity to rest and to think, she realises that at last she is able and free to be herself.

With calm relief, she envisages leaving her husband for good, turning her back finally on the frets and endless adjustments of the family circle. Why not? Once the baby is born, she and it will be free. But will they? What effect will even a hint that she may desert her home have on her grown son Ronald, her teen-age Barbara, and on the two children, Alec and Susan?

The issue is as simple and complicated as just that; and Mr. Courage's sensitive unobtrusive art, equally simple on the surface, is (deep down) a subtle blend of sympathy, humour and tenderness. It is an achievement for a young writer to evoke character with such effortless ease, to present with equal certainty the ripe and unripe moods of two parents and four children. It is more than an achievement for a male novelist to interpret so gently and so delicately the conflict in the mind of a mature woman between an impulse to grasp her first and last chance of care-free liberty and the centuries of instinct which hold her to her mate and to her young.

The small town in which the tale of *The Fifth Child* takes place, is in New Zealand. But, apart from a farming hinterland with Dominion characteristics of its own, the scene could be set in any English speaking country.

Constable & Co Ltd

Asgeir Scott, noted for his intricate book jackets, designed this one for *The Fifth Child*, published by Constable in 1948. *S20-576d, MS-0999/139, Hocken Collections*

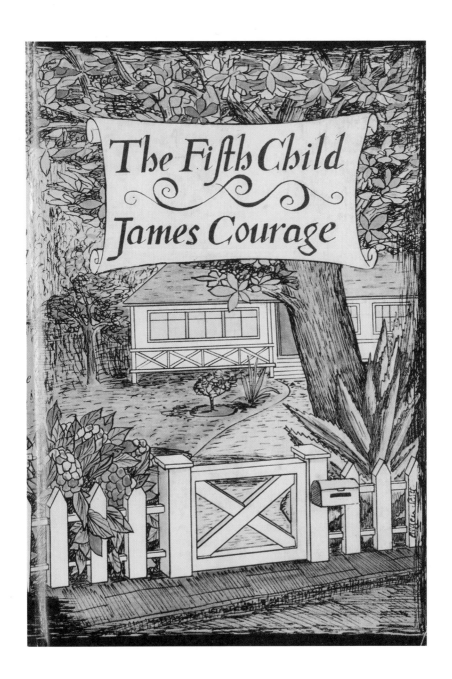

The Fifth Child

James Courage

THE FIFTH CHILD

RALPH STRAUS (*Sunday Times*): "Not for some little time have I read a novel by a new writer which has given me so much quiet pleasure. It is the simplest of stories about the most ordinary people. " Mr. Courage writes with both tenderness and humour, and I have little doubt that his book will obtain the warm welcome it deserves."

by James Courage

Constable   8/6 net

"It would be a pity if the rush of Christmas shopping or anything else has kept the reader who likes a really good novel from

Desire

Without Content

by JAMES COURAGE

"It is firmly constructed and beautifully written, its sombre theme relieved by the humanity which informs it, and by the background of hill and farm painted with economical strokes. A book not to be missed."

LETTICE COOPER (*Yorkshire Post*)

A Book Society Recommendation

10s. 6d.

CONSTABLE

ABOVE LEFT: A *Sunday Times* reviewer helps promote *The Fifth Child*, 1948.
S20-568a, MS-0999/141, Hocken Collections.

ABOVE RIGHT: A newspaper advertisement for *Desire Without Content*, with a citation from Courage's friend Lettice Cooper, 1950. *S20-542h, MS-0999/141, Hocken Collections*

2 December 1949

Heard to-day that my grandmother (I.F.P.) died on November 25th.* This is the first real break in the family circle as I know, or knew it, and I am now nearly 47. I last saw my grandmother (she was my mother's mother) about six months before I last left New Zealand, in 1935. She asked me to go up to Mt Somers to see her once more before I sailed, yet although I knew I should probably never see her again I did not go. This was cowardice: a horror of last farewells, of definite and irrevocable partings. In my youth she was probably the person I most loved and who had the most influence on my literary and artistic tastes (she was given to quoting poetry and singing snatches of songs). I wrote a poem about her – 'Old Mrs Somers' – which appeared in [the magazine] *Modern Reading* about three years ago. She is also the Mrs Kendal of my novel, 'Unhallowed Ground', which Constables have just accepted; the portrait, however, is not a complete one – it could hardly be that in the story as I have written it – and omits her humour and something of her command of life. All the same there is much of truth in my portrayal of Mrs Kendal's relationship with her son Lewis (my uncle Robert, in life).† Lewis's madness – that it, Robert's madness – laid a great deal of weight on her, of sadness and care. A partial portrait of her (my grandmother) also appears in a short story called 'Uncle Adam Shot a Stag', which was printed in *English Story* a year or so ago, but here again I had modified her character. I think I shall dedicate 'Unhallowed Ground' to her: In Memory of I.F.P.

29 January 1950

General news-bulletin about the new novel: There is no doubt now that Constable will publish it. The book's title has, all the same, caused us some wrangling. 'Unhallowed Ground' – my 2nd choice – struck Sadleir & Co as

---

* Ida Frances Peache was born in 1859 and lived most of her life near Mt Somers in Canterbury.

† In the novel published as *Desire Without Content*, Lewis is committed to an asylum after he unintentionally drowns his infant daughter in a river during a fit of madness. Lewis was an only child but Robert Somers Peache, who never married, was one of six children. He died at Ashburn Hall, a private psychiatric hospital in Dunedin.

The cover of *Desire Without Content*, published by Constable in 1950.

S20-576e, MS-0999/135, Hocken Collections

melodramatic and out-dated (Victorian in tone). I have now finally agreed on a title of their own choice – *Desire Without Content* (Macbeth Act III, Sc. 2). I didn't like this at first – it doesn't express the major theme at all – but have come round to it. The writing of *Desire Without Content* was an enormous struggle – something really of my life's blood, my very inbeing, went into it – whether this sounds pompous or not. I feel I can't write anything again for a long time yet. The well is dry – and the thought of the physical process of writing and re-writing really nauseates me.

All this writing about my struggle with the novel – my novel, rather, prompts me to put down a few random remarks about the year 1949. Well, to me it was a difficult year. In May, after much suffering from a kind of melancholia (no new complaint) I went to a psycho-therapist ([Ellis] Stungo in Harley Street). Our sessions took us on, at almost weekly intervals, until October, when I seemed to be so much improved that I ceased, with his agreement, to go to him. I can't really go into the substance of his cure or of what neuroses we uncovered (and there were plenty), but misery was greatly lessened. The relief still continues, and may, I hope, be permanent.

16 April 1950

Graham kissed my hands on saying goodbye to me. Is this boy of 23 to be my last love? Certainly I am in love with him.

18 April 1950

This morning a note came, enclosing a poem ('Colloque de Silence'). The note says – 'This is a small return for your great goodness – I am so grateful, you know, for you: but I feel I don't really give anything in return except a few moans and groans and a great affection.' In some physical pain all day – a constant ache on the right side. It makes me feel I am no longer young, and deplorably mortal.

1950–1959

24 November 1950

Up at 6.30 and shaved with the light on in the chilly bathroom. Breakfast at a quarter to eight; porridge and a vague omelette of egg and tomato, on toast. Appointment with the psychiatrist at 9.15. I arrive at 9.10 – it's at Notting Hill Gate – and we go into session at once. A book of memorial essays to T.E. Lawrence lies on the chair by the gas-fire, so we begin by talking about Lawrence. I say he had a strange craving for self-debasement, though it isn't 'strange' at all and that the same desire is in myself – a hankering for the primitive and tough. I admitted as much after a few moments, adding that I didn't enjoy the mixing-in life when I got it. F.B. (the psychiatrist) says 'Well, you ought to know – you had three months in a public mental hospital.' 'Yes,' I said, 'and I came to hate it.' Then I talk, abruptly, of weaning. My mother didn't want to suckle me because she was tired of birth & pregnancy and the rest of the clammy process. She had had an 18-inch waist before I began to enlarge it, and wanted to get back her figure, and be able to ride and hunt again. I also tell F.B. that she'd told me, once, that she nearly ran away with another man (not my Dad) when I was a year old. I don't know who the other man was. But has all this weaning and threat of loss (though I was so young at the time) induced the neurotic feeling of desertion and loneliness that torments me now? F.B. says 'Yes, but I don't think it's as easy as that.'

Felt depressed when I reached the street, so took one of the one-grain, blue sodium amytal tablets I keep in my ticket-pocket always now. Went by bus to Piccadilly Circus, had a cup of coffee at a Kardomah Café, then walked to Clifford Street, off Bond Street, for an interview with Brack, manager of Longman's, the publishers; I had asked them, through John Guest, for an editorial job.* Brack was kind and affable and showed me over the building (impressive, 18th-century house, huge stair-well, had once been degraded into a Victorian Hotel). In one of the director's rooms was a

---

* The kind and gentlemanly Noel Douglas John Brack (1902–1997) was the backbone of Longmans, where he worked for 40 years from 1928, heading the firm after 1938. For almost 30 years John Guest was one of London's top editors.

modern washbasin hidden in an ornate mirror-faced cupboard. I saw nearly every department, including the shipping-room (a clean smell of timber for the iron-banded crates addressed to Canada, Buenos Aires and Norway). I enjoyed being shown round, *en prince*, but don't see a job emerging at present. Brack advised me to write to the Employment Secretary of the Publishers' Association.

Took a bus to Victoria and arrived at my part-time job at Wilson's at one o'clock exactly. Spent an hour in the back room, opening parcels and checking them, then went downstairs and had a cigarette in the grimy little yellow-walled lavatory. Later, helped in the shop for two hours, before picking a book of Proust's letters from the shelves and doing a little reading. Amused by his evasive, flattering letters to Robert de Montesquiou.* Left Wilson's at 5.30 and came home to Hampstead by bus. Very cold feet; my nose and throat still stiff with catarrh. In the evening, listened to *We Beg to Differ* on the wireless,† though I wanted to write. To bed at 10.15. Tried to tinker with a poem I'd attempted yesterday, but became too sleepy. Took a 3-grain tablet to make sure of not waking too early (my worst and most defenceless time of the day).

25 November 1950

My cold has gone slightly to my chest. Took some of the medicine (a sort of black-coffee tinctus) the G.P. prescribed, and stayed in bed until 11.15, reading the *New Statesman* and wearing a white cricket-sweater over my pyjamas. This bedroom of mine at my good friends the Harrises is cold as only an unheated Victorian-style bedroom can be. The gas fire warms only the few feet of frozen air in front of it. If I had the courage I'd go back to my own centrally-heated flat, but I'm still terrified of being or living alone. All the same, I went to the flat to-day, directly I had got dressed. Mrs Timmons was there, washing my shirt, socks and handkerchiefs in the kitchen. She

---

* Robert de Montesquiou (1855–1921) was a French aesthete, poet and dandy.
† A BBC discussion programme.

had seen a copy of my new novel lying where I'd left it on the sitting-room sofa and asked if she could buy one. I said I'd give her a copy and thereupon wrote on the fly-leaf the following words: 'To Mrs Timmons, to whose help and comfort I owe more than she can possibly know.' This is no exaggeration: no other housekeeper (she's really a daily) would have stood by me as she has for the past six months. She then made the journey to the mental hospital (Napsbury) once a week to see me & bring me clean clothes, fruit and cake: every Wednesday afternoon from two to four we'd sit in that awful long gallery, surrounded by patients and other visitors, and talk. She's been with me for over twelve years. A mother-substitute (she is 62)? Very possibly. But I am a son-substitute for her (her own son is about 40 and, married, lives away from her). In the afternoon went to tea with Eve Disher and found her painting a jar of six magnificent yellow and pinkish roses; the picture was only roughed in on a 3-ft square canvas board.* Eve says that Leslie Hurry arrived back from Moscow three days ago, via Warsaw and Prague. He had flown out at the invitation of the Soviet Cultural Relations Committee, to look at Moscow art galleries and the city generally. They also flew him down to S. Georgia. Eve reports that he was impressed by the high place artists have under the regime, though their styles are 'guided' into 'social realism' (in other words, art immediately understood by the people).

26 November 1950

I wrote a letter to Graham, who is in Athens studying Greek orthodox religion; I asked him to pray for me when he next visited the little Temple of Nike (Victory) on The Acropolis. This Temple has been, I believe, partly reconstructed (the stones were scattered) since I saw it on my own visit to Greece in 1927. Incidentally, Graham's birthday was on Nov. 1st. He is 24. At 46, last year, I was in love with him and he (slightly) with me.

---

* Artist Eve Disher (1894–1991), best known for her portraits, had known members of the Bloomsbury Group.

28 November 1950

A bad day; depression, anxiety, loneliness, frustration – all the familiar and unholy team. Mrs T. asked if I'd like to marry 'if anyone suitable came along'. I said yes, though I doubt if this is really true; it might lead me into a worse state than I am at present.

29 November 1950

Another bad day. A session with F.B. from 10 till 11, during which I cried most of the time, being in utter misery and not knowing why, except that I feel that I belong nowhere and to nobody (an infantile wish, no doubt, but there it is). I am now writing this journal in bed, having just taken a 3-grain sodium amytal pill (known in hospital as a 'blue bomber' from the similarity in shape between these pills and a tiny-model block-buster).*

1 December 1950

In the evening called in at David's and was asked to stay to dinner. The guests were a couple of Lesbians (Terry and Margaret) and a couple of male homosexuals (one a television actor). Much amusing conversation about the seduction of 'normal' men by queers, though the constant equation of sex (physical) with love (of any kind) as usual makes me priggishly silent. All the same, the evening took me out of myself and did me good.

3 December 1950

Sunday. In the afternoon I motored to Chistlehurst with the Harrises to see old Mrs Harris (Jack's mother, aged 81) and her daughter. Slight snow-showers on the way: very cold. We took hot water-bottles in the car with us – I put mine against my stomach and held it with my hands. The daughter, aged about fifty, thin, restless, goodish-looking and faintly bitter. Strange, but I

---

* Sodium amytal had sedative and mildly hypnotic properties; '3 grains' referred to a 200-milligram pill. This highly addictive drug was traded on the streets as 'blue heavens' and used recreationally. Production ceased during the early 1980s, by which time a wide range of anti-depressants had replaced it.

could recognise at once the symptoms of some sort of neurosis similar to my own (the escape-movements, the silences, the desperate attempts *to rise to the surface*). Later I was told she had been in a mental hospital. I believe she, on her side, recognised certain symptoms in me, for she avoided noticing me when we arrived (always managing to be doing some little job). Neurotics recognise one another just as frequently as do homosexuals.

7 December 1950
In the afternoon, Ralph Arnold rang me up from Constables to ask if I had a photograph of myself which *The Sketch* could use. He said that Rupert Croft-Cooke, who reviews for the *Sketch*, wanted to pick out my novel for distinction in the next issue of the paper. I very much doubt this, as Rupert C-C. has never liked me since that incident with Stanley Allingham (yes, I even remember his name), the homosexual manservant, whom we both liked. He left Rupert and became available to me – I put it this way, as the actual incident was unsatisfactory – and Rupert was angry. However, he may now have forgiven me and decided to give my book a good notice; we shall see.

11 December 1950
A letter from Charles Brasch, from N.Z. He has, he says, mentioned me in an article he's written for *Landfall* about the N.Z. Literary Fund. Whether he's suggested I should be subsidised I don't know but I should feel anxious, had he done so, about any obligation involved. In the matter of writing, I must go my own way.

15 December 1950
I also wrote to Ngaio Marsh, whose programme on Canterbury is being broadcast to-morrow, asking if she remembers producing [Arthur Wing] Pinero's *The Amazons* in Christchurch (N.Z.), in which I played a French count.*

---

* By this time New Zealander Ngaio Marsh (1895–1982) was well known for her detective fiction and was often interviewed on British radio and TV. This programme may have had something to do with the December 1950 centenary of Canterbury province.

16 December 1950

Went to D. and D.'s in the evening. David was on the point of leaving for a party in Holland Park – a queer party, for which he was taking many pains to make up his face before the mirror, using some sort of astringent and then a skin-cream. The party, he told me, was being 'thrown' by one Fred who works for Fortnum and Mason's – 'he plucks geese, somewhere in the basement, and is very indignant if you ask him if he ever plucks chickens'. David said that he was going to leave Fred's party at 12 and go on to another – 'a drag-party given by some sluts in Bayswater'. I would give a good deal myself to be as young and as full of gusto as David (he is 25).

22 December 1950

A session with F.B. at 9.15 which meant a 6.45 rise on a freezing morning. F.B. more sympathetic than usual, and said I could ring him up over Christmas if I got 'frantic'. He made me draw (in coloured chalks) the visual impression I had of my own despair – a blackish disc with a greyish intrusion on one side, all surrounded by a circular black line. Is this a 'psychotic' picture? I suppose so.

A Christmas card from F[rank] from Buenos Aires. I was flattered and pleased to get this, as it must be 20 years ago since I met him in the Riviera Express – a meeting which developed into the most passionate love-affair I've ever had. True, the whole thing collapsed when I went out to S. America to join him, but the first months, in London, were idyllic. F.B. was asking me this morning about *fellatio*, but that was a minor pleasure to my experiences with F. (in which I usually took the passive role).

25 December 1950

A lad of 17 named Colin came to dinner with the family. Dark-eyed, dark-haired, rather blunt features, long-waisted slim body, belted trousers – all very attractive. But alas, the attraction was one-sided: he had no time whatever for me and even avoided saying goodbye to me when leaving in the evening.

26 December 1950

Boxing Day. I went to the flat in the morning and spent an hour tearing up old
letters and bills, with a dreadful, stifling sense of finality. What am I afraid
of? I ask myself this a hundred times a day and can't find an exact answer.
And yet I *am* frightened; I am frightened by my own fear, my own future, the
inadequacy of my own talents to fulfil my expectations, by the blackness and
tension that constantly engulf me, by the various physical afflictions from
which I suffer and by my own detachment and touchiness.

5 January 1951

For once, a day fairly free from neurotic anxiety. Is this the beginning of
a change? Pray Heaven it is so (if an atheist may use such an expression,
betraying his early religious training.) A session with F.B., who was late and
suffering from lumbago (in fact bent almost double). He asked me about
my sexual fantasies: I told him of the one about the Army private and his
sergeant.

> F.B.: Then you see yourself as having *power* over your sexual partner?
> *Courage*: Not exactly. I take both parts – the active and passive –
> though it is the active that assumes control at the orgasm.
> F.B.: What sort of a person is this active sergeant?
> *Courage*: A rather tough extrovert, with no sexual inhibitions.
> F.B.: The sort of person your father would have liked *you* to be?
> *Courage:* I don't think so. I don't think of my father in such connection.
> F.B.: Nevertheless, you do assume another character in imagination.
> *Courage*: Yes. If you want to draw conclusions from one isolated
> fantasy.

7 January 1951

Edward L. came to tea at the flat. He spoke of his feeling apart from other
people – most other people, in fact – when in general company, and said
that their comments on things (books, plays, people) seemed shallow, their
judgement childish, and their malice universal.

Edward: I'd rather be by myself and reading a good book.

Myself: In theory, so would I; but my own company appals and panics me with anxiety. I have no peace.

Edward: Do you find peace with others?

Myself: Very little more than without them. As a matter of fact this trouble is an old one. Though you may not know it, you helped me through some bad years with your friendship and our physical relationship (now past). I had peace through you.

Edward's eyes filled with tears and so did mine. He is under thirty and I am nearly fifty, and except for Graham he is (was) my last love. To-day I kissed him on our parting at the door: he was returning to his parents' house in Shepherd's Bush. His father is a shoemaker and Edward was born in the East End. He has an innate refinement, much intelligence, good looks and a kind heart.

13 January 1951

A letter came from Frederick Page, who is Professor of Music at Victoria University in N.Z.* and who is now on sabbatical leave in England, saying that he had just read *Desire Without Content* and praising my evocation of that magical country: in prose which he describes as 'beautiful, clear and precise'.

18 January 1951

In the evening I went to see Noel F. and talked about psychoanalysis. It is the turned-in force of the libido that is so painful in my case – the energy that can be expressed only as anxiety. I *know* this but cannot do anything about it.

21 January 1951

To the flat in the morning. Opened my old wooden box of papers and manuscripts, in search of my early autobiography to show F.B. Found some

---

* Courage met Page (1905–1983) when he was in New Zealand in 1934. Page studied and lived in London from 1935 to 1938.

old letters from Emlyn Williams, D'Arcy Cresswell and R.W. Kelton-Cramer – also 2 letters from T.S. Eliot about the autobiography (rejected, finally, by Faber), a letter from Gerald Barry and 3 from J.C. Squire. I destroyed all of these, feeling that I hated the past and must get rid of it. David Winfield came to tea. I sat beside him on the sofa and, desperately in need of human contact, held his hand and rested my cheek against his sleeve. He did not object. He told me that he was impotent with women. He is 21 and I am 47, yet in some ways I think of him as the same age as myself. He is at present living at Horsham, so as to be near his psychiatrist – a strange arrangement.

22 January 1951

A session with F.B. I told him I was no better. He asked me his opinion of him.

> *Myself*: I have a sort of affection for you – a fixation even.
>
> *FB*: That's quite normal between physician and patient you know.
>
> *Myself*: You know more about me than anyone else does.
>
> *F.B.*: No doubt.
>
> *Myself*: That produces a sort of dependence.

Later, I told him about my behaviour with David yesterday. It seemed dreadful in retrospect, but he accepted it calmly enough.

23 January 1951

A slightly better day – perhaps due to the direction of libido, as the Freudians might say. I played the piano for an hour (Bach, Brahms, a little Ravel): my life seemed to have a trifle more purpose.

A letter from Hazel Armour (from Scotland). She writes in praise of *Desire Without Content*, which she'd just read. 'I kept counting the pages, for I wished the book never to end ... a kind of magnificent and harmonised orchestration ... there is something in your courage and sincerity which brings a sense of grandeur to life.' All this is very kind of Hazel, but what is it in me that doubts her words or sincerity? I would far rather have written a book that I'm reading this morning myself –

24 January 1951

Again a slightly better day. Am I beginning to recognise my own conflicts not simply to suffer their ravaging force?

A session with F.B. I told him about Napsbury and explained my distress before going there. I also attacked F.B. for being reluctant to commit me to the place (as a mental hospital).

15 October 1952

Writer's Notes

Frank Sargeson has written to me from N.Z. – 'It seems to me that more than any of us you have wiped off the technical blot from New Zealand writing.'

And again: 'I can't work out the mystery of your prose – its easiness makes it seem to lack concentration and yet the concentration is there.'

Denton Welch writing in his journal of a young farmer who had stripped naked for a bathe – 'his flesh was white like junket with a malt surface'.* Very vivid, that. Myself, I often think on seeing a naked male body, of an anatomical chart – tinted blue, pink and red – in a textbook. 'Is all *that* inside the skin?' I overhear myself asking, though without disgust.

Up to the end of June '52, the sales of *The Fifth Child* were 6224, and of *Desire Without Content* 2915. *The Fifth Child* still sells, apparently, at the rate of one copy a month, 4½ years after publication. I haven't had a statement from Constables on the sales of *Fires in the Distance*, but they may well be below those of *Desire* ... And yet, why do I go on writing? One reason is that I believe I've written about people in Canterbury (N.Z.) as it has never been done before – just as Turgenev wrote about certain people in Russian provincial society as it had not been done before.†

---

*   Denton Welch (1915–1948) was a writer and painter.

†   Ivan Turgenev (1818–1883) was a Russian novelist, short fiction writer, poet and
     playwright.

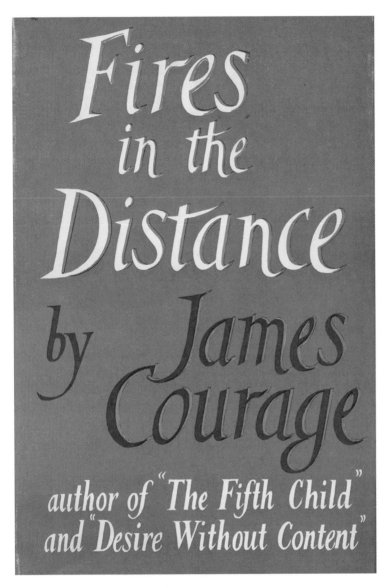

Fires in the Distance was published by Constable in 1952.

S20-576b, MS-0999/138, Hocken Collections

A name back to me from my schooldays, last night. There was a tall flax-haired youth (a prefect) in my boarding-house called Philip Boulnois. The youth was, as I say, tall, and had rather a small head for his height: he had good, rather Viking-like features and chin. The only thing I remember him saying to me, though I was allotted to him as a fag, was: 'I can see you're going to be one of the boys' – a sort of jocular compliment. I was, in actual fact, anything but 'one of the boys', ever.

After reading some of Waley's translations of Po Chü-I –

I am tired of trying to look beautiful:
I shall sit under a bamboo tree,
Not glance at myself in pools,
And be contented, once and for all, with my ugliness.*

22 October 1952

R. is at least 25 years younger than I am. Last night, as we were walking up Tottenham Court Road after the theatre, he suddenly said he wanted to eat potato chips from a fish-and-chip stall. So I bought him a fourpenny bag of hot chips, and these we ate in our fingers as we walked on slowly, arm in arm. This made me very happy. We laughed, threw away the empty bag and looked into lighted shop windows. And yet, as I say, this boy is less than half my age. There's no fool, I say to myself (as my mother used to say), like an old fool.

From Charles Brasch's letter to me after he'd read *Fires in the Distance* – 'Assurance is the word all through; you're so easy to read, so persuasive, always.'

I read these words with astonishment. It's very seldom that I write even a sentence with *assurance*; quite the contrary. There must be some technical legerdemain here, obviously.

---

* Arthur Waley (1889–1966) was acclaimed for his translations of Japanese and Chinese poetry. Po Chü-I was a Tang Dynasty government official born near the end of the eighth century AD.

'What are your habits?' the doctor asked me, referring obviously to my sexual predilections. 'Various,' I replied, 'and all of them bad.' My doctor is a Scot. 'Tell me the worst,' he said stolidly.

R., when in the R.A.F., dressed up as a girl (high heels, spotted veil, a *snood*, and two rolled socks as breasts) and took himself, with a companion similarly dressed, to a fancy-dress dance. At the gate of the camp, they were pulled up by the S.P. (sentry) on duty. – 'Oi, miss, where you bin?' R. said 'I live here, you silly boy.' 'Blimey,' the S.P. said, 'all right, hop it quick, afore the C.O. catches you up. You're on the camp all right.' R. likes kissing, caressing, but not *that*. Was once engaged to a girl named Valerie, without apparently any conception of his own homosexuality. 'We used to go dancing, but I didn't get any fire when I kissed her or she kissed me.' In the R.A.F. he was nicknamed 'the officer's bum-boy' – to his intense resentment. 'I fought one when he touched me.'

'I am grateful each time I read one of your books, for yours is a New Zealand which was in danger of going unsung. The Sargesons are all very well but there is no reason why they should be allowed responsibility, which they are only too ready to assume, for the *whole* of New Zealand.' From a letter to me from John Stacpoole, from Auckland.* H'm. Yes, and No. Still, praise is sweet.

25 July 1953
R.A. here to supper. His telling me of his drive in a pink taxi (now a private car) painted to resemble *quilting*. His innocent physical conceit – 'my hair was in a good mood that day' – his scent of *chypre* or resinous something – the delicate air of security his beauty gives him. Just before leaving, he gave me a snapshot of himself almost naked (or rather, standing in khaki shorts in some back garden) and, borrowing a pen, wrote on the back 'To Jimmy, from "your boy".' As a matter of fact this pleased and flattered me. After all, I am 50 and he 24.

---

* John Stacpoole (1919–2008) was an historian, architect and avid book collector.

Hot August days. These remind me of New Zealand – days when blue-bottles buzzed in the hot house and one could hear the mason-flies making their little clay egg-cradles in the curtains or a crack in the window-sills or the ceiling. Out of doors, a nor'wester blowing in the blue-gums and making the grass paddocks look almost colourless under the burning sky.

A story that will never be written. X., a young homosexual living in a big city, had been in the habit of paying for his sexual pleasures. He was not typically physically attractive, was unhappy and had found great difficulty, always, in finding a bed-partner to his taste (his 'type' ran to a peculiar form of toughness and was for some reason connected with Scotsmen and red hair). He had had many adventures but had made no permanent match with any one man. One night, in defending himself against a 'lover' who had stolen money from him and had tried to beat him up, he accidentally killed the aggressor. X. was arrested, convicted of murder and eventually gaoled for life. In prison X. found himself in the cell next to a convict who was, so to speak, the man of his dreams. This man, likewise a murderer and under life-sentence, became – and remained – X.'s lover. For the first time in his life X. was contented: the partnership was not based on an exchange of money and was (owing to the confinement of their prison-fates) almost as binding as a life-marriage. X.'s lover, in fact, became devoted to him. The lover was a tough amiable type: a Scotsman with red hair. Due to the wisdom (and, for once, the humanity) of the Prison Governor, the 'marriage' last for 20 years, until X. died. The Scotsman, an older man, was heart-broken.

Hell is being confined indefinitely with one's sexual partner who is only one's sexual partner.

Sex and Literature

(1) I had never experienced physical love with a man before. He was some years older than I, and I had gone to his house in friendship and an innocence mixed with indefinable curiosity.

He undressed me without haste, until I was standing naked before him, then kissed my body and put his mouth against my genitals. This excited me. He himself took off his clothes, pressing me gently against him, whispering endearments. I was not frightened but remained in a kind of trance in which I could not protest (even had I wished to). Presently he bent down and took my element between his lips, again gently and as though naturally, caressing my thighs and the globes of sex between them until my seed spurted – with what rapture – into his throat. In my ecstasy I cried aloud, holding his head against my belly.

Later he laid me on the bed, kissing me many times again; then, telling me not to be afraid and that he would not hurt or harm me, turned over my body beneath his and gently penetrated me from behind. I could feel his element inside me. He made slow tender movements, holding me close and kissing my cheeks and neck, until his arms tightened about mine and I knew that his seed had passed into me. He was gentle and kind, telling me of the pleasure I had given him.

Later we lay together, our flesh touching and softly kissed one another (another many many times). His seed was in me and mine in him, and there was no fear or harm in us because of it. We slept in one another's arms and woke happily. From that moment I loved him.

(2) It was the first time I'd been fucked. The chap was older than I was – I was 19 and he 25. He stripped me then took my cock in his mouth and sucked me off. It was grand. I cried out as I spunked. When I'd finished he put me on the bed, turned me over and buggered me. I could feel him come up my arse. No, it didn't hurt even though he was big and had held me hard. Later we went to sleep together. It was all grand and I wanted it again.

Now which of those two accounts of sexuality is the more sophisticated? The straight 'innocent', simple one, or the lavatory-wall 2nd version. Most people would say the latter, but the first is, to my mind, infinitely the more complex and the harder to write. The choice is a problem for anyone who would wish to describe such an episode (without moral bias or fear). Such is our civilisation that to write naturally about sex – normal or abnormal – is the hardest thing of all. Most writers fail when they attempt it, even clinically. One feels their apprehension in their words. Even D.H. Lawrence forces the note, from 'nerves' or bravado. Perhaps it can only be done by a very sophisticated writer, using a naïve, almost Biblical simplicity of language, without fuss or falsity.

Synonyms for penis in French: member, queue, verge.

In English: stalk, tail, stem, rod, wand, handle, stamen, organ. For anus: oeil de bronze, la bastille, la rondelle, l'oignon, le derch, le darjeau, la lune.

25 July 1953

One should be able to write of one's sexual predilections as naturally as one's taste in food.

Remembered to-day something I'd said to F. last summer as we lay on the bed together: I said 'You know, you're one of the few men I'd like to have had a child by.' After all, it was nearly twenty years since F. and I first went to bed together, so my remark shouldn't have startled him. But no, perhaps it didn't startle him – I'm wrong. Only his arm round me tightened a little. 'Yes,' he said slowly, 'I'd have liked that too.'

8 February 1954

10.30 p.m. This is written in the last few hours of my fiftieth year. I was born on Feb. 9th, 1903. I would not wish to live my first fifty years over again: they have been too painful, too full of anxiety and too lonely. J.F.C.

2 April 1954

A great day for me: Cape have accepted my novel *The Young Have Secrets*. Then I am not dead, as a writer – a fate I had feared.*

---

* *The Young Have Secrets* is the story of young Walter Blakiston, who is sent to live with his schoolmaster and is confided in by several adults in the extended family about their complex and tragic romantic lives. It would be Courage's most commercially successful novel.

5 May 1954

Wrote to my father. I find it so difficult to be natural towards him, even writing at a distance of 12,000 miles: he is still the awful parent of my childhood, with a pipe, an explosive temper and a general attitude towards me in particular of 'you'll never be a man, or a success'. And now he writes of himself – 'I am pretty feeble. I get up at midday and walk about round the house, in the sun in the early afternoon ... But at 87 one must expect these troubles.'

5 May 1954

Note, 1954

Although I'd always meant to be a writer I didn't really *get down* to writing until 1947 (when I was 44). I had, it is true, made various attempts to use obliquely autobiographical material before then, but did not know how to treat and shape the subjects – mostly dealing with New Zealand – that occurred to me. When I did begin, however, with *The Fifth Child*, one result of this long delay was that I saw my given subjects with a maturer eye than I would have had I published books (dealing with the same material) in my twenties (as would most intended writers). The subjects, insofar as they were based on early autobiography, had by that time also gained a remoteness that made it easier for me to discard inessentials in them. Furthermore, they'd accumulated a nice varnish or patina with time: most of the bitterness, for instance, was painted over with a kind of compassion – or at least a later understanding.

16 September 1954

I heard to-day – from Wren Howard, who rang me up from Cape – that *The Young Have Secrets* has been picked out to be the Book Society Choice for December ('54).* This was such staggering news that I couldn't at first believe it (after the book's vicissitudes with Constable, who turned it down pretty

---

* Wren Howard, the co-founder of Jonathan Cape, had a strong sense of design that informed the look of the company's books.

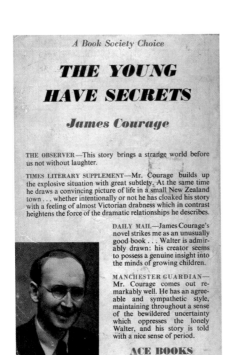

The back cover (LEFT) and front (OPPOSITE), in a pulp fiction style, adorning the second edition of *The Young Have Secrets*, released by Harborough in 1958. Jonathan Cape was responsible for the first edition of 1954 and the novel would be published again by Allen & Unwin in 1985.

John Webster collection

meanly & flatly); I must have sounded a complete zany on the telephone to Howard. I went back to the sitting-room, where I'd just been about to settle down to my tea (at 5.15 p.m.), and had a strange impulse to cry, to weep because I wanted to tell somebody the good luck and there seemed, on the instant, to be nobody – not a soul – who'd be interested to hear. Such is my isolation.

'Surprised by joy, impatient as the wind,
I turned to share the transport – oh, with whom?'*

The next day (17th) passed in a dream, though I'd hardly slept during the night. Then, on the day following I decided that the news was a complete illusion, or delusion rather, and that, a psychotic now, I was really 'for it'. I began to tremble. I went to the telephone and rang my literary agent. No,

---

* These are the first two lines of Wordsworth's poem 'Surprised by Joy'.

ACE BOOKS

H213

A DEVASTATING STORY OF DRAMATIC RELATIONSHIPS

James Courage

THE YOUNG HAVE SECRETS

A BOOK SOCIETY CHOICE

he had heard nothing of the Choice, having been away on holiday himself. I asked him to telephone to Cape, as I was now unwilling to do this on my own behalf. Twenty minutes later he rang back: he'd been unable to get any confirmation from Cape, as Howard was out. He, the agent, would however try again (I could tell that he was excited but doubtful) and telephone me before six in the evening. I spent a hideous day of anxiety: in fact I took a sedative to help me through. Then the phone rang. And yes, the news was true and I was to be congratulated. Let this all be a lesson to me, to believe in my own work and to be confident that if I do it with all my powers and my utmost skill somebody will appreciate it somewhere.

21 September 1954

Tonight R. came here to a dinner which I'd cooked for the two of us. And I thought again, as I've thought before, that he is the most beautiful young man I have ever seen. He is 24 years old, in the full bloom of a loveliness that is tender, even innocent, and certainly not intellectual. We sat talking: I did not make love to him, though we kissed one another on the lips when he arrived and again when he left, like understanding friends, which indeed we are. Only I felt, and deeply, the sadness of his physical beauty – as though I should never see him again as I saw him this evening; never, never again. (Propertius could have said all this in elegiac stanzas beyond my powers. And Propertius has been dead nearly 2000 years.)*

The cyclist – a young man – with his white shorts and pink legs – looking like a ham sandwich, from behind.

No date

Note made to cheer myself, October 1954

In the past year, my 51st, I have had the following works published:

(1) Short story, 'After the Earthquake', in *New Zealand Short Stories* (World Classics, O.U.P. [Oxford University Press]).

---

* Roman poet Sextus Propertius lived from about 55–45 to 15 BC.

(2) Short story, 'Nothing to Make Us Mad', in *The London Magazine*.

(3) Short story, 'Scusi', in *Landfall* (N.Z.).

(4) Short story, 'A Worry to His Mother', in *The Pick of Today's Short Stories* (V) (Putnam).

(5) Novel, *The Young Have Secrets*, to be published by Cape in December. This has been made the choice of the Book Society for that month.

When I think of the insecurity, loneliness and doubt I have always found myself in as a writer, and of the awful early years when I was trying in solitude to learn my craft – then surely I have a little something to comfort me now.

11 February 1955

I heard to-day that my father killed himself. He shot himself with a gun at about six o'clock on the morning of February 1st. This is a raw and terrible fact that I do not find easy to think about. It seems to mean nothing and to lead nowhere except towards madness.*

27 March 1955

To-day, for the first time, I saw myself described in print as 'the best living New Zealand novelist' (the words were in a review of *The Young* ... in the Christchurch *Press*). Was this always my ambition? I suppose so. But what a long time it has been in coming, and how much bitterness and pain – and what a warped and one-sided life – I have endured in the meantime. I would have been happier, by far, as a simple normally-orientated farmer like my own brother [John].† I am a good novelist, I might say, because I am an invert, a neurotic and an incomplete human being. But never would I have chosen such a fate.

---

* Frank Courage had been ill for some years: he had had two haemorrhages, persistent heart trouble and spells in hospital, and was bedridden by the end of his life.

† James's married brother, John Alexander Courage, farmed near Amberley and had two daughters and a son.

No date

Billets Doux [Love Letters]

'The male sexual organs are ugly, hideous – don't you agree?'

'Not necessarily. I always think of a man's body as some long pale plant with the flower and the seed-pods about half way down. Some flowers are beautiful and some not so. They vary, like the more recognisable kind of flora.'

7 November 1955

Finished the typing of my new novel, which has taken me 16 months to write. The title at present is 'After the Accident'. As usual I am very uncertain of the book's value – the subject is tricky and I may have blundered in the working-out and conclusion: but then I had the same doubts about *The Young* ... when I'd finished it (the latter book, I mean). In certain ways 'The Accident' is a better-constructed and better co-ordinated novel than *The Young* ..., though less poignant. Why then am I in so nervous and anxious a state?

Because I fear rejection; also I have *faked* certain scenes in the narrative of the new book. I am not really interested in a heterosexual love-affair, as depicted. It doesn't *involve* me. In so far as I've treated it at all intimately it is a concession made to the public – a concession for which I despise myself.*

23 May 1956

To Dr Mascall for a general urinary examination. I asked him about the present incidence of V.D. 'Oh,' he said, 'it's practically a back-number since penicillin came in, we can hardly get enough specimen cases of syphilis to

---

* This novel was published as *The Call Home*. There are many parallels between the book's characters and Courage's immediate family. Will, a shy would-be Lothario who took refuge in drink, was based on James's brother John. Like Will, as a young man John learned to fly an aeroplane. 'Boy you ought to have your neck wrung. Referring to me as you did, what with the booze and the girls,' John wrote. 'However I got a jolly good laugh out of it.' John Courage to James Courage, 17 September 1957, MS-999/146, HC.

John Courage and his racing car. John inspired at least one character in James's
writing. *S20-569c, MS-0999/178, Hocken Collections*

show our students. Gonorrhoea is slightly more prevalent – largely due to a
number of "rogue" cases who float about, promiscuous and untreated – but
even this disease may soon become only a medical memory. We consultants
will be out of business.'

June 1956
Let me note here that my mental health has been better during this month
than for at least twelve years past. For once, the long analysis I have been
undergoing has appeared to be getting somewhere – I seem to have made
a human relationship with at least one person (the psychiatrist) that does
not cause me misgiving, pain and anxiety. This has never – and I repeat that
sad word never – happened to me in my whole life hitherto, and this simple

statement of neurotic isolation is true. I am not a religious man but – God help me to persevere, to recover, to live with less anguish. In the course of my life I have uttered the words 'I love you' to about six people. I have never heard them uttered to me in return – never, not once.

30 July 1956

Publication day of *The Call Home*. I felt sad and anxious all day, as though this were to be my last book. Only one letter came (from B.C.) wishing me and the book well. Seán O'Faoláin's review in last week's *Listener* (he'd reviewed the book in advance) gave me some trouble to digest. On the whole, I think it is good, but the tone is cool and could, with one small push, have gone over into sourness. But he makes the perceptive remark, nevertheless, that the book must have been difficult to write (little does he guess *how* difficult), while admitting that 'this is a novel to be respected, admired, and quietly enjoyed'. Hmm ... I get lots of respect and admiration but precious little enjoyment.

23 September 1957

An interview this afternoon with Dr Larkin at the St Marylebone Hospital of Psychiatry* – perhaps the most disturbing and in some ways terrifying interview I've ever had in my life. Larkin had in front of him the report on the intelligence-and-association tests I underwent at the same Hospital about two months ago (one morning when I happened to be very depressed). I had gone to him this afternoon, however, not to hear the result of these tests but to ask him – since my present and private psychiatrist had

---

* Sydney-born and educated, Edward Henry Larkin (1908–2002) moved to England to train as a thoracic surgeon, but became interested in mental illness. During World War II he was a colonel in the Royal Army Medical Corps and was appointed reader in psychiatric medicine at the Royal Army Medical College. He also oversaw the rehabilitation of shell-shocked soldiers.

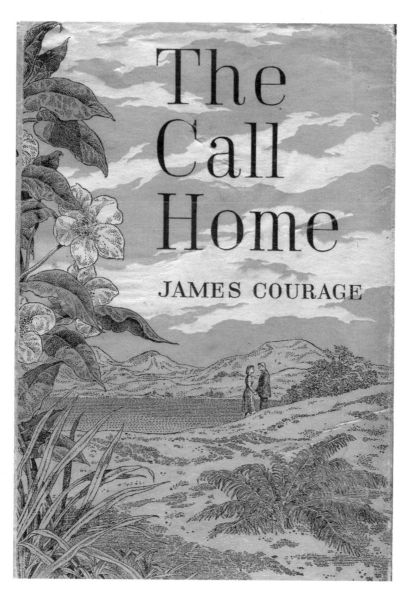

The bucolic jacket of *The Call Home*, published in 1956 by Jonathan Cape, evokes the New Zealand landscape as effectively as Courage's writing. *Rachel Scott collection*

recently hinted that his treatment had not so far 'worked' with me – what I was to do, so desperate did I feel about the future. Larkin, however, after some slight hesitation, evidently decided to go straight to the findings of the tests.

'You know you're a bit dotty, don't you?' he said.

'No. Do you mean psychotic?'

'Well, let's say you've a character-neurosis, slightly schizoid, which no amount of psychiatric treatment will alter, in the sense of turning you into a normal, well-balanced human being – even if you've ever been one.' He then went on to tell me that my intelligence and true personality (according to him, an aggressive, virile, unpredictable one – in fact, 'slightly mad') indicated a degree of near-genius, but that I had so repressed and screwed myself down in the past that I had limited myself to talent only; in a word to the scope of published writings. Where was the other side of me – the Van Gogh, crazy side that was undoubtedly present even if I wouldn't acknowledge it?

I heard this diagnosis in a state of depression and stupefaction, having really only caught the words 'slightly mad'. When I could speak I asked if all this meant that *no* therapy would work: must I go on in the state of melancholia and anxiety-tension in which I lived at present?

'No,' said Larkin, 'I don't think so. On the contrary I'd consider you an excellent subject for a psychotherapy with considerable limitations of aim.'

I told him I'd had eight years or more of psychotherapy from private practitioners: was it my fault that it had failed?

'No. Neither yours nor the therapists, who have been slightly off the beam, or so it appears.'

'What am I to do, then? Can you give me a therapist here at the Hospital?'

'Eventually we hope to. But it isn't easy to arrange a long-term course for you. You are, however, on our list, I assure you.'

'Have you a say in the choice of psychiatrist to whom I'll be allotted?'

'Certainly I have. You should know that.'

– All this, of which I've given only the gist, was interlaced on his side with jokes and somewhat obscene asides on homosexuality; remarks very typical of Larkin's brash Australian character. Passing over these here (if I'm being what he called 'prissy', I can't help it), I now reach the second and no less surprising half of the interview.

'I've a suggestion to make,' he said. 'I think we might try an experimental technique on you: I think we'll try a hallucinatory drug, if you agree?'

'Do you mean lysergic acid?'

'I did, yes. You could have it here at the Hospital.' He pressed a bell-push suspended above his head and one of the nurses appeared at the door.

'We want to give Mr C. a dose of L.S.D., nurse. When could it be done?'*

Most of the staff, it seemed, were away on holiday but it could be done in ten days.

'All right,' Larkin said to me. 'You arrange it with the Nurse.' And after a few more observations the interview ended.

So it appears that I am 'slightly mad', slightly schizoid, and that one way to help me may be through the use of a hallucinatory drug – or at least for purposes of prognosis. I find all this highly disturbing, however much it may explain of the past.

11 January 1958

Finished typing and revising the book (I supposed I must call it a novel) to which I've now given the title of 'In Private'. No other book I've written has given me such trouble, such doubts, and such hard labour (blood and tears, my God) as this one, no doubt because the *persona* of the book's supposed first-person narrator is not precisely my *persona* and I've had to alter my style accordingly. But – apart from this – the subject-matter of the book was extremely hard to deal with, or at any rate to deal with with artistic integrity and detachment. Outside prejudices and assumed disapproval kept getting

---

* LSD rose to prominence during the 1940s, when it was marketed as a cure for schizophrenia, criminal behaviour, alcoholism and sexual distress.

in the way – not to mention the defences and infantile repressions of my own mind. Homosexuality, in fact, is both a valid human theme and a clinical phenomenon: and the line between the two is very difficult to preserve in balance, so to speak. I doubt very much if I have succeeded – or succeeded in this, my first attempt, to tackle the subject head-on: I may need a second try, later.

Still, I have finished this present book. It took me about nineteen months, with a long gap of about four months somewhere in the middle. Now I must get an outside opinion of it – dreaded process – first from my agent and then, presumably from a publisher or publishers. I very much doubt if Cape will accept the book, whatever its integrity and whatever the quality of the writing. We shall see.*

21 January 1958
A letter from my agent (Paul Scott) –

'I've now read "In Private" and my *own* feeling is that you've succeeded in communicating something of what must be the reality of this particular kind of life. I don't like homosexual novels *qua* sex, because being the sort of chap who doesn't care a great deal who goes to bed with who or what I'm always left with the conviction that if one ignores the aberration one is left with Boy Meets Girl (Boy), Boy Gets Girl (Boy), Boy Loses Girl (Boy) and this is just the stuff of romantic novels. But you have overcome this, dear James, by writing a novel that is also a novel, and by starting off on the premise that the homosexual man is still in a man in the world (not only in the homosexual world).

'In fact I like this one more than I've liked books "of this sort" and I think we should publish and be dammed because it stands up in its own right as a piece of writing.'

Well, so far, so relatively good, or at least satisfying. I am over one hurdle.

---

* 'In Private' would be published by Jonathan Cape as *A Way of Love*.

12 January 1959

Publication day of *A Way of Love*. This book had given me immense trouble to write (or induced in me immense guilt, which may amount to the same thing) and I had got to the point, last week, of wishing I could withdraw it before publication (it was accepted by Cape almost exactly a year ago). Even now, and after a good review in yesterday's *Observer* ('Mr Courage is an artist who has made a modest contribution to literature ... '), I feel as though I had thrown myself, as a homosexual, on the hostile mercy of the world: committed myself irretrievably to perdition, as it were; an anal outcast. So be it. The book, I've already been informed by K. and E.M., is extremely 'courageous' (E.M. added 'outrageous', regarding the love passages). I don't feel it to be courageous so much as foolhardy, an indiscretion. Yet what have I to lose? I couldn't really be much unhappier (*or* nearer mild psychosis) than I have been for ten years or so: this long awful torture of Oedipal guilt which clouds and twists my life and outlaws peace of mind. This depression, anxiety, inertia, passivity. Even a prison sentence couldn't be a worse fate (punishment) than those.

The book itself, which cost me so much, is sad, sad, sad. I didn't really feel this when I was writing it – it seemed 'realistic' – but I see it now, and other people have already seen it. Again, so be it. Homosexuality, for all its flippant and amusing sides, is a tragedy for the individual (who cannot change his true inclination, try how he may). It cuts him off from the vivid involuntary force and drive of life – he has no part in its continuation – his love (his physical, sexual love) is sterile – his happiness precarious.

Have I said all this in *A Way of Love*? Much of it, yes, by implication at least. Much else I have hidden or glossed over. Yet I suppose I had to write the book, had to publish it, had to feel as I do. It was *in me* and had to come out.

JAMES COURAGE

has also written

The Young Have Secrets

'The best, most vivid and sensitive study of a small boy's thoughts and actions I have read. Mr. Courage has written one of the best novels of 1954.' NEWS CHRONICLE

'An admirable novel, blending objectivity with insight, and written in a crisp prose.' DAILY TELEGRAPH

'Well deserves to have been chosen by the Book Society.' SUNDAY TIMES

'Mr. Courage builds up the explosive situation with great subtlety. At the same time he draws a convincing picture of life in a small New Zealand town.' THE TIMES LITERARY SUPPLEMENT

The Call Home

'Mr. Courage remains a writer well above the average who can handle small domestic incidents and relationships in a very telling way.' TIME AND TIDE

'Mr. Courage once again proves his ability to evoke the landscape of New Zealand. His characterization is sound his dialogue natural.' OBSERVER

'The writing is taut, precise and occasionally vivid.' SPECTATOR

'A gracefully written book, gently and firmly shaped, and satisfying to read.' TABLET

A WAY OF LOVE

It requires considerable detachment in a writer to assume that a passionate friendship between men is as valid a subject for a serious novel as any other in our modern world. James Courage, in this notable book, has done just that, without apology or satire. His main character is an architect in London who here writes his own story—what he calls the 'little history' of his relationship with a younger man. It is a relationship which works itself out in the needs and ambitions of both partners, yielding no small benefit to each. Their wider social life is depicted with honesty, but it is their emotional interchange and its delicate adjustments that give the narrative its particular intimacy, value and flavour. The characterization of the minor persons in the book is acute and often humorous, and the story's happily unforced outcome has psychological implications which (without being insisted upon) are by no means confined to overt homosexuality or to this particular relationship.

This is a dignified novel upon an important subject.

'Most novels about sexual inversion are marred by sentimentality or flippancy. . . . Mr. Courage has avoided these extremes. He is sympathetic without being sloppy; entertaining, but not satirical. . . . There is much to recommend this book. Mr. Courage is an artist and has made a modest contribution to literature as well as to the understanding of an urgent social problem.' OBSERVER

15s. net

This striking orange and white design graces the jacket of the English edition of *A Way of Love*, published in 1959 by Jonathan Cape.

S20-576c, MS-0999/132, Hocken Collections

JAMES COURAGE

a way of love

1960–1961

PRIVATE

Diary of a Neurotic

Each is his own origin of ill and end, his own Time and place.*
—Byron, *Manfred*

---

*   Courage misquoted. Byron wrote: 'The mind which is immortal makes itself/Requital for its good or evil thoughts,/Is its own origin of ill and end,/And its own place and time ...'

10 May 1960

On the Couch

'When in doubt, shout,' the analyst tells me whenever I fall silent or relapse into tears on the couch. 'You've got to be a child, here with me, and a child expresses himself by shouting, screaming, biting, kicking. Go ahead.'

'But I'm not a child.'

'I don't want any intervention by the intellect or reasoning powers. Affect is all. Bring it out.'

Impossible exhortation. To-day however I tried once again: the desperate efforts of a fifty-seven-year-old man to behave like a frustrated unhappy infant I undoubtedly once was and whom I just as undoubtedly retain within me as an almost total stranger. To please the doctor I tried to shout, even to scream, shutting my eyes against the sight of the lime-green wall at the foot of the couch and opening my constricted throat with all the breath in my chest. What happened?

Noises came out, certainly. Stifled howling yells that at once shamed me as an adult and that sounded maniacal in this small room at the hospital. The yells appeared to be without content, quite senseless. 'No, I can't do it,' I said in distress, and was silent.

'But you are doing it,' Dr L[arkin] leant forward in his chair behind my left shoulder. 'Don't let up. Try again.'

I put my hands over my face, wanting only to cry, as I did so often in these sessions. 'I can't,' my voice repeated.

'Yell. You can do it.'

'It means nothing,' I sobbed.

'Leave the meaning to me. If necessary I'll do the interpretations. Simply shout.'

'Shout what?' I prevaricated as an adult.

'I want the noises to be oral – or anal if you wish. All this is on the pregenital level, you see. Try again. The little child must use his own language.'

I tried again. Without question the noises were oral. I discounted the anal part, the language of the sphincter. That could wait. I tried instead to keep my mouth open and to howl a protest – indeed, a succession of protests. Again the sounds struck me as so ridiculous and in some way utterly beside the point of my mental suffering. In a word, and if 'affect' was all, as Dr L. postulated, then the required affect (emotional release) was not getting through. I sweated, trying again and again: outbursts of infantile din. I stopped after some minutes, exhausted, longing for the end of the session. 'This is the hardest work I've ever attempted,' I complained at last, in tears. Unperturbed, Dr L. got up, carrying his notes. 'Blood, sweat and tears. We shall try again next time, when I see you on Friday.'

17 May 1960
'Why did I finally break down?'

'The return of the repressed. You were trying to live always on ground with mines and explosives underneath the surface. Unconscious dynamite.'

'Including my "unholy terrors"?'

'Those more than all. The infantile terrors begun by the bad mother. Great terrors indeed to the weak ego.'

So we came back to the bad mother. My mother, I realised, though I had no recollection of the original terror, the bad object, as such. The mother I remembered had been a selfish, inwardly harassed or absent-minded woman, whose face, so to speak, was permanently turned away from me, her eldest child. Something had been very wrong, certainly, since as a boy I had always felt – what? – lost, abandoned, rejected. But all this had taken place on the far side of the world, in New Zealand; the obverse of my adult life, its antipodes. For years I had hardly thought about my childhood, still less my early infancy. I had not wanted to think about them, since their atmosphere disturbed me with a kind of guilty panic. Now the atmosphere must be brought back, abreacted with Dr L. I did not want to abreact it. Anything *but*, I found. Not that, not that, ever! Above all, I disliked resurrecting memories of my parents, particularly my mother (herself an ingredient of what I have called atmosphere).

'My mother herself, if she were privy to this analysis, would call my neurosis complete nonsense,' I told Dr L. 'She'd say everything was done for me as a baby that could be done. To her my illness would be my own fault for my wrong living.'

'Naturally that would be her reaction,' Dr L. said calmly, as though he'd known as much all along. 'The parents put their own guilt on to the children. But the fault in the first place was overwhelmingly on her own doorstep.'

'And on my father's?'

'Later, yes. Both parents, in their separate ways, rejected you.'

I was in no state to argue; I sank into silence. How could they have rejected *me*, my heart kept demanding of the wall at the end of the couch. The insistent thing of the neurotic, surveying his childhood under analysis. Why was I so bad, so unworthy of love? Hopeless questions. Besides, my teeth kept hurting me, producing panic.

'What must I do?' I asked of Dr L. in a terror I felt must be childish. 'What can I do?'

'When in doubt, shout, as I've told you. Fight back at that bad mother, the tormentress you've internalised. Give her the toothache, which she so thoroughly deserved. Shout, bawl, yell –'

'Shut up,' I yelled, this time in anger at Dr L. himself. 'Don't bully me. I can't stand it from you, you bastard!'

'There, you see,' he said, pleased rather than alarmed, 'you can do it when you try.'

'You're not offended?'

'Don't spoil it by apologising. It's the apology that makes me cross. Call me what you like, and sound as though you mean it. Make the rafters ring.'

'All right you stupid bloody sod.'

'Good. That is music to my ears.'

But not, somehow, to mine.

18 June 1960

A bad day to-day. Anxiety, terror and desolation of the soul. I try so hard in analysis, yet seem to get more depressed, more hopeless. I have to keep remembering Dr L.'s words of diagnosis when I first went to him as a patient, two years ago: 'You suffered a fairly complete early rejection by both parents ... It was too much for you: it has given you a depressive illness of long standing. Alleviation is going to take some time. Don't despair.'

Curiously enough those seemed to me the very first words of compassionate understanding that had ever reached me. For once, I thought, somebody realised my trouble and might help. Even so, they had had to give me four treatments with lysergic acid (L.S.D.), a hallucinatory drug, at the hospital before a diagnosis became plain. Some time I must write about my experience under the drug: very strange, the return to childhood.

On Sunday evening S. came to supper here.* He is under treatment himself (though not by Dr L.) for neurotic trouble, and we can talk as one patient to another. S. and I understand one another very well, after three years of intimate friendship (he used to come to the hospital and 'collected' me after my drug sessions, bringing me home when I was groggy). *His* first breakdown came during the war: he was wounded at Dunkirk, then later sent to an Army Neurosis Centre where the doctors detected deeper than physical wounds, and advised psychiatric treatment in civil life. That was at least fifteen years ago, but S. has been a patient since: for at least ten of those years he attended group therapy sessions at the Tavistock Clinic,† then, since these were ineffective, started private treatment with a Freudian analyst.

29 June 1960

I thought back to my four years at Oxford, when bad depressions had first hampered me. I imagined my difficulties were my own fault – a matter of

---

*   Stuart Hurrell, the 'S.' of this excerpt, would be Courage's lover and helpmeet until the latter's death in 1963.
†   Opened in 1920, the Tavistock became Britain's most famous psychiatric clinic.

weak character, sexual deviations, even of excessive masturbation. Psychiatry never occurred to me: in fact, I knew absolutely nothing about it.

11 July 1960

'Melanie Klein's work on infantile traumas has enormously extended the range of analysis and its length of time, you see.* The whole depressive, persecutory position has to be worked through as well – the first two or three infantile years, when so much damage can be done – and, in your case, was done.'

'I can't remember any of that. The early mother-part. Nothing before about five or six.'

'Remembering doesn't so much matter –'

'It's hopeless – all too long ago –'

'No,' Dr L. pulled me up. 'The bad objects – the breast that poisons and persecutes – is still there with you. Vomit it out on me.'

I had a fantasy, as so often, of that enormous black breast like a thunder cloud: perhaps a breast with a baleful eye in place of the nipple (this came up under the hallucinatory drug, the L.S.D.). The whole thing is frightening, profoundly threatening my life with annihilation. All of which I repeated again now to Dr L. 'The bad breast ... '

'Vomit it up! Tear it in pieces,' he said strongly. 'Get rid of it on me.'

'I don't know why you took on my case at all,' I flared, using any weapon I could. 'It's hopeless.'

'If I'd considered it hopeless I wouldn't have taken you on. I had complete access to your dossier, you know; notes on former attempts at your treatment by others; all that.'

This was an unwelcome surprise to me. 'All the same, by now you must have detected symptoms that hadn't been unearthed before. My psychotic traits.'

---

* Author and psychoanalyst Melanie Klein (1882–1960) focused on child development and was a key figure in the development of object relations theory, which explores the process by which individuals develop a psyche. Courage read her books and made notes from them.

'I have found nothing that wasn't noted before –'

'My paranoid feelings?'

'What I *have* found is that you'd never adequately worked through your repression. Never, in analysis.'

'I was always much too afraid – and too much in need of present help to risk bringing out aggression from the past.'

'Precisely. Let's go ahead then.'

'Where I distrust and fear you is' – I stopped because I couldn't put this into words – 'I fear your condemnation of my homosexual, passive side. I feel you've never accepted that without conscious censure. It's immensely important.'

I could sense Dr L. lean forward in his chair behind me. 'I made it clear at the beginning that I didn't intend to disturb your sexual deviations. To do so would be a cruelty to anyone of your age. Also quite futile.'

'Then you accept me as I am?'

'I hoped you'd realised the fact long ago.'

'No. I suppose I don't because of some reflection from my father's attitude – or what I assumed it to be.'

'Certainly,' Dr L. went back to his notes. 'Your tremendous projection of an unloving, even a brutal, father,' he observed. 'You never get round that relic of the past.'

'Nor would you, if you'd felt the continual disapproval I experienced in early life.'

'Well, now's your opportunity to fight back,' he took up. 'Disapprove of me, make me squirm.'

'I don't know anything, or enough, about you personally, to abuse you.'

'That doesn't matter. Give the id its head – say anything you like.'

'You don't get me better, you f—g bastard,' I retorted, as strongly as I could manage. 'I hate you.'

'Good. But you trail off every time – you lose heart – you don't carry it through.'

'I don't because I don't feel any strength to.'

'Your original strength was crushed. The crushing began very early. Go on, nevertheless. The strength can be revived.'

14 July 1960
My father had always hated my playing the piano: it was a girl's prerogative.

15 July 1960
My father was an anti-intellectual if ever there was one, never opening a book or looking at a picture.

S. came to see me last night, as he does every Friday ('our evening'). As usual we began by talking about our analyses and our progress therein, if any. We drank whiskey and soda, our customary consolation and aphrodisiac. I had lent S. a book by Quennell on Byron last week, and presently we talked about Byron.* S. said he'd hardly ever read such a diagnosis of a repressed homosexual – 'every reaction to and in his marriage showed it'.

'Nobody would have believed a word of that at the time. Byron may never even have admitted it to himself.'

'If his autobiography hadn't been destroyed we might have known more. The manuscript may've been burnt for just that reason, come to think of it.'

'No Freud in those days! If a man had a mistress or kids he was ipso facto a hetero – or at least not predominantly a homo.'

'Interesting to imagine,' S. said drowsily, 'how Lord B. would've behaved if he'd been analysed by your Dr L.' The idea amused us a good deal, sitting on the sofa with our drinks. 'But would he've been any happier I wonder?'

'Given the mores of his day, probably not – though he had the money to lead a concealed life if he'd wanted to. In any case there must have been times when he loathed his Countess G., conscious or unconsciously, simply because the poor creature was female.'

'Unless she was a mother-figure, of course,' S. said knowledgeably. 'After all, he didn't have any children by her.'

---

* Peter Quennell (1905–1993) was a biographer, literary historian, editor, essayist, poet, and critic.

'In any case,' I said, 'you enjoyed the book.'

18 July 1960

'I'm afraid of women.'

'Of their sexuality, yes. Your mother's severe rejection of you on the oedipal level.'

19 July 1960

'I'm ashamed of my narcissism,' I told Dr L. 'Afraid that all the time you're despising me for it.'

'Why?'

I couldn't explain. The narcissism was part of the homosexual make-up, I attempted, and as such had been attacked by my father, though he had no conception of its meaning in any such terms. 'He simply regarded me as no good, ineffective, a sissy – no proper son for him to have engendered.'

'Because you didn't want to work with him on the farm?'

'That, partly. But my whole personality was wrong, a mistake, as far as he was concerned.'

'He was blaming you for being the damaged personality you already were, through no fault of your own.'

'I didn't even want to ride a horse,' I brought out, shrinking from memories that scared me with shame. 'Much less to dirty my fingers in labouring on the farm.' I put my hands over my face. 'These things seem so trivial – I hated the smell of sheep, for instance – yet they overwhelmed me with guilt all the years of my childhood. I can't talk of them now without cringing in fear. How did I come to be born in such an environment?' I burst out. 'How, how? Nothing of it was in accord with the real me, nothing at all.'

'You had other qualities.'

'Not strong enough to bolster me or as a basis for fighting my parents, my father, ever. I simply retreated further into my narcissistic ego, trying to make it impregnable against enemies.'

22 July 1960

'Why should I be so afraid of you?' I said.

'Why do you think? Answer carefully.'

'There's something sexual mixed up with it – though I've no idea what. Except that I always imagine you're condemning me for my sexual practices – suckings and lickings – and will punish me.'

'That's simply a rationalisation. Go and suck an elephant if you wish. Nothing wrong in it. The bigger the better.'

The idea seemed wonderful. 'All the same I'm afraid of you. You're going to bust me open – my rectum – something like that.'

'Yes, go on.'

'I put up a terrific resistance against you for it ... Is it against incest? I've nothing against incest as such.'

'Go on. The unconscious –'

'If it's unconscious then I'm fighting you incestuously, on that level. As my father.'

'It *is* unconscious, just as it always was originally, vis-à-vis your father. Also of course in fighting and despising you for your unmanly traits *he* was fighting homosexual feelings towards you in himself.'

'I'm quite certain he never felt them as such!'

'Of course not. They were deeply unconscious too.'

I took all this in slowly. 'I want to love you,' I confessed at what seemed to be a tangent, 'to give you everything, to be accepted – nothing would be better. A longing to be completely passive in your hands, like a child. But not be bust or disintegrated, as I so deeply fear. You're like some immense hostile penis that could split me – and I don't mean rectally –'

'That big penis is inside you already, busting you. Incorporated, as hostile. Think of it –'

'My super-ego?' I suggested.

Dr L. leant forward. 'Yes – now this is an important point for you to understand. Two ideas to connect: the hostile, destructive penis of your father and the incorporated hostile super-ego (which you project on to me, and fear for unconscious reasons) – and the super-ego that is so tyrannical inside you, – the father's penis –'

'A bad object, like the bad breast?'

Dr L. was checked a moment. 'That also. Both of them. But one thing at a time. We're on to a very important point, after all these weary months –'

'I didn't mean to make them weary –'

'Weary for you, not for me, I meant ... But you begin to see now why there's this negative transference (or part of it)? This fear of me, and great resistance? It has a sexual undertone, unconscious – I want you to understand –'

'Don't go too fast. This is new to me, you know.'

'Of course – and rather too much to take in. We'll have to work through it.'

'I was going to say – interpretation's not enough, is it?'

'Not in your case, anyway. Far from it.'

'Then I've got to defy that big cock of yours inside my mind –'

'Defy me, fight me. I'm the big cock. Don't just give in, passively.'

'You won't hurt me?'

'Swear at me for hurting you ... '

We went on. 'This is a very fruitful session,' Dr L. said several times – and, true enough, I felt a sort of reality or validity when we spoke (how shall I put it?) on a sexual level, however unconscious.

27 July 1960

The guest was W., a youngish man who is a child-therapist at an L.C.C. [London County Council] clinic in Middlesex. He is himself also a victim of some deep-seated mental trouble and is having treatment from a Viennese-trained analyst, a woman, to whom he goes for five sessions a week. As fellow-neurotics we of course talk shop: an inescapable social obsession. He began almost as soon as he had sat on my sofa and I'd lit his cigarette for him.

'This masochistic need to suffer – none of us can get round it ... I have physical symptoms all the time ... I think my prostate's enlarged and I get attacks of cystitis without any trace of a cause – at least according to the bloody G.P. I go to.'

'Has he taken tests?'

'He's taken the lot! All negative,' W. said in his soft Scottish accent. 'For months he used to put his big fat finger into my rectum and prod away at the prostate. I had to stop *that* when I found I was enjoying it like mad!'

I asked if his analyst had had any comment. 'She had! She asked me if I was an anal masturbator. All my Edinburgh Puritan reactions rushed out and I said 'No, certainly *not*' in a prim voice, not in the least understanding how one could masturbate anally anyway. She had to explain how the infant retains his faeces out of pleasure of being able to move the mass up and down at will: the sensitive rectum-lining responding with every satisfaction to the stimulus.' W. drank his coffee and began to wolf the sandwiches. 'So then,' he went on, 'I realised I was having a lot of fun under the name of anal masturbation, without knowing I'd practiced a form of it all my life, felt alone in my overt sexual delights. Very shaming, my dear. Especially my ignorance.'

'Did the explanation cure you of prostatitis or whatever it was?' I laughed.

'For a while; then it came back. A libido-fixation of the lowest infantile sort,' W. admitted, 'but dreadfully compulsive. And of course my old Viennese girl plugs away at it now when I'm on the couch. I feel terrible when I think of my age and not being married, you know.' He evidently regretted this fact profoundly, and sighed. 'My super-ego troubles me, there.'

'Mine troubles me too. Same guilt.'

'Both of us, then. I don't need the sex, but the mother ... It's come out in analysis that I was in love with my elder sister – she set the standard for me, emotionally, in my childhood.'

2 August 1960

I returned last night from spending the bank holiday weekend with my sister (Patricia) at Churt in Surrey. 'Do you remember how we used to cry at home when school loomed ahead?' 'I do indeed,' she said grimly. No more than I, I think, does she recollect our childhood with pleasure (she is eight years younger than I). A preoccupied, guarded, defensive tone comes into her voice when we reminisce about New Zealand and our parents. 'I'll never forgive mother,' she once remarked. 'She was beastly to me before I finally left home. Ugh!' And she shuddered. 'Mum's selfish, you know, and protests that she's always loved her children, but she's never loved anyone – least of all Dad. The marriage went wrong from the start.' I agreed. 'I hated going to school,' I said now. 'I used to cry because I was utterly caught in despair between two insecurities – home and school.'

4 August 1960
Went to W.H.'s flat yesterday afternoon and sunbathed with him on his terrace, three floors up and not overlooked by neighbouring windows (the terrace has a view of tree-tops, ponds and a church spire, a view which must be unique in London). W.H. was already lying out on a towel, wearing only a pair of white briefs. I undressed, put on my own bathing-slip and lay back on a long chair. He was going away for a holiday to Menton in the morning, he told me, and would be away for ten days. His rehearsals for a new production – of Wilde's *Importance* – began in a fortnight, and a copy of the play lay beside him on the terrace.

9 August 1960
I began to talk about those two predominantly rational elements that always obsess me in depression: the fact that I have no steady practical job (in my father's constantly reiterated sneers, I am 'a waster') and the fact that, because of my sexual deviation, I have not married. 'The thought of both these failures tortures me – even to confess them to you hurts me –'

'Guilt,' Dr L. intervened.

'Guilt in the highest degree. And a need to be ill, due to guilt,' I added with what I considered a placating honesty. 'I even resent your trying to wean me from my guilt.'

'You realise that unconscious resentment?'

'Oddly enough I do. The need to suffer isn't all that unconscious, whatever Freud declares.' I paused, then launched words at Dr L. belligerently: 'In any case, don't you attempt to push me towards "work" or to marriage either. If you do, I warn you you'll get an unresolvable negative transference. I'd take your exhortations as highly traumatic, in this situation.'

'I wouldn't do any such thing. Certainly not.'

'You might.'

'As regards "work", why does your writing not satisfy you there? After all, you've written many books, you're an artist –'

'None of that would've impressed my father in the least, you see. He always regarded writing as so much playing at life. No occupation at all for a man.'

'And marriage?' Dr L. took up.

I hesitated. 'Marriage is beside the point, in reality-terms. An expedient, as far as I'm concerned –'

'Many of your deviation have married.'

'If ever I do, I must come to it as a matter of free choice – not be driven to it out of guilt, as a neurotic solution –'

'Of course.'

'And not be forced into it to please you.' I finished what began to smell like an argument.

'That's understood,' Dr L. conceded. 'In any case I want you to see that your writing (incidentally a prolonged defecation on your father) and your active homosexuality have been great standbys to your ego: profoundly necessary to its survival in the past ... Any attempt on my part to rob you of either would amount to callous cruelty. I wouldn't do it.'

I felt mollified, lying on the couch with one hand over my face (guilty, even now, despite Dr L.'s benevolent tones). 'You're not foxing me?' I asked.

'Why should I?'

'You see how deeply distrustful I am, still.'

He began to speak of this attitude: the effect on me of my long period of condemnation in childhood – we always come back to that – and how my guilt had been created, engendered, by my parents' guilt towards me, projected as disapproval. 'Your mother's guilt because she felt in herself she had failed to give you something, as she had indeed, and her dissatisfaction with her own love-life in marriage; and your father's guilt because he had castrated you from the first, turning you into less than a man. Both parents took it out on you as a result of their unconscious attitudes – and the experience was utterly too much for your balance. The seeds of your illness were sown. That's why you're here now – forty – fifty years later. You couldn't take the risk of blasting your mother to hell – or of telling your father what an inhuman bully he was.'

'Unthinkable. To me it was always *I* who was wrong: a failure at school, a sissy, a disappointment to everyone – except, probably, to my grandmother. She loved me, or seemed to. My mother's mother, that was, my Uncle B.'s mother.'

'Your Uncle B[ob], who seduced you,' Dr L. observed.

'That's true.' I'd told him of this months ago: a sexually guilt-laden event when I was fourteen, an event which had brought on my first breakdown at school. My Uncle B. had subsequently developed overt schizophrenia and had died many years later in an asylum. 'In my case,' I returned now, 'I have got to continue to express my resentment against you.'

'Every time,' Dr L. concurred and got up, the session over. 'A little at a time, every time. We'll continue on Friday.'

17 August 1960

I felt, as Dr L. had promised, a little stronger after yesterday's outburst; but only a little; the relief didn't last; the despondency and anxiety came sneaking back (a kind of fog that drops a bleak tint over everything, even over food, and that puts a sort of menace into sunlight itself). Those are so often the times when I want to die – when I read in the papers about the death of strangers and say to myself, 'They're at peace, they're out of it, they don't have to contend any longer with – with what? The struggle, I suppose, not to be overcome by the pain of the mind ... Something like that ... ' And I remember my attempt at suicide, three years ago, when I took so many capsules of sodium amytal, not caring whether I ever woke up. But that was before I started going to the hospital or began analysis with Dr L.

(up till then I'd had years of what might be called supportive treatment or 'cosmetic' therapy – most of it superficial and all of it quite ineffective). Well, I still don't know whether I'm any better, however much insight I've gained meanwhile through Dr L. H'm.

19 August 1960

My tremendous guilt over the failure, the progressive shipwreck, of my life since I left Oxford (at the age of twenty-four) – my whole session with Dr L. this morning was concerned with this. Of very deep importance: so much so, that my resistance makes me almost mute when I have to talk about it, to try to explain. Fear and guilt literally stifle me, even when Dr L. intervenes, as he did to-day:

'But thousands upon thousands of young men come down from Oxford and don't find themselves tormented with guilt because they embark on lives of pleasure, autonomous lives, lives devoted to the arts and non-profit-making activities.'

'In England, yes.' Impossible to explain my colonial background by contrast. 'I was brought up in New Zealand,' I said.

30 August 1960

A note from Mrs B., bless her.* I'd seen her on Sunday evening and tried to explain, over coffee and biscuits in her flat, something of my sadness of heart. Subsequently I wrote her a little letter to thank her for her kindness in listening (incidentally I'd given her an outline of my analytic treatment, as I saw it). Her answer reads, in part: 'Does it help you to remember that in spite of this early trauma you own achievement in life is very considerable? And your sympathetic approach to your friends must mean a great deal to them, you know ... I'm sure you are on the verge of a very great relief – so hold on!' A kind woman. Dr L. thinks I ought to marry her, though there's been no emotional exchange between us (her and me, I mean). But marriage, at this stage, would be a neurotic solution.

---

* Margaret Bassett, a close friend who lived in Courage's neighbourhood.

6 September 1960

M. came to see me last night. The usual thing happened. When he told me of his other loves, afterwards, I burst into tears, though he did his best to comfort me ('I've always liked you … you're different from the others … but you needn't be so possessive'). I tried to tell him how hardly these semi-rejection situations bore on me ('childhood memories' etc) but didn't get very far: I couldn't admit to him that I was ill – he might not wish to see me again. He simply knows, from past experience, that I get 'upset' over personal relationships very easily, and ought to have 'more sense' … All the same, he has a Teutonic lack of tact that I find antipathetic, also a kind of grossness or coarseness (he's always wondering why he offends people). Our evening was only a partial success, despite some physical gratification (the entire range of perversion almost).

I had to tell Dr L. all this during our session to-day at the hospital. I showed much guilt.

'Your homosexuality is a block here we haven't yet worked through,' he said. 'It's a big resistance to me: you're so defensive about it.'

'I try not to let it be.'

'You don't really accept your deviation, you see. You may do so intellectually – but not with me –'

'Don't make me feel guiltier than I am,' I burst out. 'How can you do otherwise than condemn me for it – as a psychiatrist you must be against any such pathological aberration, ipso facto.'

'Oh no. For you it's the norm, on the instinctual plane, the sexual plane. I can't condemn you for it – how could I? No, no, of course I couldn't.'

'It's the only gratification I can get. And any love's better than none at all.'

'Of course. And I accept it here. But we'll have to work through your guilty resistance sooner or later. It's most important, a high defence against me … '

8 September 1960

Last night a young man of 27, A.C. by name, arrived to see me, without warning. He was in distress, though he took some time to tell me so and to bring out his reason for calling. In brief he wanted me to tell him how he could arrange for some 'personal analysis', either under the National Health or privately. The question brought back to me my own problems over the same matter, twelve years ago. I told him he could go to his G.P. and get a 'referrer' to the local clinic, as I did, or he could contact a private analyst ('but you must go to a Freudian') and pay for treatment (A.C. told me he had some money due to him and could do this). I asked him about his symptoms and wasn't surprised to find them much the same as mine – depression, much anxiety, homosexual guilt, tension, stomach pains, inadequacy feelings in his job (he's an architect with quite a creditable post in the Office of Works – Historical Monuments section). 'I've known for a long time that I couldn't go on in the "state" I am,' he finished, adding that he'd at last brought himself to the point of coming to me for advice ('you know about these things').

'I'll do all I can to help you,' I told him, and began by giving him a drink and sandwiches. I had an immediate compassionate desire to alleviate his loneliness and pain, to give him love, even to embrace him (yes, and with tenderness). 'I know very well exactly what you're going through,' I assured him. 'A desperate lack of human contact, amongst other things.'

'Yes,' he said, almost in tears.

'Well now, relax. You're safe here.'

He explained that he had been walking about the West End by himself, fighting off the compulsion to pick somebody up for companionship. ('It's for that, more than for sex, though the need for bodily contact is mixed up in it as well. But the kind of pick-up I'd get might be dangerous and wouldn't be more than a temporary solution anyway – however much it seemed to fulfil a need.')

I knew this neurotic need (how well I knew it), and told him so. He brightened under my eyes: a good-looking, thin, attractive boy (less than half my age), with a helm of black hair springing beautifully from a good forehead, rather pale, and with a wide mouth. 'You're not alone in all this,' I assured him, and fought off an impulse to take him in my arms, to comfort him against his fears (and perhaps assuage my own). But to do this would, I knew, be a breach of trust (tantamount to an abuse of transference in analysis) and might add an interpersonal difficulty to his already sore troubles. 'I realise exactly how you feel,' I added and sat fast in my chair facing him across the room (I'd put the portable electric fire between us in case he was cold). 'I'm glad you came to me.'

'There was nobody else I could come to,' he said after a time, reminding me that we'd first met five years ago in T.'s room in Hampstead.

'I thought then what a self-contained person you were,' I remarked.

A.C. smiled ruefully. 'I remember telling you later that I wasn't neurotic,' he said. 'Everyone else was, but I wasn't! How wrong I was.'

'Anyway, you acknowledge it now.'

'I'll go to Dr F. in the morning, first thing, and get a letter. Are you sure he'll be sympathetic?'

'Certain to be,' I said, though I wasn't sure (despite the fact that it was this identical Dr F. who'd once arranged for my initial treatment). 'I remember him, myself.'

A.C. was worried. 'It'll be a strain telling him why I want psychiatric help.'

'Yes. I'll think of you.' (I would indeed.)

'I'll go to the surgery at ten o'clock and see him early, to get it off my chest.'

After a time he said he must go home to write some letters. And nervously, impulsively, he embraced me at the door. 'You've helped me a lot.'

This morning he rang up to say that he'd seen Dr F. and all was well. 'I've got a letter to Dr B. at the hospital, and an appointment in a fortnight.' And he thanked me again, 'I'll let you know what happens. I feel better already.'

19 September 1960

'Your resistance is still high,' Dr L. said calmly. 'Tell me where you consciously identify your resistance.'

'The area where it is highest?'

'Yes.'

'I don't know – about sex, I suppose – I'm overcome with shame there, however much I know I needn't be.'

'Yes,' Dr L. said again, leaning forward. 'If you'd tell me about your sexual fantasies it would encourage the transference. Let us try.'

'Sometimes I've felt it might be a help,' I admitted. 'Just to confess my passivity – acting out a sort of hateful coquettishness towards you – offering my body –'

'Yes, go on.'

I went on. All the perverse fantasies I could think of – excretal and genital. 'These things are part of my mind,' I excused myself, aware of a slight relaxation of my rigid abdominal muscles. 'And I'm sure you don't mind –'

'You must not apologise,' Dr L. impressed it on me 'Say whatever comes to your mind here.'

I delved aloud further into the fantasies – the oral compulsions that emerged as fellatio ...

'The breast,' Dr L. murmured. 'Do not be ashamed.'

The masochistic anal day-dreams ... again and again.

'These derive from infantile experiences and fantasies,' Dr L. absolved me. 'Again, you must not feel guilty of them as an adult.'

'I do, always.'

'The super-ego does. That all-powerful super-ego of yours –'

'Don't you think I *ought* to be ashamed of them?'

'You see,' Dr L. commented at once, 'you are trying to draw me in on the side of your super-ego, against your ego. I will *not* be drawn there: I am an enemy of your condemning conscience ... '

A.C., the lad who came to me for advice about analytic treatment, telephoned last night. He'd been for his first interview at the local clinic, where a woman-doctor had been most helpful and even 'rather impressed because I had some true ideas of therapeutic procedure – thanks to you'.

I've been thinking about this conversation this morning, telling myself that I wish to heaven I'd taken A.C.'s step *when I was his age*. I was deeply frightened, unhappy and bewildered (even then, some of the repressed was pushing up, bent on making a return). I was twenty-eight or nine and had no notion what was wrong with me save that I blamed my homosexuality for most of it. And I was very much alone, having withdrawn myself and being unable to talk to anyone about my emotional troubles. Psychotherapy just did not occur to me (I imagined it dealt only with what I'd now call psychosis). So I began to get lost.

30 September 1960

'This morning I'm going to do a little necessary interpretation. I've put off doing this lately, as you hadn't been well and had had enough to deal with.' He blew his nose and leant forward behind me. 'This resistance and defence of yours,' he said, 'is a sexual resistance against succumbing to me.'

'In the transference?'

'Of course. Even to yourself you won't admit that you want my penis in your rectum.'

'But I have admitted it,' I said uneasily.

'Not with any conviction.'

'No, because I don't see any value in a transference on that basis. Not here.'

'Why not?'

I hesitated. 'Because I'd be passive, not active.'

'But that's your sexual orientation – a masochistic one also, let's admit. You can't help it.'

'You don't blame me?'

'Why should I?'

'Because in such a situation I'd be confessing myself no better than a hysterical woman.'

'You won't accept your feminine deviation, will you! You're so diffident about these sexual questions.'

'It's very hard for me and always has been,' I reminded him.

'There you have two components of much of your difficulty,' Dr L. said. 'The father whose cock you want and won't admit to wanting – and the hostile, cruel father who is your super-ego and against whom I'm always trying to get you to rebel here.'

I became confused, lost in a sort of fog. 'You mean,' I clutched at sense presently, 'I can come along here and say to myself "I can grasp that great big comforting cock and it'll be all right"?'

'Why not?'

'Because in actual fact you won't give it to me, you can't in this clinical situation.'

'That doesn't prevent your wanting it. And you can and must abuse me when you don't get it.'

I held myself taut on the couch. 'It's quite true,' I admitted. 'If I could come here feeling there was some sexual bond – a secret love – between us I'd feel a much surer foundation of confidence and trust than I ever do now. I could hold on to that big cock to save myself.'

'Of course. The cock is a breast also.'

I waited a moment, confused again. 'I'd certainly feel a warmth,' I admitted, 'even a kind of love for you then. I mean the love would rise out of being allowed to feel passive to you here, without shame. I could accept my need.'

'Why is it so hard to accept – why is it productive of so much resistance and defence?' Dr L. returned. 'Why?'

'You know very well,' I countered. And presently I rushed into confession: 'I'll tell you something – it's only when I've sensed some inkling of love *from you* here, in the past, that I've known a relief from anxiety. But always I've got to sense that loving attitude *first* – your counter-transference, if you like – before I can respond. It's like a tentative sexual approach on your side which makes me feel valuable, lovable, desirable ...'

Dr L. waited in silence, listening.

'You must have a tricky time keeping track of your counter-transferences,' I relieved my tension by saying. Dr L. gave a grunt of disconcerted laughter, then remarked: 'I do my best.'

'You'd better!' I said. 'And don't you lose sight of the counter-transference in my case! It's too important to me. Absolutely essential.'

We went back to the main subject, or rather I took up again, with more self-tolerance, the idea that the transference could be valid on a passive basis – i.e. that I was allowed to build up a rapport with Dr L. on an implicit homosexual love-feeling (not so implicit, either). For the rest of the session we discussed our relationship, with a good deal of sexual detail. (I've given above only a sketch of our conversation. In actual fact many of my remarks were repetitive, obscene and remonstrative, going over the same ground again and again to reassure myself that I understood Dr L.)

1 October 1960
The improvement I felt after yesterday's session – and it was a real gain in confidence – did not last over this morning. It began to seem a delusion. The underlying anxiety is too great to be so easily dispelled.

3 October 1960
Dr L. leant forward. 'Well now, you know that over the past few months I've been trying to exploit the negative transference here – trying to get you to attack me. I want you to go on doing that.'

'On the excuse that you're refusing me sexual contact?'

'Just say what you feel. But I'd like it to be active – verbal eroticism. You're f—g me, not me you.'

'No,' I said, 'that's just where I fail. I want to remain in a passive state to you: I'm safer there ... You've got to let me stay like that,' I begged. "till I gain a little strength from feeling I'm safe in such a love-situation. You mustn't rush me ahead. I'm weak.'

After a moment Dr L. said: 'This passivity, you see, has been the bane of your life – and of your sexual role, of course. Always your passivity, your masochism.'

'It was a natural development,' I argued, 'from what happened to me very early on: my aggression never got a proper start, through no fault of my own.'

'True enough.'

'Well then –'

'But there are homosexuals who are pugnacious, sadistic,' Dr L. reminded me. 'That's the other side, which I want to encourage. The combative urge.'

I felt nothing of such an urge, I told him.

'You do feel a little of it. In fantasy.' He said. 'You've told me so.'

'Well, my fantasies are different now. I want to stay passive here – to extract love from you on that level.'

'Because you've had so little love in the past,' Dr L. told me with cruel truth. 'Now you want love, tenderness, consideration – as well as the erotic satisfaction.'

4 October 1960

'Oh, and another memory – the anxiety I always felt at having to go to bed. My mother would say goodnight to me in the drawing-room before dinner – the last time I saw her for the day – then the nurse would whisk me upstairs and into what was a perpetual evening nightmare: lying alone, the nurse gone and my mother out of reach ... Stark panic, as I remember it.'

'What age would you be then?'

'Two to four, about. Are such incidents important?'

'Indeed. But your mother's general inadequacy of response was more important still. Her selfishness.'

'I remember that cold face,' I said in fear.

'Precisely. A cold face that did too much to you – it castrated you, robbed you of half your power.' Dr L. leant forward behind me. 'Now do you see why you never developed the aggression, the genital drive you ought to have had? It was all inhibited, resulting in a failure of development – a fixation – a regression, not a progression.'

5 October 1960

What am I so guilty of when I'm Dr L's presence? The answer always seems to amount to the original accusations flung at me by my father – that I was a waster, that I ran away from helping him on the farm (as the eldest son of a farmer my obligation was to succeed him), that I was no *man* but an effeminate mistake (though I am not overtly, in the least, effeminate), that I concerned myself with 'artistic' flummery with no importance and certainly of no money-value, that I'd never be able to support myself in adult life. And so on, interminably. I had no armour against these onslaughts, except to retreat despairingly into myself. From the age of five (and following on what I now see as my mother's rejection) until the age of nineteen I was never once off the defensive, in this fashion: determined to protect myself, distrusting others, obsessed with an underlying inferiority (made worse by long persecution at a brutal school and by a growing realisation that my homosexuality was reprehensible, a matter of taboo as something unnatural, guilty, unthinkable) ... Is it small wonder that I now project all these outside hostilities of attitude on to Dr L. or that my power to fight him is so puny and inhibited? The wonder is rather that I can stand up to him at all and am not more crushed than I am in the face of my involuntary embodiment of these persecutors out of the past.

7 October 1960

I went on to tell him I'd had a letter from a stranger who wrote glowingly about my last book: 'It is certainly the best homosexual novel of our epoch – great courage and ethical integrity', and so on.

'Yes,' Dr L. said. 'Well, that was gratifying.'

'I may have considerable reservations about such praise,' I laughed, 'but it helped my ego to feel that *somebody* felt that way. For a few minutes I'd actually defeated my father.'

11 October 1960

'The resistance always seems to spring from one fact: my guilt about my homosexuality.' I trembled.

'Even now?'

'Very much so. All the oral and anal acts involved – the sucking, licking, biting. Even my queer fantasies I tend to hide from you, out of guilt.'

'But these things – these acts – are as "natural" to you as is normal sex to a heterosexual. No less, no more.'

'I wish I could accept that.' I waited. 'You know, when I had that good period a week or more ago, I think it arose because for once I felt guiltless, sexually, with you. I needn't defend myself any longer. What chance of survival would I have had in a hostile world? None at all, without money, security, confidence – just what I didn't possess.'

'Indeed,' Dr L. admitted thoughtfully. 'Go on.'

'No-one would've supported me, except possibly my grandmother – the only person I felt loved me for myself. And her I hardly saw. She lived in the mountains, a hundred miles away from the farm. And after her son, my uncle, had seduced me – and had been found out – how could I appeal to her? My guilt inhibited me, though the seduction wasn't really my fault.'

'No,' Dr L. said.

'Do you know what my uncle called me? I was this timid boy – delicate and small even at fourteen – and he called me "White Mouse". He seduced me in a cave, a limestone cave. I was terrified. For six months afterwards I lived on the verge of a breakdown, then collapsed at school. But I couldn't tell anyone *why*. I thought I'd go to prison, be hung.'*

'Who "found out" your uncle's seduction of you?'

'The tutor who was teaching him at home. My uncle was about nineteen or twenty at the time, only five years older than I ... Is this all important?'

'If you feel it important to you,' Dr L. said.

'I do, because it confirmed my guilt at a critical age ... It castrated me even more emphatically than my mother had done, and made me even more guilty in my father's eyes (though he didn't know of the seduction).'

---

* Courage's uncle influenced the character of lighthouse keeper Mark in *The Young Have Secrets*. On page 177 he told Walter, 'You sit there like a mouse – a white mouse – and listen to your elders.'

17 October 1960

'When I'm in bed with another man it's always his cock I find the greatest comfort but somehow it is not his cock I seek and worship, it's my own, transferred.'

'Unconsciously it is your own,' Dr L said. 'That's just it. The homosexuality is a narcissism, erotically transferred to another man's body.'

7 November 1960

A strange episode last night, the very measure of my regression. I went to see Mrs B. and cried in her arms. My isolation and insecurity had become altogether too much for me to bear alone, after a dreadful day. She was very kind, let me clasp her against me, stroked my hair and shoulder, kissed me on the forehead. It was a coming-home, of a kind.

'You see what an unloving mother did to me,' I tried to explain, my head in her arms (she sat on top of a table by the fire, with me on a low chair). 'You're very good.'

'Not wholly good. I'm often selfish.'

'I've never broken down like this before, not with a woman.'

She comforted me, my tears falling on her dress and wrists. It was a great relief to me to give way, to feel I was a child again, to be soothed maternally. Yet I was ashamed of my weakness. 'You mustn't let this embarrass you,' I brought out.

'It doesn't. I don't know sometimes how you manage to carry on. So unhappy.'

'I've been in an unbearable state these last few days. Partly the analysis – it's raised up all my childhood anxiety and despair and they won't rest.' How I could I tell her? 'I go about with a void inside me ... No help, no love ... Just what I felt as a kid, only worse because I'm not a kid any longer.'

She let me cry for a long time, holding me while I trembled. I was afraid she would cast me off; I had to give a stumbled explanation about wanting 'the good mother' but being afraid of further relationship. 'The sexual side is always so difficult for me,' I said, against her breast. 'It has never worked out.'

She did not answer directly. 'You know, you're a valuable person,' she said. 'You're very human – people like you – and I respect you – I feel affection for you.'

'Dear Margaret ... ' I broke down again. 'This isn't fair of me, but I can't help it.'

'Why isn't it fair?'

'I don't know – it puts an obligation on you somehow.'

She said something about not being a young woman (I think she is a few years younger than I). 'I've had two husbands, you know.'

'Yes.'

'And I've got a son.'

'I feel jealous of him.'

She kissed me on the forehead. 'You mustn't.'

Later we sat in separate chairs and talked of other things for half an hour. Then I had to go.

'Bless you and thank you,' I said, holding her against me. 'I mean for letting me cry.'

'I'll be in to-morrow evening. I get back from the office about six ... '

I kept waking up in the night and making sounds like a child. Groans also. What had I done? Given way to a tenderness I felt ashamed of because in my childhood, there had been a taboo on tenderness? I've no conscious memory of my mother holding me or of her ever kissing me. But I had wanted both, so much. And now I had given way, I thought, with an odd feeling of shame, reproach and fear. The feeling still persisted this morning.

16 November 1960

My dentist asked me yesterday in confidence:

'Tell me, what is this four letter word that has been causing such trouble in the *Lady Chatterley* case?'*

---

* In 1960 Penguin Books was tried, under the 1959 Obscene Publications Act, for publishing an unexpurgated paperback edition of D.H. Lawrence's novel *Lady Chatterley's Lover*. The publisher was acquitted.

'F-U-C-K,' I spelt out for him.

'Well, but every schoolboy knows that one,' he said. 'I thought it might have been C-U-N-T.'

'That also of course. Also S-H-I-T and A-R-S-E.'

He seemed gratified at hearing the worst. 'Absurd,' he said all the same. 'They mean so little, except when they're written down. They're just names for things everyone has in his mind.'

'Particularly in analysis,' I remarked. 'Though you might not know about that. Or not much.'

'I don't. But what Puritans the English are.'

He went on with his work, but a little more gaily than before, almost light-heartedly, as though wanting to whistle a tune. The release of having had a mild sex-talk (in the absence of his secretary, by the way) had given him quite a fillip. I had the feeling too that most of his patients must be women, of whom no such questions concerning Lady Chatterley could be asked. I was even flattered that he'd asked me to explain something, one man to another.

'I'm Irish,' he said, intent on fitting my dental plate which had become loose. 'Like Oscar Wilde and Bernard Shaw,' he added, and went on: 'How Shaw would have laughed over a harmless decision about printing the word fuck in an English book.'

18 November 1960

'I can't be aggressive.' And I switched to telling him that my feelings for Mrs B. had certainly some slight twinge of aggressive-heterosexual instinct.

'Yes,' he took up with interest. 'A little genital urge, I think.'

'Vestigal, anyway ... When I was in my teens I had some dealings with girls – I've never told you this. I used to kiss them and hold them, but I hadn't any real cock-feeling, and no erection.'

'No,' Dr L. accepted.

'It was all a try-on – all the other boys were at it too, and I had to conform, even outdo them.' I thought of dances, letters, sittings on beds with pink girls. 'Thank God I didn't marry one of them – it would certainly've been a tragedy.'

'Your ego preserved you there.'

24 November 1960

'I hope you're writing a new book,' Miss W. said to me at the end of the interview at Cape's yesterday afternoon. 'No,' I said, embarrassed by the question. 'Or only notes for a book, not a novel.' My conscience had insisted that I answer *something*, that I mustn't seem idle, but I could not confess that I was writing unpublishable notes on a mental illness. It was an effort to talk to Mr R.D., the editor who had the manuscript of my novel in front of him and who asked me about points of punctuation and phrasing. I wanted to leave everything to R.D. and Miss W. (a young woman, thin, dressed in black, her eyes lengthened with dark pencil). They could settle it all: I couldn't really care. So I agreed to Miss W. doing certain revisions. 'All right,' I said. 'You do the changes for me.' She and R.D. complimented me on the book, which had (or seemed have) aroused much interest and sympathetic feeling ('We're tired of angry young men as heroes'). I said 'Thank you' in an automatic way.

In the evening I was very unhappy again – I even rang up my neighbour overhead (Miss F.) to ask if I could come up and talk. She had gone to bed (and told me 'I didn't sound very well'). I went out to post a letter and saw – yes, this was a blow – saw *my Mrs B.* with her arm linked with that of a middle-aged man I didn't know. We just greeted one another in passing, but my heart was hurt; my foster-mother was being unfaithful. Masochistically I shut myself in my shell and cried.

3 December 1960

S. was here last evening. We talked of our problems, over the usual glass of whiskey. He has much of my own troubles, fears, panics, dread of the future but his aggression is much healthier than mine (he works it off in militant trade union activities) and he has very little of my frightful superego. 'I would really like to have been a whore,' he tells me, with much regret for the past. 'If somebody bold and uninhibited had seduced me good and proper when I was twenty – who knows?' He goes into day-dreams of promiscuous experiences with blond, slim young men – all of whom would have made him extremely unhappy and inflamed his neurosis. I told him so and he eventually agreed.

'One always imagines sex is the answer,' he sighed. 'It isn't of course ... I was a long time in finding out my mistake. But half these kids I meet now are still in the fantasy stage I was. I'm sorry for them, poor young bastards.'

7 December 1960

I have many friends. I have my sexual relation with S. I have my filial relation with Mrs B. – more, in fact, than have many neurotics in my state.

7 December 1960

To dinner last night with Mrs B. I was withdrawn to begin with but gradually thawed over the meal. I took her a bunch of violets, a present to my foster-mother. My heart sank, however, when she told me her real son (aged 26) was due to arrive for coffee. I had not met him before and was vaguely jealous and apprehensive. His name is J.

He arrived at nine, having come through the fog carrying a suitcase full of liquor 'for Christmas'. He did not kiss his mother, in fact their greeting seemed casual, rather impersonal though good-natured. His attitude to me was well-controlled, I thought, rather than cordial. He rather baffled me, like a big selfish handsome dog. I made futile attempts to analyse him as he talked. The voice had curious 'common' Army overtones or inflections. The physique excellent, broad in the shoulders, slim, compact. But the face, with its square regular features, was not really as pleasant as it ought to have been: the eyes and mouth cruel, rather predatory, the little moustache a conceit. His manner had great or apparent self-assurance. Yet I was convinced there was a weakness.

'I do hope I haven't made him afraid of women,' his mother said when he had gone (I stayed on for ½ hour). I knew what she meant. 'There was a female in his office who pursued him,' she added. 'I met her and found her impossible.'

'Why impossible?'

'Nine years older than he – and *impossible*, although she knitted him pullovers. But she's fading out of the picture now.'

'No younger women?'

'None that I can see or hear of, though at 26 you'd think he would have found *somebody*. All the girls he used to be so gallant with are married now.'

Yes, I thought, there's trouble somewhere, but I couldn't expound it to her or define it in psychological terms. Was J. homosexual? I could see no evidence of this, but there are types who betray nothing, even to another homosexual: they are not true inverts. Perhaps infanto-homosexuals? Perhaps the type whose sex-partner is 'normal' – except that there must be a penis in place of a vagina, due to early shock? I don't know. So I said nothing to Mrs B. about my suspicions.

'You've got a big son of your own,' I said teasingly when I kissed her a foster-son's 'good night' on the cheek. The soft skin made me think I was kissing my mother – yet there was a faint stirring of sexual feeling also, unless I deceive myself.

15 December 1960

After a depressed day yesterday I went out to a small party given by B. and R., a 'queer' gathering of seven or eight. I lost some of my depression simply by talking, and was helped by an attitude of respect on the part of the younger guests towards me as a writer. One young man (Nicholas by name) praised two of my books, particularly the last (*A Way of Love*), which he had recommended to his friends with gratifying results ('they were impressed'). My ego expanded, helped thus from without against the superego's cruelty within. For a time I became human, even warm: I could feel at ease, my muscles relaxed, I talked naturally ... Another guest (G.) was carrying a rubber bottle with a glass nozzle, in his hand. Seeing him sniffing at the nozzle I asked him the reason. He had asthma, which he thought was 'nervous in origin'. He asked my opinion.

'How long have you had it?'

High Street
Princes Risborough
Buckinghamshire.

December 29th 59

Dear Mr Courage
        I have rarely enjoyed a book so beautiful as "A Way of Love".
It is with a heavy heart that I have come to the last page - but this
novel will rest in my bookcase, a friend, a leaning post in times of
stress.
        Thank you for the pleasure you have given me.   The book is
beautifully written - never to be forgotten.

                Sincerely,

                Leslie Hermon

                Leslie Hermon

A letter of appreciation from a fan. *S20-542c, MS-0999/118, Hocken Collections*

'Oh since I was ten or so. I don't know why.'

'According to some psychiatrists,' I suggested, 'asthmatic symptoms amount to a suppressed cry for the mother!' I pointed to the nozzle. 'You're carrying your mother about with you.'

He laughed, with high scorn, as at a rather malicious joke aimed at his self-respect. Yet a few minutes earlier he had been attacking R.F. (in absence) for indulging in alcoholic bouts because of despair: 'What's he got to worry about? He's in a good job and he's young ...' No conception of R.F.'s very severe neurotic pattern, which is killing him and is not being treated analytically. No compassion, either. In fact, complete and hostile ignorance of 'psychology'. Sad and terrible in a man of G.'s age (forty to forty-five). He looks like a rather faded baby, with gray-blond curls and fair skin.

11 January 1961

My father was a hard, selfish, condemning swine, with almost no friends – and that's the truth. He was an uncultured, sneering, ignorant, provincial New Zealand farmer whom I saw as my enemy (and unfortunately internalised as such), the enemy of my sensibility, my tenderest feelings, the values I valued – all my little artistic leanings, my inarticulate puttings-forth towards poetry, my terrified shy hunger for evidences of love from my environment (and God knows I got few enough) ... My bad father remains an internal tormentor – and whether I call him conscience or superego matters not. He is anti-me, anti-life, anti-love. He deserves only the hell he has given me.

Have I exaggerated my father's character here? No, I don't think so. With the exception of my eldest sister, my brothers and sisters considered the old man was a tyrant, a bad-tempered unsympathetic monster, to be spoken of only with a half-apologetic laugh (as though he were listening). Even Patricia, my mildest sibling, once said, on looking at a photograph of the N.Z. homestead, the hills, the scene of our childhood: 'You know, it could all have been quite beautiful if it hadn't been for those old devils Dad and Mum. They spoiled it for us, our parents.'

21 January 1961

I should have adopted Dr L., as a corrective-good-parent, when I was in my early twenties. I could then have *lived* my life more effectively instead of being lived by it – or rather by neurosis, anxiety, panic, despair. I ought to have begun treatment when, on coming down from Oxford, I tried to face the responsibility of adult existence with what I now see to have amounted to an infantile incapacity to do so, a psychic paralysis almost, anyway an illness of mind. I should have put myself under psychotherapy *then*. Such an idea, however, never once occurred to me: I knew nothing of psychiatry (except that I assumed it dealt with 'mad' persons, quite unlike my precious self). Nevertheless, as I know now, the state of psychological theory and of clinical practice was at that date relatively primitive, based on the earlier Freudian discoveries. The English school, and Kleinian concepts, arrived later in history. Assuming I had been 'treated', the analysis would have been in Oedipal terms and, as such, a whole or partial failure. Masochistic obstructions would hardly have been recognised, I think. Yet I might still have gained something – some sense of rapport with an impartial human being, some conviction that my guilt was not as inevitable and crushing as it seemed, some psychological perspective on my 'queerness'. Who knows?

8 February 1961

I am whistling a little tune, to keep up my spirits. The underlying anxiety keeps coming back, like pains (and I have pains in my belly and bowels this morning). And I keep thinking of Dr L., a saving figure in the present, somebody behind me, kind and just, an ideal parent.

'I love the man, I love him,' I said aloud to myself at one point this morning. And I felt the spontaneous words to be true and full of longing and tears. Nobody else in my life has ever had this validity for me, or has even approached it. He has not, I tell myself, thrown me over: he has patiently endured my torments of childlike fear and recrimination. He is still there, leaning forward at my shoulder to point out the terrible relevance of the past. What can I feel but gratitude to an ally who has defined the undefined demons that have threatened my life with collapse and dementia? Whether I can call my resultant response 'love' or transference does not matter.

23 February 1961

Saw my Mrs B. last night and was affectionate with her, calling her 'chicky' and 'darling' rather self-consciously and adopting a protective manly attitude that rather surprises me. When I'm with her I have a sense of security, a kind of peace even (for a while). Last night she told me how she was recurrently seeking a kind of pattern in her life, that was always getting disrupted or out of true in some way. The pattern was broken or shaken by 'frivolous' non-integrating factors like social parties and too much work that did not personally involve her interests (I fancy her job came in here). She could never quite consolidate her pattern-in-embryo, so to speak.

'You and I had better take a flat together and look after one another,' I heard myself suggest, not quite seriously, at one point. 'Your life is too public and mine's too private.'

'We'd have to balance them out,' she said, but speculatively, as though only a remote hypothesis which I couldn't interpret as encouragement. In fact the flat idea was dropped, though I wondered whether I had sown a seed that she would wake in the night and think about. I want to be 'of consequence' to somebody, a protective figure, a mother. But I am so afraid, always, and the alteration in my life frightens me in prospect, throws me into conflict. Irreconcilable aims, in every direction.

4 June 1961

Worry, not least about the situation last night with S. He said he wanted us to relinquish (anyway for a while) our more intimate relationship: 'If you don't mind.'

'Of course I mind. Very much,' I retorted.

'It's not you, and not your fault. It's in me. This passive sexual business gives me such conflict. Not at the time – I enjoy it – but later, when I'm calm.'

'Yes.' I've known this for some time, and have even explained it to him (analysis of infantile sado-masochism, etc, and his being put in a resented passive role, etc). 'This was bound to happen, though I'm not going to accept it myself masochistically, as a rejection' (all the same I was doing just that, inside). 'I'll hate losing our good times,' I added.

'It's my aggression that the trouble. It's been coming out lately, perhaps as a result of analysis. Anyway I don't want us, you and me, to end in a blazing row. We've far too much in common, to finish as enemies. I must tell you all this –'

'Yes, it is better to,' I said. 'But I'm sad, all the same.'

'You mustn't take it as personal –'

'Well, it makes me think I'm a bad lover.'

'No, nothing like that,' he broke in. 'But I don't want any sex for a while, with *anyone*. I'm in a chaotic state – a stage of my treatment, I suppose – and I want to be surer where I'm going. I mean, whether I want to be passive or active, or just opt out of sex altogether.'

'Yes,' I said. 'That could happen, for you.'

'Could it?' I think he was surprised at such an abandonment of object-relations on his part.

'It could happen,' I repeated. 'Though analysis should be working just the opposite way, for you, after all. I mean, towards improvement and consolidation of psychosexual bonds. No narcissistic withdrawal.' (I heard myself describing my own dilemma.) Surely you see that?'

'Yes,' S. meditated. 'But I've got to struggle through it myself, with my chap.'

We went on talking. But inside me I was sad, as I'd told him. My liaison with S. has meant a lot to me over four or five years and I'm grateful to him. Very grateful. And something within me kept saying, 'This is your last explicit affair – there'll be nobody else. Anything sexual from now on will be different for you.' How could I not be sad and in fear? Loss of a link, loss of libido, shadow of a lifetime of inhibited and imperfect relationships. Yes, it hurts and dismays me.

All the same, I'm fonder of S. than of anyone, and I must consider his feelings, his own neurotic entanglements, his own struggle to sort out his own severe conflicts. In fact, it is only because I'm under treatment myself that I can understand what his mechanisms are. Otherwise, we might well end, S. and I, in that 'blazing row' – an explosion of mutual rejection-resentments – which he's anxious to avoid (and so am I, even more so) … Curiously enough I feel something like love for him – perhaps more so now than ever before.

In the evening S. came here. A khaki shirt, open because of the heat: a torso like a labourer's. For once he was not ambivalent about wanting sex. We went to bed.

Better for him than for me. I had to summon ten workman-fantasies to achieve an end. Not very successful. But S. was more potent than for a long while: 'I just am that way tonight. It must be the hot weather.'

We smoked cigarettes in bed afterwards. 'I wonder what lovers used before cigarettes were invented,' S. remarked.

'They had their little lamps – Psyche and Eros – to reveal themselves in the dark.'

'H'm, not very satisfactory,' said S., not much given to poetic overtones. 'Messy too.' He smoked his cigarette. 'You know, *this* ought to be the answer – lying here in peace. If one had this every night … but it doesn't work out … one has too much withdrawal … what you call a failure of object-relationships. But, to live with another man would be – what? –'

'A nice breach of the law, for one thing,' I joked.

'I wasn't thinking of that …'

I kissed his belly and genitals – 'One of the best local views, down there' – and got up to wash. 'Why aren't you always like this?' I asked later. 'I mean why don't you want sex more often?'

'All you think of is my body,' he mocked.

'Nothing of the sort, you exasperating bastard.'

A playful scrimmage – yes, at my age – ensued. 'You'd better go home,' I said.

'Want to turn me out, do you?'
'Stop it, be yourself!'
'You know I don't mean it.'
He left at midnight.

1961–1962

4 November 1961

Letter from Frank Fleet, from Buenos Aires, yesterday. More than 30 years since our affair, yet we still write (I'd written to him for his birthday on October 10th). 'One loves but once and that for the first time' – yes, but I remember only too well the psychic disturbances the whole thing caused me: the guilt and the infantile dependence I showed (though I didn't recognise the source then), the mad hunger for love, which he couldn't ever fill, and so on. I was pretty ill at the time, though my defences hadn't broken down as they did later. I had near black-outs (and no idea that psychiatry would have an explanation), particularly on the sea-voyage to S. America. Frank was more stable than I, outwardly at least. He had some intention of marrying and carried it out four years or so later. Now he's not only a father but a grandfather. Yet he has an alter ego (or rather an alter id) which has been very largely mine over the years. The private life, in a separate compartment from wife and children: in many ways his real life. I think he has suffered much from the division, having often spoken to me in letters of his 'deadness of emotion', his 'philosophical attempts at acceptance', his 'stoic rigidity' and so on. I advised him, six years ago, to have analytic treatment but (out of fear that 'people would know') he did not have it. And now I imagine he never will.

I believe his life to have been much happier than my own – though he regards mine as a successful accomplishment ('you haven't given in' – he meant to the limitations of the passive – 'you've become something'). He has a wealthy wife, a home etc – far more of an 'accomplishment' than my books, from the psychic point of view. He has in fact made a better compromise with neurosis than I have (I doubt if he even recognises himself as neurotic, merely as difficult). His wife loves him jealously (she calls him Bunny and will hardly let him out of her sight). As far as I know she has no inkling of his homosexuality: in fact she regards his sexual tepidity as a sign of spiritual worth, sensibility, higher organisation than other husbands, and so on. True of course but based on false or at least unperceived reasons (the cart before the very big horse). I could tell her that Frank had great potency and considerable emotional heat in his true direction (that it is and was his true direction I've no doubt: his confession to me that only with a male love-partner was he unreserved, that he couldn't give himself emotionally to a woman, try as he might, was indicative of much). So, in Freudian terms, his libido is as thwarted as mine, though in a different way.

14 November 1961

A fan-letter for me this morning. Two foolscap pages in large rather characterless hand from a man, age unknown, who describes himself as a Display Artist. He has read all my books but writes about the queer one: 'It's difficult to express appreciation of such a fine work, indeed almost impossible ... I like everything about this book ... I like the brevity of your descriptions, terse and vivid, conveying exactly what is required ... and the admirable treatment, sensitively handled with tender intimacy. It's so human. You have given life and compassion to a story which *could* have become a bawdy sensational theme ... Each time of reading only convinces me more of your talents as a most skilled and accomplished writer ...' And so on.

The address is Invercargill, though I can only guess that this is the N.Z. town I once visited at the age of nineteen or twenty (and a dreary place it was). The air-mail envelope has neither stamp (N.Z.) nor postmark. Cape forwarded the letter, having (I deduce) put on the English stamp (which remained unfranked, thus only confusing me more). The postman did not collect a surcharge, at least not from me, and there's no Postage Due stamp. A fine puzzle. The letter *could* have come from Scotland, but in that case the airmail envelope was not necessary – and is there a Scottish Invercargill, anyway? It doesn't matter, except that I feel I must acknowledge such a welcome blast of praise.

To return to the fan-letter. Of course I lap up these saucerfuls of praise out of the blue. They nourish my ego's anaemic fortitude, and the more lavish they are in adjectives the better. But one curious fact upsets me all the same: these fan-letter-writers all have, in my case, some more or less evident kink (e.g. to-day's lies in the lack of stamps and proper address – as though there were an unexpressed grudge behind the admiration – a craving to get something as well as give it. I've noticed this before.) Of course the theme of the queer book was in itself an invitation to the lonely, the kinky and the inverted to send me cris de coeur [cries from the heart] – and that is what has certainly happened. But I do wish a few of the more normal would also write, occasionally. Their praise wouldn't have me making such allowances against my pleasure in their letters as such.

Fan-letter again. 'Over two years ago I suddenly discovered you as an author ...' The word 'suddenly' pulled me up. I could – but won't – postulate situations of discovery. Well, at least I am read; somebody reads me: thus giving substance to a thought that often occurs – 'Who, in the world, is at this instant reading a book of mine, and what is he/she thinking?' I suppose this happens to every writer – or at least to those whose work isn't strongly popular in tone. One wants to know who one's readers are, why they read novels, and so forth. And the disapproving ones, the hostile ones – what goes on in their minds? Do they give up in the middle of the book, with bouts of sickness, headache, etc? Vaguely one wishes they did. Better that than indifference: 'I don't care for his books,' as they turn on the wireless instead or make a cup of tea as a relief. Luckily they don't often write letters of complaint or hatred – at least they don't to me (I've had only one such letter in ten years – from a woman, about *The Young Have Secrets*).

15 November 1961
The N.Z. interviewer, Mr R., turned up to see me yesterday afternoon, so arranged by telephone. Very much a man's man, thick black eyebrows, solid body, not unattractive in a rather coarse-fibred fashion. His father taught me history and maths at College ('The only master in that ghastly place with

a sense of humour,' I told him yesterday. He was taken aback, obviously, by this view of his Dad – and to be frank, Dad was a rattish man, suspected of randiness on the rumour of having begotten ten children somewhere in the poorer suburbs. My remark was a form of ingratiation for which I despised myself.) I sat Mr R. on the sofa and gave him tea while he asked me questions – or rather switched the conversation back to questions, when it grew too dispersed. He made pencilled notes in his reporter's book, asking me about my novels and stories. No very personal queries. My life-story appeared, I suspect, rather odd to him, nevertheless. I was resolved, however, not to bring in the extenuating dimension of neurosis, since this would have meant nothing to him (a married man with a son and a successful career in journalism). Instead I did my best to talk lightly, to engage his interest without solemnity – a kind of ironical detachment of which I was not very happily conscious. I could see that this approach worked best for me, all the same.

'Now what about inspiration?' he asked, poised.

'I'm wary of the word, in a literary sense. Inspiration of a sort is fine, but what counts in the result is perspiration – the effort of working-out in words over a longish period.'

He made his notes, a little at odds ('I'm not a literary chap and haven't read your books'). 'Thank you. Yes, a second cup of tea – nice of you to take the trouble.' And he added: 'An interview in such a relaxed atmosphere is always much easier for me, you understand –'

'I can't imagine that anything I've told you will be of vast interest to syndicated press readers. I'm a most untypical New Zealander (as much so as Patrick White is an untypical writer in Australia) –'*

'Yes, but I think all this will shape into a nice little story. I'll write it up and read it over to you on the phone to-morrow if you like.'

---

*   Australian writer Patrick White (1912–1990), a novelist, short-story writer and playwright, won the Nobel Prize in Literature in 1973. From 1941 until his death he lived with his male partner Manoly Lascaris.

He rang up at 9.30 to-day and having thanked me again for the tea, rehearsed his piece. It came out surprisingly glib. Apparently I am 'a man of great personality and charm, who tends to be whimsical about his writing. Not inspiration but perspiration is his line ...' and so on. H'm. I feel a fraud and rather a shallow kind of playboy, caught in such an incarnation. And what an article I could perpetrate about myself: the 'personality' and awful 'charm' would be revealed as neurotic defences for a harassed ego – a facetious mask for passive masochistic fears of rejection by a stronger man (Mr R.). In a word, it is all false, my attitude, so neurotically conditioned, that I sweat with shame in its contemplation. I took in Mr R. thoroughly, I can see. But –

'Yes,' I said on the phone. 'You've got it all in beautifully. Thank you.'

'I'll send you a cutting when it comes out.'

'Do – if the editor uses it, that is.'

I could hear that I'd implanted a professional doubt he found chilling. However, the conversation ended most amicably. In fact I'm not a little surprised, considering my abnormal state, that I got through as normally as I did (without, that is, having used any alibis of illness to exonerate myself before Mr R.). The depersonalisation technique of irony as a standby. Despicable but useful. 'Charm' as an overdraft, etc. As for 'whimsy' – ush.

21 December 1961

To Mrs B.'s last night, bearing a box of Fortnum's soft-centre chocolates (her teeth are as rocky as mine). No reciprocative gift, I noticed. In fact I had a suspicion she was glad I hadn't asked her to see me over Christmas: I am difficult to mix with her other friends, creating a social block of which I'm most unhappily conscious (the neighbours' child who simply will not play at the party). Anyway we had coffee and talked. I had moments of boredom, even of an odd disassociation on a depressive base. What was I to chat about? Large areas of my private life are forbidden ground. My queer friends etc.

10 January 1962

A telephone call last night from an unknown young man (a teacher of French, he said, to boys of 11 to 16 in a secondary school at Bushey), who wanted to tell me how identical his life and circumstances were to the lad named Philip in *A Way of Love*.

Myself: 'I hope you don't for that reason take the book as a libellous statement.'

'Oh no, nothing like that; but I was astounded when I came across it (in the Public Library). I felt I was reading about my own life ... I even know somebody named Bruce ...'

'Well, it was kind of you to ring and tell me,' I said, at a loss and feeling something was expected on my side.

'I looked you up in *Who's Who* and found your number. I hope I haven't disturbed you?'

'Not at all ... Are you happy as a teacher?'

'Fairly, yes. I'm living in rooms ... I'll ring you again some time.' A nice, slightly provincial voice.

I should find all this flattering and in a sense I do. But the fact of having written books and receiving such phone-calls counts not at all against the constant damnation of the superego. It hates me implacably as a writer (a profession denigrated & scorned by my father as playing at the serious business of life – or rather, earning a living); so much so that I've dried up, I can't write creatively any longer. *A Way of Love* was good but not good enough, not deep enough, not sincere and personal enough. Even so, I'd like to be remembered by it, and by *The Young Have Secrets*, as the best I've been able to do within my limitations. Nobody else but I knows the struggle I had to defeat the interior prohibitions and write them at all. An almost absolute ban.

23 January 1962

Ego-support – a letter this morning from N.Z., the admirer who wrote before. Diffuse praise about *The Visit to Penmorten*, which he'd just acquired.*
Also, again, about *A Way of Love*; 'This book I've loaned out to a number of people – to those in sympathy & those against. The reaction in *every* case was most favourable, and in many instances you gained a wider & more tolerant attitude towards ... this problem than hours of lecturing and explaining would ever have done. A wonderful tribute to your creative powers.'

23 April 1962

To dinner on Saturday evening with the D.'s. A.F. was there & spoke of my novels. He'd thought the homosexual one 'very fine', yet he's a married man of presumed normal sexuality (4 children). Again I felt guilt – and a sort of relieved astonishment that he and B.D. (host) could speak of the book (and the implied nature of its writer) with toleration and candour. I never get over the shock of surprise.

31 July 1962

Charles Brasch telephoned last night (when A.C. was here), partly to say goodbye & partly to ask if I'd heard of 'the ban'.
'Ban? What ban?'
'Your *Way of Love* has been banned by the Customs in New Zealand.'
'Well, who's responsible?'
'Oh, some nasty-minded little official. But there'll be a row. I'll kick up a stink when I get back. I'll do everything I can, depend on me. I'll suggest they might ban Shakespeare's "Venus & Adonis" also.'

---

* Set in the Cornish village of St Ives, *The Visit to Penmorten* tells of a young man's recovery from a nervous breakdown, his complex relationships with some of the town's inhabitants – including a male couple – and his eventual engagement to a young woman.

'No, don't go as far as that! The book (mine) isn't good enough to make a fuss.'

'But it's the principle. Anyway there'll be a run on such copies of the book as are still in the libraries; in fact it will be "lent round" in all directions.'

'I don't know whether to be depressed or what.'

'Be angry. Anyway I'll do what I can. I'm flying home on Wednesday, but hope to be back in 2 years.'

'If we're both still alive. Anyway, my dear C., good luck to you.'

I feel nervous about the ban to-day, but not at the moment depressed by it. Even if there were a court case in N.Z. I wouldn't be there. But slight paranoid feelings do arise apropos of the N.Z. background, even so. A bit mephitic, though only what I'd expect; 'that dreadful book', and so on. All the same I regret that it wasn't much more 'dreadful'. It was too timid by far, a mouse of a novel.

I told Dr L. about C.B. & the ban.

'Well, you've got somebody to speak for you – you've got friends.'

'C.B. owns a paper out there.' An exaggeration for prestige sake, but at least C. is the editor of a magazine. In fact he's the one person, possibly, in N.Z. who could speak with literary authority and be heard. Incidentally I've just realised that I must be the first N.Z. writer – N.Z. born, I mean – who has had a book banned in his own country.* Invidious distinction. What next?

---

* Courage was not the first. Jean Devanny's novel *The Butcher Shop* was banned in 1926.

This jacket evokes the Cornish seaside village depicted in *The Visit to Penmorten*, Courage's last novel, published in 1961 by Jonathan Cape. *Rachel Scott collection*

7 August 1962

At the D.'s yesterday, B.D. gave me a type-script left with him by C.B.;
a re-appraisal of *AWOL* [*A Way of Love*] intended obviously for print in
N.Z. Written by a woman, on the occasion of the book's ban. A critical
assessment, a fair-minded attempt to break through her own (and others')
'unconscious defences against homosexual trends latent in us all' and to
see the book more clearly. Did C.B. commission this, I wonder? Anyway she
says the book is 'too slight & in scope too restricted ... A wider canvas and
a bolder brush were needed.' (Yes, agreed, but she also says that the novel
doesn't purport to be anything but 'a straight account of a homosexual
love-affair'. She can't have it both ways, big & small.) All the same she does
arrive at: 'In one sense this is Mr C.'s best book, in that he has more to
say in it than in his others, and he is calm, sure, and stringently honest.'
I suppose I must be content with that, but I'm not, I'm depressed by the
whole thing, book & reappraisal together. Not a good morning. Courage,
courage again, God help me. Don't give in, don't give up, fight.

24 August 1962

Last night, a stranger who gave his name as Leigh Hunt rang up to ask
where or how he could get copies to read of my first two N.Z. novels:
Fifth Child and *Desire Without Content*. Told him to get his local (Ealing)
Public Lib. to send a request note to other Libs., 'who must have copies'.
He thanked me: a pleasant manly voice. He said incidentally that he'd
also read *A Way of L.*, on wh. I wanted to ask his opinion, but didn't. I felt
nevertheless that this was the novel he'd begun on, before seeking the
others (in hopes of further homo revelations, no doubt). For a few minutes
I felt a real writer, with a body of work behind me; a stay against paranoid
spasms of worthlessness.

Stood in an enormous smelly queue for the Dispensary. I really hate
people at such close quarters, I told myself, fuming, while a man behind me
muttered: 'Did I come fourteen thousand miles for this?' I assumed he was

a New Zealander, but carefully didn't encourage an affinity on that score (he might know about the ban on *Way of Love* anyway and I was in no mood for snide marks about morality).

1962–1963

10 December 1962

J.K. here last evening – a dark talkative S. African, a bio-chemist, who tried to explain how computers work. I remain ignorant.

12 December 1962

Certain reality factors have made to-day's state much worse, or initiated it. Notably the reading of a book, *The New Zealand Novel* by Joan Stevens, which C.B. sent me from N.Z. at my request & which arrived yesterday afternoon. This Joan Stevens, who's Associate Professor of English at Victoria University, writes towards the end of her survey (p. 131): 'Obviously the present writer does not have as high an opinion of J.C.'s novels as many articles do.' This is putting it mildly: she has hardly a good word to say for my work, notwithstanding the fact that she chooses one book (*The Young Have Secrets*) as a discussion-subject for the Adult Education Service (whatever that may be). In general she describes my books as 'unsatisfactory, good only in parts, unconvincing, etc'; in fact she begins, on the very first page of the text, with a crack at Pamela Hansford-Johnson, who as an English critic had described the background of *The Young* as 'excellently done' – 'How does she know?' Miss Stevens retorts in a nasty accent (disregarding the obvious fact that P.H-J. was speaking of technical ability rather than verisimilitude). And she doesn't miss a chance to denigrate my characters or subjects (admitting only 'a high professional polish' and a certain deftness of construction occasionally). Yet in at least one respect she is right, I must admit: too much of the normal-love-affair-parts of my work are disguised 'sentimental romantic fiction'. I hate the truth of this: my failure *there*, as I was unhappily conscious while writing, was and is due to my neurosis – I was working outside my range – I was *faking*, as a concession to conventional novelist's subject-matter. I know this and admit it. Yet I was hurt at having it pointed out in a critical way. Only when I'm writing of homosexual love am I truly at home – and how could I fit *that* into the N.Z. background I knew? I couldn't. Publication was difficult enough to achieve as it was, outside N.Z., without adding the obstacle of depicted perversion. Miss Stevens almost touches this point when she says: 'Abnormality in mental and emotional states seems to interest [him] as material for fiction ... *A Way of Love* deals with a love affair between two men.' Yet she doesn't let the inference play back over the earlier (N.Z.) novels. Perhaps for obvious reasons she dare not: or didn't critically follow up the hint, or even wasn't conscious of it.

15 December 1962

'Criticism, as so often, functions as a mask for moral prejudice.' I read this last night and thought of Joan Stevens' criticism of my novels. Implicitly she condemns me for pathological traits – 'abnormal states' – she dislikes & fears. The N.Z. superego. Whether the book is good as literature is secondary to its given tone – no, this isn't quite what I mean, but it must do. Incidentally, irony & humour both escape Miss J.S., in my work. I find that her strictures have rankled with me far too much.

22 January 1963

A copy of *Landfall Country*, N.Z. anthology, came to-day (postman rang bell while I was having breakfast). As usual I get a slightly schizoid sensation when seeing my name in print: some other me has been at work. The story C.B. has included in *L.C.* isn't one of my best: in fact it's too much like a chapter from a novel, but it was one of those stories the *London Magazine* published so I suppose it has merit of some kind. *L.C.* is a big fat book, but is well-printed (as it should be for 45/-) & I'm glad to have it. I'm wondering whether this is the last time I'll see anything of mine printed or reprinted.

23 January 1963

Young W.H. told me, incidentally, that he had, as far as he was able, run through D.'s private papers and had destroyed diaries, also a packet of letters marked 'To be burnt on my death' (letters from whom?). I commended W. for this act of compassion to D.'s memory. There were also other diaries, belonging to J.N., in the flat. Erotic, I gather, and incriminating. W. had sealed these in an envelope for J.N. to collect. I thought here of this journal

of mine, which must one day be destroyed in similar fashion (perhaps by S.).
Well, all this is as it should be, I suppose, though part of my mind revolts
at the necessity for covering up the evidence of a man's homosexuality – or
indeed his heterosexuality, come to that. Such a necessity simply indicates
the neurosis of our repressive civilisation. The fact that D. had led a singularly
'blameless' erotic life doesn't alter that reflection.

17 April 1963

F.B. came in for an hour or so last evening. Rather boring and I exhausted
myself in trying to contain what I now recognise to be aggression or at least
hostility. F.B. told me about a fancy-dress queer party that he'd been to in
a Putney house which happened to have an R.S.P.C.A. clinic next door, a
propinquity which had prompted the host to instruct in advance: 'Don't any of
you dizzy cows go to the wrong door or you'll be neutered like cats, drag and
all.' Two of the guests had been dressed as nuns, wimple included, and one
as Marie Antoinette. There were also 2 naval ratings – one of them false and
one real ('tubby') – and a real naval officer ('holding hands in a corner with
something fetching in black leather trousers and a flowered shirt'). All this
seemed far away and only momentarily amusing, save for the R.S.P.C.A. touch.
A hectic gaiety to cover the segregated despair of the invert: I know it all, as
does F.B.

18 March 1963

Saw S. distantly in the street yesterday but avoided him as he was with a
crowd of second-rate youths I haven't much time for (nor, to be truthful,
has S., I fancy). Told myself that S. was *with* them but not *of* them and that
only I know his mind and body. True enough, but the fact is that I don't
really like S.'s friends much, though they're the best he can manage given his
environment and character, etc. Yet if he were an intellectual I would not like
him as much and would probably quarrel with his opinions about literature,
interior decoration, music and so on. So, let him stay as he is, with mediocre
chums for the weekend at the pub. I am not married to him.

May 1963

Phillip Wilson mentions the 'ludicrous ban' in N.Z. on *Way of Love* but doesn't comment further.* I wish Whitcombe & Tombs would do an edition of *Young Have Secrets*, by arrangement with Cape, and include it among their N.Z. classics. I suppose this may ultimately happen, even if not in my lifetime. *The Young* must have gone to near 60,000 [copies], including the cheap edition. I don't think W. & T. likes my work very much, especially after the ban nonsense.

22 May 1963

To N.'s and G.'s last night to view their travel pictures – colour transparencies – of Egypt, shown on small screen. G. worked the slides & gave commentary. I found this absorbing & admired G.'s aplomb. The films led up to Abu Simnel temples, which quite bowled me over: the effects of yellow sunlight – dawn & evening – on the reddish sandstone – superb. The pyramids smaller than I'd imagined; rather pathetic heaps of dung-coloured stone in huge bleakish landscape. But one's eye is spoiled for size by modern city-building. N. was keeping his distance after our last erotic encounter, but offered wine, crystallised fruit, coffee, biscuits, cigarettes. I caught him for a moment alone later, in the kitchen. Asked when I was to see him again, as he & G. fly to Paris for Whitsun, but he was evasive: 'odds & ends to do'; adding, however: 'You're here and I'm here' (i.e. locally) 'so we're not all that apart.'

But at the back of my mind was ancient Egypt and Time's hurrying chariot – not least because I'd caught sight of myself in the kitchen mirror and noticed how thin my hair was and the signs of age on my skin. I also noticed, earlier, that of the five of us present (B. & R. were also there) four wore glasses and only R. was young (he'd let his sideboards grow and looked raffish & Spanish low-class). I suppose I was at least eight years older than

---

* New Zealand novelist and short-story writer Phillip Wilson (1922–2001) worked for the *New Zealand Listener* for a time.

any of them. Yet I wanted us all to be young – almost willed us to be so – not a gathering of middle-aged homosexuals, including N.

8 June 1963
S. rang at 6 last evening to say he'd had a gastric attack (diarrhoea) and couldn't come in later.

Me: Really, S., you are a chump. You always get something towards the end of the week, blast you.

S: Well that's a nice way to speak to an invalid.

I spent the evening alone, reading, but was conscious of underlying depression (rejection) wh. is more marked this morning: the usual lack of contact as a self-reproach: deep sense that I've missed something in life – security, wife, child, home – for which I've only myself to blame (once again, not true). The plight, of course, of the homosexual – though more so of the ageing one. (I refuse to write the word queer, as being derogatory.)

12 June 1963
S. rang about eight and said he'd been conscious that he might have been curt when I'd rung him the evening before. I was touched, though we hadn't much else to say except to make an appointment for Friday. But I felt a rapport which I was badly in want of. Later, went for a stroll in the fine evening. This hot weather brings out too many beautiful young men for my comfort: with a sort of impotent craving I see their bodies, thick hair, lips, skins rich in sun-colour. Temptations wh. cause torment from the vigilant super-ego. Yet I have S. and am grateful.

13 June 1963
Aches again in left leg, beginning when I woke up at seven. Thoughts of a blood-clot and so on. Would I fear dying? Yes and no. I don't want to suffer physically, yet my life is and has been such a torment, mentally, and the future seems (often) so nightmarishly bleak that – no, I can't

finish that sentence in any way that seems to avoid self-pity or masochistic attitudinizing of one kind or another.

14 June 1963

Confused session at 10, in which I did my best, without much progress. Yet Dr L. appears to think I'm improving, if only because I have (with him) less guilt about the homosexuality.

15 June 1963

S. was in distant mood at first, as I expected. He complained of feeling 'ticklish' – meaning un-calm, irritable – 'I want to be soothed'. I did my best, allowing for my own difficulties. Massage, tenderness, discussion of his problems (mainly libidinized passivity), attempts to draw out his affectionate response by sexual means. Up to a point successful, but I had to give out more than I was willing to do and even so, S. excused himself for not being able to take some lead – as he occasionally does or can – in bed. He came twice, once to masturbation-cum-fellatio, and once to masturbation ('you've got a wonderful touch on the knob' – i.e. glans). I came once, but not satisfactorily, against his buttocks. But it wasn't a very easy evening, all together. I had to woo S. against resistance (though he says this isn't great, it was considerable): he wanted it and didn't want it; fluctuations of the spirit, hesitations and conflict.

I told him A.C. was coming to lunch to-day.

S: 'I suppose you'll go to bed with him in the afternoon.'

I wanted to deny this, knowing it wasn't true, but kept quiet (wondering if I'd got a jealous rise out of S.) except to say (in Dr L.'s tones): 'There's your masochism, wanting me to reject or slight you. Isn't it?'

'Could be, I suppose.'

S. went at 11.45, with his newly-cut hair well combed and neat. He said he was getting bald on top but I reassured him – 'only a little thin'.

17 June 1963

Session at 10, as usual. Told him about S. and me on Friday night: the fellatio, the arse-licking, the lot: tried to make it as little apologetic as possible: 'That is my sex and you can take it or leave it.' All the same I'm very uncertain within, and almost want condemnation (a legal-social reaction), in other words the old wrong mechanism persists as the 'natural' one for me – the character thing.

Talked a little of S. here: how his analyst didn't drive *him* in the sessions.

Dr L.: 'But S. has a longer time than you – he's younger.'

I hated being reminded of this and said: 'S. has had ten years of treatment and even now can't bring out real aggression on the couch – or so I believe.'

'There you are then.'

More infantile anger (inhibited) then the session came to an end. At least I think I can see where I'm going, in a blinkered sort of fashion. No masochism.

ACKNOWLEDGEMENTS

I FIRST BEGAN TO explore James Courage's archive in 2005, the same year the embargo on his personal papers expired. Over the years the staff at the Hocken Collections have been unfailingly helpful and good humoured as I ordered files multiple times to check details and to digitise the evocative photos nestled inside.

I could not have put this edition together without the dedicated and careful work of Natasha Smillie. She transcribed page after page of diaries, navigating her way through some challenging material, especially in relation to the times when Courage suffered from severe depression.

I would like to thank Christopher Burke for our many enjoyable discussions and his insights when I supervised his PhD thesis on Courage's writing and sexuality. Will Kerley got in touch from England to provide valuable information on the London performance of *Private History*. I have also been fortunate to have the ear of Virginia Gray, Courage's niece, who gave her blessing to the project and told me about the extended family. Vincent O'Sullivan made valuable suggestions on the penultimate version of the manuscript, provided details on the connections with Katherine Mansfield and kindly arranged for Dunstan Ward to translate one of Proust's poems. John Webster lent me the magnificent pulp fiction-style edition of *The Young Have Secrets*, and Les O'Neill helped with photographic work. Anna Paris, Greg Rawlings and Jeffrey Vaughan offered wonderful guidance and support at various points.

Rachel Scott at Otago University Press has enthusiastically championed this project from the very start. I am most grateful to her and the rest of the Otago University Press team, especially Fiona Moffat for her fantastic design work and Anna Rogers for her editing skills.

Chris Brickell

INDEX

Bold denotes illustrations.

Published by Otago University Press
533 Castle Street
Dunedin, New Zealand
university.press@otago.ac.nz
www.otago.ac.nz/press

First published 2021
Copyright © Chris Brickell
The moral rights of the author have been asserted.
ISBN 978-1-99-004803-6

Published with the assistance of Creative New Zealand

Editor: Anna Rogers
Design and typesetting: Fiona Moffat
Printed in Hong Kong through Asia Pacific Offset

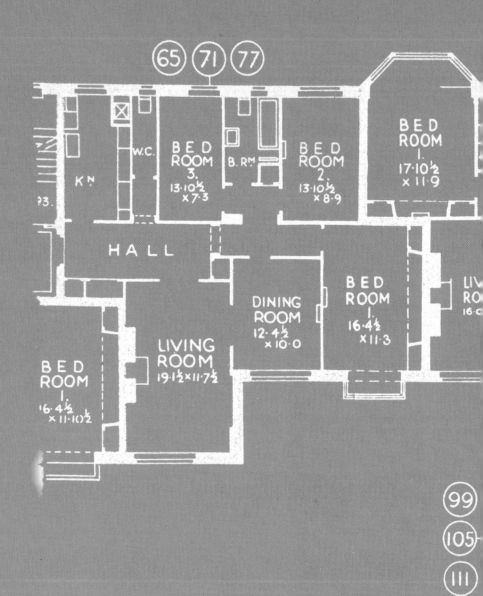

65 71 77

K^N

W.C.

B.R^M

BED ROOM 3.
13·10½ × 7·3

BED ROOM 2.
13·10½ × 8·9

BED ROOM 1.
17·10½ × 11·9

HALL

DINING ROOM
12·4½ × 10·0

BED ROOM 1.
16·4½ × 11·3

LIV RO
16·0

LIVING ROOM
19·1½ × 11·7½

BED ROOM 1.
16·4½ × 11·10½

99

105

111